NAGANUMA'S

Practical Japanese

(Basic Course)

with 2 cassette tapes

by

Naoe Naganuma

Director, Tokyo School of the Japanese Language, Tokyo

and

Kiyoshi Mori

Lecturer, Sophia University, Tokyo

The texts are voiced by Messrs.
Yoshinori Nakamura, Muneo Kimura,
Seiji Washio, Mrs. Sachiko Hasegawa
and Miss Noriko Muramatsu, instruc-
tors of Japanese at the Tokyo School
of the Japanese Language on two
Kaitakusha cassette tapes.

Foreword

A few years ago, by the request of the Nippon Columbia Co. I wrote the texts for the three records of beginning Japanese entitled " Practical Japanese (Basic Course)" for those who want to learn spoken Japanese systematically.

The records were accompanied by a pamphlet showing the Japanese texts with English translations, but it was obviously not sufficient for raw beginners. It needed explanatory material on grammar and construction patterns. Exercises were also wanted. I mentioned then that I would prepare such materials in the introduction of the pamphlet, but the work was very slow until Mr. Mori came to the rescue.

Mr. Mori not only arranged the material on hand very efficiently, but also added much more of his own.

In this book I have tried to offer a short all-round course of beginning Japanese giving minimum essentials of structural patterns and vocabulary. But the principal aim has been to present basic structures gradually and systematically. Although vocabulary items are secondary, special attention was paid to their selection.

In consideration of advantages of classroom procedures each lesson is presented as a connected whole instead of a series of disconnected sentences, and so there are a few cases of less important words creeping in. Such words should be lightly treated.

The advantage of this book is that it is accompanied by the tapes which give good models of actual speech. By repeating after the tapes any number of times, trying to reproduce exactly as it is spoken the student will be able to master the contents of the book in a comparatively short time. The grammar notes and glossary will solve most difficulties of the student.

However, to get most out of the book the student is advised to engage a tutor who will give thorough drill on the texts which are especially designed for oral question-and-answer drills.

Language is mainly for communication and its mastery is dependent more on skill than theory. At first the student should learn the language instead of learning about the language. This means that he should learn to use the language for communication which can only be achieved by constant practice. Merely being able to recognize the meaning of a sentence is not enough. It should be practised until it can be reproduced without delay.

The texts are mere "memos." The real objective is to be able to use the contents freely and easily.

In preparing this book thanks are due to a number of people who have been kind enough to help me in various ways. In particular, I want to thank Miss Tsuruko Asano, Mr. J. W. Cravens, and Mr. A. A. Milne for their many valuable suggestions, and Miss Sumie Yamaki for the most painstaking job of the preparation of the manuscript for the press and proof-reading.

Naoe Naganuma

THE TABLE OF CONTENTS

NAGANUMA'S
PRACTICAL JAPANESE

(Basic Course)

Ichi

(Greetings)

A : Ohayō gozaimasu.

B : Ohayō gozaimasu.

A : Ikaga desu ka ?

B : Genki desu.

A : Sore wa kekkō desu. Sā, hajimemashō.

(Main Text)

A : Kore wa hon desu.

  Sore wa isu desu.

  Are wa mado desu.

  Kore wa tsukue desu ka ?

B :   Hai, sō desu.

— 1 —

A : Sore wa kaban desu ka ?

B : Iie, sō ja arimasen.

A : Are wa nan desu ka ?

B : Doa desu.

A : Kore wa pen desu ka, empitsu desu ka ?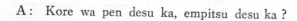

B : Empitsu desu.

(For Memorizing)

1. Kore wa [tsukue] desu ka ?	1.	Is this a [desk]?
2. Hai, sō desu.	2.	Yes, it is.
3. Iie, sō ja arimasen.	3.	No, it isn't.
4. Sore wa [pen] desu ka, [empitsu] desu ka ?	4.	Is that a [pen] or a [pencil]?
5. [Empitsu] desu.	5.	It's a [pencil].
6. [Are] wa nan desu ka ?	6.	What is [that over there]?

doa (′–)   hon (′–)   pen (′–)

heya (–′)   uchi (–′)

hako (– –)

hagaki (– – –)   hasami (– – –)

(Closing Remarks)

A: Hai, kekkō desu. Kyō wa sore dake desu.

B: Arigatō gozaimashita.

A: Dō itashimashite.

B: Sayōnara.

A: Sayōnara.

Ichi — Lesson 1

Greetings (Aisatsu)

Ohayō (gozaimasu) [- - - -] literally means *You are early*. Therefore, it is not usually used after about 10 a. m. When speaking to equals or inferiors **gozaimasu** may be omitted.

gozaimasu [- - - - -] the polite form of **desu**, *to be* (See Lesson 25, Grammar 202.)

ikaga [-'-] means *how about*. In this sentence a word meaning *your health* is understood. When used as an ordinary question, the sentence means *How about it, Do you care for it*, etc.

desu ['-] *is, are*, etc. The final **u** is usually mute in standard speech. (See Grammar 5.)

ka [-] a particle or a postposition of interrogation

genki ['- -] *energy; high-spiritedness; pep*

sore [- -] *that* (See Grammar 2.)

wa [-] a particle or a postposition which shows that the word or words preceding it is usually (but not always) in the nominative case

kekkō ['- - -] *fine, splendid, good*, etc.

sā ['-] an interjection meaning *now, well then*, etc.

hajimemashō [- - - - - -] *Let's begin.*

Main Text (Hombun)

Glossary

kore [- -] *this* (*thing*)
hon ['-] *a book*
isu [- -] *a chair*
are [- -] *that* (*thing*) *over there*

mado ['-] *a window*

tsukue [- - -] *a desk*, pronounced as [ts'kue]

hai ['-] a sign of agreement: *yes, that's right, you're correct*, etc. In familiar circles **ee** ['-] is frequently used instead, and when a male subordinate answers his superior in a more or less formal or stiff way, such as a private answering an officer, **ha** with a jerk is used.

sō [- -] *so*

kaban [- - -] *a bag; brief-case; satchel; travelling bag.* A handbag or a vanity-case is not called **kaban**.

iie [- -'] *no*, a sign of disagreement

ja arimasen [- - - - - -] the negative form of **desu**, *is not, are not*, etc. **Ja** is a contraction of **dewa** which can be used in more formal speech. Some fastidious women may prefer **dewa**.

nan ['-] = **nani**, *what* (See Lesson 4, Grammar 26.)

doa ['-] *a door*

pen ['-] *a pen*

empitsu [- - - -] *a pencil*, pronounced as [empits']

Grammar

Nouns, Number and Gender

1. Nouns in Japanese have no number nor gender, that is, there are no singular or plural forms of nouns as such. Nor is there any distinction between masculine, feminine and neuter genders.

Nouns are not preceded by articles such as *a*, *an*, and *the*. Therefore, **hon** may mean *a book* or *books*. The context alone will determine which is meant. It is possible, when necessary, to express plurality by the use of suffixes or other devices which will be dealt with later.

"Kore," "Sore," and "Are"

2. These are pronouns. **Kore** refers to what is close to the speaker; **sore** to what is close to the person spoken to; **are** to what is removed from both the speaker and the person spoken to.

Particles

3. In Japanese there is an important group of words called particles. They resemble English prepositions such as *in, on, of, at, from*, etc., or conjunctions such as *because, but, since,* etc., in that they show the relation of one word, phrase or clause to another or connect the different parts of a sentence. However, as they are sometimes called postpositions they always come after a word as if they were a part of it. One of the beginner's faults in speaking Japanese is giving too much emphasis in pronouncing particles. They should be pronounced with the preceding words without a pause between, but not loudly.

"Wa"—a Particle of Topics

4. **Wa** has no English equivalent. It shows that the preceding word or words are the *topic* of the sentence—the thing you are talking about. Most often the topic of a sentence becomes the subject of the sentence.

"Desu"—a Copula

5. The English verb *to be* (*is, are, am,* etc.) is sometimes called a copulative verb, because it acts as a copula, connecting two parts of a sentence as a kind of equal sign.

> *This is a book.* → This = a book
> *I am a student.* → I = a student

In Japanese **desu** (pronounced as [des']) serves the same purpose. Since nouns in Japanese have no number nor gender, **desu** can be used for any of *is, are,* or *am.*

"Ja arimasen"—the Negative of "Desu"

6. The negative of **desu** is **ja arimasen** (or **dewa arimasen**).

> **Kore wa isu ja arimasen.** *This is not a chair.*
> **Iie, sō ja arimasen.** *No, it isn't.* (Lit. *No, it is not so.*)

You may think it is strange that the negative of a single word should be two words and so long. The reason is that **desu** is a contraction of **de arimasu.**

the Particle "Ka"

7. **Ka** is a particle of interrogation. By adding **ka** at the end, a sentence or a phrase may be changed into a question.

> **Kore wa isu desu ka?** *Is this a chair?*
> **Are wa to desu ka, mado desu ka?**
> *Is that over there a door or a window?*

The Omission of Subject Part

8. The subject in a Japanese sentence is often omitted, if it can be safely guessed from the situation or context.

    (1) **Kore wa tsukue desu ka?**   *Is this a desk?*

    (2) **Hai, sō desu.**   *Yes, ...is so.*

    (3) **Iie, sō ja arimasen.**   *No, ...is not so.*

The sentence (2) or (3) is given as an answer to the question (1). So the subject in (2) or (3) can be safely guessed to be the same as that in (1). In such a case, the subject is very often omitted. See the note on **genki** in "Greetings" and the answer to an alternative question in this lesson.

Alternative Questions

9.   **Kore wa pen desu ka, empitsu desu ka?**

          Is this a pen or a pencil?

Notice that *or* is not outwardly expressed in the Japanese sentence. It is implied in the two sentences, *Is this a pen?* and *Is this a pencil?* put together with the omission of the second *this*.

Interrogative Sentences

10. In Japanese a statement (a declarative sentence) may be converted into an interrogative sentence by adding **ka** at the end. This **ka** is often dropped when there is an interrogative word in the sentence, but it is not recommended for beginners to follow until they become fairly fluent in speaking the language with proper intonation.

      Is that over there a window?   **Are wa mado desu ka?**

      What is this? |**Kore wa nan desu ka?**

                                   |**Kore wa nan desu?**

Sometimes the sense of interrogation is expressed by raising the tone of the last syllable of the sentence. The same advice to refrain from using this form holds good until the student becomes fairly proficient.

For Memorizing (Ankiyō)

heya [-']   *a room*
uchi [-']   *a house; home*
hako [- -]   *a box*

hagaki [- - -] *a post-card*
hasami [- - -] *scissors*

Closing Remarks (Owari no Kotoba)

kyō ['-] *today*

sore dake [- - - -] *that much,* **dake** means *only*.

Arigatō (gozaimasu) [-'- - -] literally means *rarely exist.* The idea of the sentence is *Such an act of kindness as you are showing me is rarely met with,* hence *I am grateful.* However, the basic thought is rather that it is the grace of Providence (Buddha) that I meet with such kindness which I appreciate. This accounts for the frequent use of **arigatō** when it may seem quite uncalled-for from a western viewpoint. When speaking to equals or subordinates **gozaimasu** is often omitted.

gozaimashita [- - -'- -] the past form of **gozaimasu**. **Arigatō gozaimashita** refers to a completed act whereas the present tense **Arigatō gozaimasu** only refers to a present act or one that may be expected to continue.

Dō itashimashite ['- - - - - - -] literally means *why* or *how come.* The idea of the sentence is *Why do you say such a thing (when there is no reason for you to say)?.* It corresponds to *Don't mention it, Not at all, You are welcome, That's all right,* etc.

Sayōnara [- - -'- or - - - - -] literally means *well then* or *in that case.* In this case, *I'll take my leave, I hope you will be all right,* is understood. The vowel of **yō** was originally long, but it is often pronounced short as **sayonara**.

Ni

(Greetings)

A : Konnichi wa.

B : Konnichi wa.

A : Ii otenki desu nē.

B : Sō desu nē.

A : Ogenki desu ka ?

B : Ee, okagesama de.

A : Sā hajimemashō. Ii desu ka ?

B : Dōzo yukkuri itte kudasai.

(Main Text)

A : Kore wa akai empitsu desu.

Kono empitsu wa akai desu.

Sore wa aoi kami desu.

Sono kami wa aoi desu.

Are wa shiroi kabe desu.

Ano kabe wa shiroi desu.

Sono kami mo shiroi desu ka ?

B : Iie, shiroku wa arimasen. Kuroi desu.

A : Kono tokei wa ōkii desu ka ?

B : Iie, ōkiku wa arimasen. Chiisai desu.

(For Memorizing)

1. Kore wa [ōkii] desu.
2. Kono [tokei] wa [chiisaku] wa arimasen.

1. This is [large].
2. This [watch] is not [small].

ii ('-)	warui (-'-)	takai (-'-)
hikui (-'-)	yasui (-'-)	atsui (---)
usui (---)	karui (---)	omoi (---)
furui (-'-)	atarashii (---'-)	

(Closing Remarks)

A : Hai, kekkō desu. Kyō wa kore de oshimai desu.

B : Arigatō gozaimashita.

A : Sayōnara. Mata ashita.

B : Sayōnara.

Ni — Lesson 2

Aisatsu

Konnichi wa [-----] literally means *today......* implying *Today is a good day.* It is used between 10 a. m. and evening.

ii ['-] *good; correct.* It is often used in the sense of *all right.*

otenki [-'--] *weather*, and **o** at the beginning which makes the word polite and may be omitted. (But not in **Ohayō gozaimasu** in which **o** is an essential part.)

nē ['-] anticipates the agreement of the person spoken to, and corresponds to disjunctive questions such as *isn't it ?, haven't you ?*, etc.

ogenki [-'--] means (*You are*) *well.* **O** at the beginning makes the word polite and is used in reference to someone's health other than the speaker's. But it can be omitted when speaking to equals and inferiors.

ee ['-] *yes* (See the note on **hai** in the Glossary of Lesson 1.)

Okagesama de [------] literally means *Thanks to your* (or *Buddha's*) *shadow* (implying protection). After this are omitted the words which mean *I am well.* The idea of the sentence is *Thanks to your concern over my health which is apparent in your question, I am well.*

dōzo ['--] *please*

yukkuri [--'-] *slowly*

itte [---] from **iu**, to *say*

kudasai [----] literally means *to condescend* suggesting the idea of *please condescend to do me a favor.* When used at the end of a sentence, it makes the sentence polite.

Hombun

Glossary

akai [---] (*a-A*)* *red*

kono [--] *this* (before a noun) (See Grammar 13.)

aoi ['-] (*a-A*) *blue; green; pale.* The leaves of plants are **aoi** in which case the word means *green.* The sky is **aoi**, so in this case it means *blue.* On the other hand navy blue is never **aoi**, and is expressed by a different word. In the case of a complexion, it means *pale.*

kami ['] *paper*

sono [--] *that* (before a noun) (See Grammar 13.)

shiroi ['-] (*a-A*) *white; fair* (in case of the complexion)

kabe ['] *a wall*

ano [--] *that...over there* (before a noun) (See Grammar 13.)

mo [-] *too; also; either* (in a negative sentence)

kuroi ['-] (*a-A*) *black; dark* (hair)

tokei [---] *a clock; watch*

ōkii [--'-] (*a-A*) *large; big*

chiisai [--'-] (*a-A*) *small; little*

Grammar

True Adjectives

11. There are two kinds of adjectives in Japanese, true adjectives and quasi-

---

* In this book true adjectives are marked by (*a-A*).

adjectives. In this lesson true adjectives only are treated.

The dictionary form of true adjectives, that is, the form which is shown in dictionaries, ends in **ai, ii, ui,** or **oi.** No true adjectives end in **ei.** Used attributively, that is, before a noun, the dictionary form is used without modification.

akai empitsu	*a red pencil*
shiroi kami	*white paper*

Used predicatively, that is, when a true adjective is used in the predicate part of a sentence, it requires **no** or its corruption **n** between a true adjective and **desu,** e.g.,

Kono kami wa shiroi n(o) desu.

This **no** is often dropped altogether.

Kono kami wa shiroi desu.

Although some grammarians still refuse to recognize its correctness, the tendency of the present generation, especially of the younger generation, is toward dropping this **no** altogether as far as common, conversational speech is concerned, and we may say that the practice has become universal enough to be accepted as being grammatically correct. The author has decided to follow this popular practice.

The Negative Form of True Adjectives

12. When converting the construction [*true adjective*] x (**no**) x **desu** into its corresponding negative form, we must change the **i** ending into **ku** and put **wa arimasen** after it, e.g.,

Kono kami wa shiroku wa arimasen. *This paper is not white.*

"Kono," "Sono," and "Ano"

13. These are pre-nouns which always stand immediately before nouns. They are never used alone.

"Mo" — a Particle of Repetition

14. **Mo** is a particle which adds the sense of *also, too.*

Sono kami mo shiroi desu. *That paper is white, too.*

Unlike the English word *too,* **mo** is not added, but takes the place of **wa.**

In a negative sentence:

> **Kore wa hon ja arimasen.** *This is not a book.*
> **Kore mo hon ja arimasen.** *This is not a book, either.*

Ankiyō

warui [-'-] (a-A) *bad ; wrong*
takai [-'-] (a-A) *high ; expensive*
hikui [-'-] (a-A) *low*
yasui [-'-] (a-A) *cheap ; low-priced*
atsui [- - -] (a-A) *thick*
usui [- - -] (a-A) *thin*
karui [- - -] (a-A) *light* (not heavy)
omoi [- - -] (a-A) *heavy*
furui [-'-] (a-A) *old*
atarashii [- - -'-] (a-A) *new ; fresh*

Owari no Kotoba

de [-] a particle meaning *with this much*
oshimai [- - - -] *an end*
mata [- -] *again*
ashita [- - -] *tomorrow*, pronounced as [*ash'ta*]

Exercises (Lessons 1—2)

A. Here are ten English sentences numbered from 1 to 10, and Japanese sentences lettered from a to j. Match up the sentences by finding the Japanese equivalent for each of the English sentences.

1. Good morning.
2. Good afternoon.
3. Good-bye.
4. How are you ?
5. I'm quite well.
6. That's good.
7. Are you quite well ?
8. Yes, quite well, thank you.

a. Arigatō gozaimasu.
b. Ikaga desu ka ?
c. Ee, okagesama de.
d. Dō itashimashite.
e. Sore wa kekkō desu.
f. Ohayō gozaimasu.
g. Konnichi wa.
h. Ogenki desu ka ?

— 12 —

9. Thank you very much.   i. Genki desu.

10. You're welcome.   j. Sayōnara.

B. There are several words in each of the following ten groups. Construct a sentence by arranging properly all the words in each group. Then read them aloud.

1. wa desu kore tsukue
2. desu sore mado wa
3. are ka desu wa kaban
4. nan desu sore ka wa
5. wa ka ka sore tsukue isu desu desu
6. ka kami kore desu wa akai
7. ano shiroi wa kabe desu
8. desu mo sono shiroi kami
9. ōkii ka sono desu kami wa
10. wa ōkiku iie arimasen

C. Here are eight sentences, each one with a blank or blanks to be filled in. Choose the correct word required to complete each sentence.

1. Kore ___ hon desu ___ ?   2. Hai, ___ desu.

3. Iie, sō ___ ___.   4. Sore ___ mado desu ___, doa ___ ka ?

5. Mado ___.   6. Are ___ shiroi kabe ___.

7. Sono kami ___ *(also)* shiroi desu ___?

8. Iie, ___ wa arimasen. Aoi desu.

D. Practise converting rapidly from one statement to the other until you become fairly fluent. In class, the teacher may give one statement and the students the opposite form.

Conversion Table 1

Affirmative Statement	Negative Statement	Meaning
hon desu	hon ja arimasen	*book*
tsukue desu	tsukue ja arimasen	*desk*
tokei desu	tokei ja arimasen	*watch*
hako desu	hako ja arimasen	*box*
genki desu	genki ja arimasen	*peppy*
sō desu	sō ja arimasen	*so*

Conversion Table 2

Affirmative Statement	Negative Statement	Meaning
akai desu	akaku wa arimasen	*red*
takai desu	takaku wa arimasen	*high, expensive*
atarashii desu	atarashiku wa arimasen	*new*
ōkii desu	ōkiku wa arimasen	*large*
warui desu	waruku wa arimasen	*bad*
yasui desu	yasuku wa arimasen	*cheap*
aoi desu	aoku wa arimasen	*blue*
furui desu	furuku wa arimasen	*old*

E. Here are five affirmative sentences. Turn them into the negative. The negative of **desu** *is* **ja arimasen** *after a noun, and* **-ku wa arimasen** *in the case of a true adjective. Read aloud your answers.*

1. Kono hon wa atsui desu.
2. Hai, sō desu.
3. Sono tokei wa omoi desu.
4. Ano empitsu wa yasui desu.
5. Kono kami wa usui desu.

F. What is the Japanese equivalent of each of the following sentences? Don't try to translate each word.

1. This box is large.
2. Is that a window, too?
3. No, it isn't. It is a door.
4. Is that pencil over there red?
5. Yes, it is.
6. What is this?
7. It is a watch.
8. This watch is not low-priced; it is expensive.
9. Is this a chair or a desk?
10. It's fine weather, isn't it?

San

(Greetings)

A : Komban wa.

B : Komban wa.

A : Ikaga desu ka ?

B : Genki desu. Anata wa ?

A : Watakushi mo. Dewa, hajimemashō.

B : Dōzo hakkiri itte kudasai.

(Main Text)

A : Anata wa seito desu.

Watakushi wa seito ja arimasen. Sensei desu.
Anata wa donata desu ka ?

B : Watakushi wa Buraun desu.

A : Watakushi wa Nipponjin desu.

Anata wa Amerikajin desu ka, Igirisujin desu
ka ?

B : Watakushi wa Amerikajin desu.

A : Ano kata wa donata desu ka ?

B : Shumitto San no okusan desu.　Ano kata
wa Doitsujin desu.

A : Anata no otomodachi desu ka ?

B : Hai, sō desu.　Watakushi no tomodachi desu

A : Sono bōshi wa anata no desu ka ?

B : Iie, watakushi no ja arimasen.

A : Donata no desu ka ?

B : Suzuki San no desu.

(A Short Conversation)

B : Suzuki San desu. Watakushi no tomodachi desu.

Kono kata wa Yamada Sensei desu.

C : Hajimemashite.

A : Dōzo yoroshiku.

C : Watakushi koso.

(For Memorizing)

1. [Anata] wa donata desu ka ?
2. Watakushi wa [Buraun] desu.
3. Ano kata wa watakushi no [tomodachi] desu.

1. Who are [you] ?
2. I am [Brown].
3. He is a [friend] of mine.

kutsu (–′) uwagi (– – –) zubon (–′–)
chokki (– – –) kutsushita (– – – –) gaitō (– – – –)
waishatsu (– – – –) nekutai (′– – –)

(Closing Remarks)

A : Dewa kyō wa sore made.
B : Oyasumi nasai.

San — Lesson 3

Aisatsu

Komban wa [– – – – –] literally means *this evening* ...... with *a good evening* understood.

anata [–′–] *you*

— 17 —

watakushi [- - - -] *I*, often shortened to **watashi** in familiar speech

dewa ['-] *then; well then; in that case.* **Dewa** has the above meaning only when it is used at the beginning of a sentence. It may be contracted to **ja** or **jā**.

hakkiri [- -'-] *clearly; distinctly*

Hombun
Glossary

seito ['- -] *a student; pupil*

sensei [- -'-] *a teacher; master.* Also used in referring to doctors. But teachers seldom use *sensei* in personal reference except when speaking to children. **Kyōshi** is used to refer to one's own teaching profession.

donata ['- -] *who; which person* (polite)

Nipponjin [- -'- - -] *a Japanese.* **Nihonjin** is also used. This is a combination of **Nippon**, *Japan* and **jin**, a person. **Jin** means *a person, man,* etc., and is used after the name of a country, a region, a city, etc. to express nationality, citizenship, birth place, etc. Thus, **Igirisujin**, **Doitsujin**, **Furansujin**, etc. will mean a native of England, Germany, France, etc., while **Kantonjin** will mean a Cantonese, a native of the province of Kwangtung.

Amerikajin [- - - - - -] *an American*

Igirisujin [- - - - - -] *a Britisher; Englishman*

kata [-'] a polite term for *a person.* Hence, **kono kata** means *this person;* **sono kata** means *that person, the person in question, the person we are speaking of,* etc.; **ano kata** means *that person over there,* i.e. *he* or *she.*

Shumitto San *Mr. Schmidt*: **San** means *Mr., Mrs.,* or *Miss.* As the Japanese language disregards gender, only context or situation decides which of the three **San** means. But **Shumitto San no okusan** definitely means *Mrs. Schmidt.* When the speaker has a housewife in mind, **Shumitto San no goshujin** (*Schmidt's husband* = Mr. Schmidt) is also possible and it means Schmidt's husband, i.e. Mr. Schmidt. In English one may say "I am Mr. Brown," or "I am Miss Green," but in Japanese **San** should never be used after one's own name, since this word is a mark of respect.

no [-] *of,* a possessive particle (See Grammar 16.)

okusan ['- - -] *a wife; Mrs.; the mistress* (of the house). This is an honorific term, and it should never be used for one's own wife. One often hears the master of the house use **okusan** referring to his wife when speaking to maid servants. In this case he means *your* (maid's) *mistress*. He will never use the term to outsiders, but use **kanai**.

Doitsujin [- - - - -] *a German*

anata no [-'- -] *your; of yours*

otomodachi [- - - - -] a combination of **o**, an honorific prefix denoting politeness or respect, and **tomodachi** which means *friend*, so that **otomodachi** means *your friend*, *his* or *her friend*.

bōshi [- - -] *a hat; cap.* There is no distinction made between *a hat* and *a cap.* When it is necessary to distinguish specific names such as *a felt hat*, **nakaorebōshi**, *a hunting cap* (*tweed*), **toriuchibōshi**, etc. are used.

donata no ['- - -] *whose*

Grammar
Personal Pronouns

15. Unlike English pronouns Japanese pronouns have no case distinction such as *I*, *my*, *me* according to their positions in a sentence. Since they are the same as ordinary nouns, they may be treated as a variety of nouns. It is for the sake of convenience that we use the term here.

1st person	**watakushi** (or **watashi**)	*I*
2nd person	**anata**	*you*
3rd person	**kono kata**	*he, she* (this person)
	sono kata	*", "* (that person)
	ano kata	*", "* (that person over there)
Indefinite person	**donata**	*who*

Since **kata** does not show the difference of sex, it can be used for both *he* and *she*. However, because this word is a polite term, it should be used for a person to whom respect is to be paid. It naturally follows that these words cannot be used in all cases when the English *he* or *she* is used.

"No" — a Possessive Particle

16. The particle **no** placed between two nouns usually makes the first noun the modifier of the second noun. Thus, **Watakushi no tomodachi** means *self's friend*, *a friend of myself*, *my friend*, *a friend of mine*. This **no** usually corresponds to *of* or *'s*.

anata no otomodachi	*your friend*
Shumitto San no okusan	*Mr. Schmidt's wife*

— 19 —

Possessive Pronouns

17. Possessive pronouns such as *my*, *your*, *his*, *her*, etc. in English find their equivalents in Japanese in compounds consisting of personal pronouns and the particle **no**.

Thus, **watakushi no** corresponds to *my*, **anata no** *your*, **ano kata no** *his* or *her*, **donata no** *whose*, and **Suzuki San no** *Mr. Suzuki's*.

The Predicative Use of Possessive Pronouns

18. In English when possessive pronouns are to be used predicatively, *mine*, *yours*, etc. are used instead of *my*, *your*, etc. In Japanese there is no change in form between *my* and *mine*.

Kore wa watakushi no hon desu.	*This is my book.*
Kore wa watakushi no desu.	*This is mine.*
Kore wa anata no desu ka?	*Is this yours?*
Iie, ano kata no desu.	*No, it's his* (or *hers*).

A Short Conversation (Mijikai Kaiwa)

hajimemashite [- - - - - -] *for the first time.* **Ome ni kakarimasu** (*I see you.*) is omitted.

yoroshiku [- - - -] *well.* This expression literally means *I hope you will treat me in the way you think fit.* **Negaimasu** (*I request you*) is left out or understood.

koso ['-] an emphatic particle meaning *the very*. The expression literally means *I should be the very one who should say so.*

Ankiyō

kutsu [-'] *shoes; boots*

uwagi [- - -] *a coat:* literally an outer garment, usually refers to a suit coat or a sports coat. But a jacket is a **jampā**.

zubon [-'-] *trousers*

chokki [- - -] *a vest; waistcoat.* This word comes from the English word *jacket*.

kutsushita [- - - -] *socks; stockings*

gaitō [- - - -] *an overcoat.* **Ōbā** which comes from the English word *over-*

coat is coming into popular use.

waishatsu [- - - -] *a whiteshirt ; dress shirt.* A short sleeved, open neck
shirt is called **kaikinshatsu**.

nekutai ['- - -] *a necktie ; cravat*

Owari no Kotoba

made ['-] *to ; as far as ; until*

Oyasumi nasai [- - - - - - -] literally means *Go to sleep* and **Gokigen yō**
which means *in good health* is omitted. Therefore, sometimes the latter is
used for the same purpose. Sometimes **Oshizuka ni** which means *peace-
fully* is used. In this case **oyasumi nasai** is understood. **Nasai** is the
imperative form of **nasaru**, a polite verb for **suru**, *to do.*

Exercises

*A. Read aloud the three Japanese sentences in each of the following five
groups, and pick out the one which fits best the situation described in English.
Be sure you know what all the Japanese sentences mean.*

1. *When you meet your acquaintance about 11 in the morning :*
   a. Ohayō gozaimasu.   c. Komban wa.
   b. Konnichi wa.

2. *When you are introduced to someone :*
   a. Arigatō gazaimasu.   c. Hajimemashite.
   b. Okagesama de.

3. *When your teacher speaks too fast :*
   a. Dōzo hakkiri itte kudasai.   c. Dōzo yukkuri itte kudasai.
   b. Dōzo yoroshiku.

4. *When you want to start working :*
   a. Hajimemashite.   c. Mata ashita.
   b. Hajimemashō.

5. *When you want to stop working :*
   a. Kyō wa sore dake desu.   c. Oyasumi nasai.
   b. Kyō wa ii otenki desu nē.

B. Read aloud the following questions, and give your answer to each of them.

1. Anata wa donata desu ka ?
2. Anata wa seito desu ka ?
3. Anata no sensei wa Nipponjin desu ka ?
4. Anata no kutsu wa shiroi desu ka ?
5. Anata wa Amerikajin desu ka ?

C. *Fill in the blank or blanks of each sentence with a word required to complete the sentence.*
1. Kono kata wa Shumitto San ____ okusan desu.
2. Sono kata wa watakushi ____ tomodachi desu.
3. Ano pen wa anata ____ desu ka ?
4. Iie, watakushi no ____ ____.   Suzuki San ____ desu.
5. Kono bōshi wa ____ku wa arimasen. Furui desu.

D. *Read aloud the following sentences. Then, turn them into the negative. Be sure you understand the meaning.*
1. Kono hasami wa watakushi no desu.
2. Sono pen wa kuroi desu.
3. Sō desu.
4. Ano ōkii heya wa anata no desu.
5. Watakushi no empitsu wa akai desu.

E. *What is the Japanese equivalent of each of the following sentences? Don't try to translate each word.*

1. Who is that ?
2. She is Mrs. Brown.
3. Is she a German ?
4. No, she is an Englishwoman.
5. Is Mr. Brown your friend ?
6. Yes, he is.
7. Is he a student ?
8. No, he is a teacher.

F. *What would you say when,*
1. you want to say it's fine weather ?
2. you want to ask if the other person is ready ?
3. you bid farewell, hoping you'll see the other person tomorrow ?
4. you meet someone in the evening ?
5. you are introduced to someone ?

Shi

(Greetings)

A : Konnichi wa.

B : Konnichi wa.

A : Warui otenki desu nē.

B : Sō desu nē.

A : Samui desu nē. Sā, hajimemashō.

(Main Text)

A : Goran nasai.

Koko ni tsukue ga arimasu.

Watakushi no tsukue desu.

Kono tsukue wa yuka no ue ni arimasu.

Tsukue no ue ni kago ga arimasu.

Kago no naka ni nani ga arimasu ka ?

B : Ringo ga arimasu.

A : Ikutsu arimasu ka ?

B : Hitotsu, futatsu, mittsu, yottsu, itsutsu,
      muttsu, nanatsu, yattsu, kokonotsu, tō——
      tō arimasu.

A : Mado wa doko ni arimasu ka ?

B : Asuko ni arimasu.

A : Mado no soba ni nani ga arimasu ka ?

B : Tēburu ga arimasu.

A : Tēburu no shita ni nani ga arimasu ka ?

B : Nani mo arimasen.

A : Soko ni hon ga arimasu. Atsui hon to usui hon desu.

Atsui no wa jibiki de, usui no wa Nippongo no hon desu.

Koko ni shimbun mo arimasu ka ?

B : Hai, arimasu.

A : Nippongo no shimbun desu ka ?

B : Iie, Eigo no shimbun desu.

(A Short Conversation)

A : Sono ringo o kudasai.

B : Ikutsu agemashō ka ?

A : Hitotsu kudasai.

(For Memorizing)

1. Koko ni [tsukue] ga arimasu.
2. [Tsukue] no ue ni [kago] ga arimasu.
3. [Kago] no naka ni [ringo] ga arimasu.
4. Ikutsu arimasu ka ?
5. Hitotsu, futatsu, mittsu, yottsu, itsutsu, muttsu, nanatsu, yattsu, kokonotsu, tō—— [tō] arimasu.
6. Nani mo arimasen.

1. Here is a [desk].
2. There's a [basket] on the [desk].
3. There are some [apples] in the [basket].
4. How many are there ?
5. One, two, three, four, five, six, seven, eight, nine, ten—— there are [ten].
6. There's nothing.

7. Atsui no wa [jibiki] de, usui no wa [Nippongo] no hon desu.

7. The thick one is a [dictionary], and the thin one is a book (in Japanese).

Shi — Lesson 4

Aisatsu

samui [-'-] (*a-A*) *cold*. Note that this refers only to cold weather or a person feeling the cold weather. A different word (**tsumetai** (*a-A*)) is used to refer to a cold object.

Hombun

Glossary

goran [- - -] a polite verb meaning *to see ; look*
koko [- -] *here ; this place*
ni [-] *at ; in*
ga [-] a nominative particle (See Grammar 22.)
arimasu [- - - -] *there is ; there are* (See Grammar 20.)
yuka [- -] *a floor*
ue [- -] *on ; on top of ; over ; above*
kago [-'] *a basket*
naka ['-] *in ; inside*
nani ['-] *what* (*thing*)
ringo [- - -] *an apple*
ikutsu ['- -] *how many*
hitotsu [-'-] *one*
futatsu [- - -] *two*
mittsu [- - -] *three*
yottsu [- - -] *four*
itsutsu [-'-] *five*
muttsu [- - -] *six*
nanatsu [-'-] *seven*
yattsu [- - -] *eight*
kokonotsu [-'- -] *nine*
tō [- -] *ten*
doko ['-] *where*

asuko [- - -] *that place over there ; yonder.* More formal pronunciation is **asoko.**

soba ['-] *by ; close-by*

tēburu [- - - -] *a table*

shita [-'] *under ; below ; beneath*

nani mo [- - -] *nothing* (followed by negative) (See Lesson 12, Grammar 91.)

soko [- -] *there ; that place*

to [-] *and*

no [-] *a thing ; one*

jibiki [- -'] *a dictionary*

de [-] connective of **desu**, *being ; is (are)...and*

Nippongo [- - - - -] a combination of **Nippon**, *Japan* and **go**, *language.* One often hears **Nihongo** for the same meaning. This is the combination of **Nihon** and **go**.

shimbun [- - - -] *a newspaper*

Eigo [- - -] *the English language*, being the combination of **Ei**, *British* or *English* and **go**

Grammar

"Koko," "Soko," "Asuko," and "Doko"

19. Here is another set of place nouns which have similar relations to those among **kore, sore,** and **are**. **Koko** means *this place*; **soko** means *that place close to the second person*; **asuko** means *that place over there which is away from both parties.* **Doko** means *what place (where)* or *which place.* They are nouns, so that **ni** is used after them to express such adverbs of place as *here, there* and *over there.*

"Desu" and "Arimasu"

20. Since both of these words may be rendered into English by the same *is* or *are*, confusion sometimes arises. **Desu** is a copula and serves to connect the subject and the predicate. It shows the identity of the subject and the predicate linking the subject of a sentence with a predicate noun or an adjective in stating a characteristic or quality of the subject. In the sentence *A is (am,* *are*) B, **desu** is used to denote the idea of an equal sign.

Kore wa bōshi desu.   Kore (*this*) = bōshi (*a hat*)

Anata wa seito desu.   Anata (*you*) = seito (*a student*)

Sore wa shiroi desu.   Sore (*that*) = shiroi (*white*)

21. Arimasu is a verb which means *to exist, lie, be in a place*. Therefore, the sentence beginning with *there is* or *here is* is usually rendered with **arimasu** since it describes the existence of something. **Tsukue wa koko ni arimasu** means that *the desk lies* (or *exists*) *in this place*, hence *the desk is here*. The formula **tsukue** (*desk*) = **koko** (*here*) does not apply in this case. (The exception to this will be dealt with later.)

It is a safe rule to follow that if the verb *to be* (*is, am, are*) in a sentence can be replaced by *exist* or *lie*, **arimasu** should be used.

This is a desk. (equal)   **Kore wa tsukue desu.**

The desk is here. (exist)   **Tsukue wa koko ni arimasu.**

There is a desk here. (exist)   **Koko ni tsukue ga arimasu.**

The above statement holds good only when the subject of a sentence is an inanimate object such as a book, a chair, a box, etc., but does not apply to living creatures such as human beings or animals. This question will be dealt with later.

"Wa" and "Ga"

22. Since **wa** and **ga** are apparently used after the subject of a sentence, the difference between the two is one of the puzzling problems in learning Japanese. The solution, however, is not very difficult, although there are some difficulties in applying the rules, due largely to the difference of viewpoint.

The fundamental difference between the two is in the position of emphasis they lay. **Ga** emphasises the subject of a sentence whereas **wa** emphasises the predicate.

    (a) **Kore wa hon desu.**   (b) **Kore ga hon desu.**

The first is the answer to **Kore wa nan desu ka?** (*What is this?*) or a statement requiring an emphasis on the predicate. In this sentence one is more concerned about whether this is a book or a pencil than whether this or that is a book.

The second sentence is the answer to **Dore ga hon desu ka?** (*Which one is a book?*). In this case the questioner knows what a book is and wants to find out whether this or that is a book. So the answer is naturally **Kore ga hon desu** (*This is* a book).

> **Koko ni tsukue ga arimasu.** *There is a desk here.*

> **Tsukue no ue ni nani ga arimasu ka?** *What is there on the desk?*

23. Negative sentences usually take **wa** because emphasis in such cases naturally falls on the part of the negation.

> **Kore wa mado ja arimasen.** *This is not a window.*

> **Kono kami wa shiroku wa arimasen.** *This paper is not white.*

> **Sono kaban wa anata no desu ka?** *Is that bag yours?*

> **Sore wa watakushi no ja (=dewa) arimasen.** *That is not mine.*

24. **Atsui no wa jibiki de, usui no wa Nippongo no hon desu.**

> *The thick one is a dictionary and the thin one is a Japanese book.*

This sentence consists of two parts joined together by **de**. (See Grammar 30.) It contains a contrast of two things. In such a case the particle used is usually **wa**.

"Ni" denoting a Place of Existence

25. The existence of an inanimate object is expressed by **arimasu**. The place of existence is accompanied by the particle **ni**.

Koko ni tsukue ga arimasu.	*Here is a desk.*
Doko ni arimasu ka?	*Where is it?*
Asuko ni arimasu.	*It is over there.*

"Nani" and "Nan"

26. They are the same word meaning *what*. **Nan** is the euphonic change of **nani** when it comes before a word that begins with **t**, **d**, or **n**.

Kore wa nan desu ka?	*What is this?*
Asuko ni nani ga arimasuka?	*What is over there?*
Hako no naka ni nani ga arimasu ka?	*What's in the box?*

"Ue," "Shita," "Naka," "Soba," etc.

27. Relative positions are expressed by such words as **ue**, **shita**, **naka**, **soba**, etc., followed usually by **ni** in the construction pattern [Noun] x **no** x [**ue, shita, naka,** etc.] x **ni**.

$$\text{Empitsu wa hako } \underline{\text{no}} \left\{ \begin{array}{l} \text{ue} \\ \text{shita} \\ \text{naka} \\ \text{soba} \end{array} \right\} \underline{\text{ni}} \text{ arimasu.}$$

Ue, **shita**, **naka**, **soba** are nouns meaning *top*, *underneath*, *inside*, *vicinity* respectively. Therefore, they follow the above construction pattern something like the English *on top of.*

Position of Numerals

28. In English modifying numerals precede nouns such as *two apples*, *three windows*, etc., but in Japanese numerals come after nouns.

> **Ringo ga hitotsu arimasu.**   *There is an apple.*
>
> **Mado ga tō arimasu.**   *There are ten windows.*
>
> **Doa wa futatsu arimasu.**   *There are two doors.*

Special attention must be paid to the fact that no particles are used after numerals.

"No" meaning "One"

29. **No** roughly corresponds to the English word *one* or *ones* and is used to substitute for nouns in order to avoid their repetition.

> **Shiroi no wa watakushi no desu.**   *The white one is mine.*

"De"—a Connective of Two Sentences

30. In combining the two sentences **Atsui no wa jibiki desu** and **Usui no wa Nippongo no hon desu**, the **desu** of the first sentence is replaced by **de** which roughly corresponds to *being* or *is...and.*

> **Kore wa anata no de, are wa watakushi no desu.**
>
>   *This being yours, that is mine.* or *This is yours and that is mine.*

Countries, People, and Languages

31. People and languages are expressed with the suffixes **jin**, *person* and **go**, *language*, put after the name of a country.

Country		People		Language	
Chōsen	*Korea*	**Chōsenjin**	*Korean*	**Chōsengo**	*Korean*

Chūgoku	China	Chūgokujin	Chinese	Chūgokugo	Chinese
Roshia	Russia	Roshiajin	Russian	Roshiago	Russian
Furansu	France	Furansujin	Frenchman	Furansugo	French

Mijikai Kaiwa

o [-] a particle indicatitg a direct object (See Lesson 6, Grammar 41.)
kudasai [- - - -] *Please give me.* (when used after a direct object)
agemashō [- - - - -] *I'll give you.*

These two will be dealt with later in more detail.

Exercises

A. *Look at the picture on page 24 and answer the following questions.*
1. Kono heya ni nani ga arimasu ka?
2. Doa wa ikutsu arimasu ka?
3. Mado mo hitotsu arimasu ka?
4. Ringo wa ikutsu arimasu ka?
5. Ringo wa doko ni arimasu ka?
6. Hon wa doko ni arimasu ka?
7. Kago no naka ni nani ga arimasu ka?
8. Tsukue no shita ni nani ga arimasu ka?
9. Isu wa tsukue no soba ni arimasu ka?
10. Shimbun wa tēburu no shita ni arimasu ka?

B. *Here are sentences with blanks in each of them.   These blanks should
be filled with appropriate particles.   Pick up the proper one from among*
ga, ni, no, to, wa *and* **mo.**
1. Soko ___ tēburu ___ arimasu.
2. Tēburu ___ ue ___ nani ___ arimasu ka?
3. Shimbun ___ jibiki ___ arimasu.
4. Tēburu ___ soba ___ isu ___ arimasu.
5. Isu ___ shita ___ nani ___ arimasen.
6. Kago ___ doko ___ arimasu ka?
7. Yuka ___ ue ___ arimasu.
8. Kago ___ naka ___ ringo ___ tō arimasu.

C. *Make a complete sentence by arranging properly the words in each of the following groups.*

1. arimasen no nani mo hako ni naka
2. ga mado kono ni arimasu heya ikutsu ka
3. wa arimasu no anata bōshi ni doko ka
4. no hon jibiki kaban ni naka to arimasu ga
5. kutsu no desu ano wa donata ka

D. *Give the Japanese equivalent of each of the following sentences.*

1. What is there in that large box ?
2. There are dress shirts in it.
3. Are they yours or Mr. Kubota's ?
4. They are not mine. They are my friend's.
5. Where are her scissors ?
6. They are under the red book.
7. How many chairs are there in this room ?
8. There are six.
9. There isn't anything on the floor.
10. Where is my blue dictionary ?
11. It is under the newspaper.
12. There are two small baskets under the table.

E. *What would you say when,*

1. you are going to retire for the night ?
2. you want to say that it is so ?
3. you meet someone on an awful day ?
4. you meet someone when it is cold ?
5. you want to get one (apple, etc.) ?

Go

(Main Text)

A : Koko ni dai ga arimasu. Donna iro desu ka ?

B : Chairo desu.

A : Kono dai wa marui desu ka ?

B : Iie, maruku wa arimasen. Shikaku desu.

A : Dai no ue ni kabin ga arimasu. Marui rippa
na kabin desu.

Kono kabin mo chairo desu ka ?

B : Iie, chairo ja arimasen. Aoi desu.

A : Kabin no naka ni kirei na hana ga arimasu.

Minna onaji iro no hana desu ka ?

B : Iie, iroiro no iro no hana desu.

Akai hana ya kiiroi hana ya murasaki no hana
ga arimasu.

Shiroi no ya momoiro no mo arimasu.

A : Kusa ya ki no ha wa donna iro desu ka ?

B : Midoriiro desu.

A : "Gray" wa Nippongo de nan to iimasu ka ?

B : "Nezumiiro" to iimasu.

(A Short Conversation)

A : Jōzu desu nē.

B : Iie, heta desu. Kore de ii desu ka ?

A : Sore wa machigai desu.

B : Naoshite kudasai.

A : Shōchi shimashita.

(For Memorizing)

1. Donna [iro] desu ka ?

2. [Chairo] desu.

1. What [color] is it ?

2. It's [brown].

3.	Marui rippa na [kabin] desu.	3.	It's a round, splendid [vase].
4.	[Akai] hana ya [murasaki no] hana ga arimasu.	4.	There are [red] flowers and [purple] flowers.
5.	[Shiroi] no ya [momoiro] no mo arimasu.	5.	There are [white] ones and [pink] ones, too.
6.	["Gray"] wa Nippongo de nan to iimasu ka?	6.	What do we call ["gray"] in Japanese?
7.	["Nezumiiro"] to iimasu.	7.	We call it ["nezumiiro"].

Go — Lesson 5

Hombun

Glossary

dai ['-] *a stand*

donna ['- -] *what sort of; what* (adjectival) (See Grammar 32.)

ıro [-'] *color*

chairo [- - -] (*a–D*) *brown*. This is made up of **cha**, *tea* and **iro**, *color*.

marui [- - -] (*a–A*) *round*

shikaku [- - -] (*a–B, D*)* *square*. This is composed of **shi**, *four* and **kaku**, *angle* or *corner*. It is a noun, but it has been used in an adjectival sense so much that it is fast developing into a true adjective, **shikakui**.

kabin [- - -] *a flower vase*

rippa [- - -] (*a–B*) *fine; splendid* (See Grammar 33.)

kirei ['- -] (*a–B*) *pretty; clean* (See Grammar 33.)

hana [-'] *a flower; blossom*

minna [- - -] *all; altogether*

onaji [- - -] *same*. Sometimes it is prolonged as **onnaji**.

iroiro [- - - -] *variety*

ya [-] *and* (See Grammar 36.)

kiiroi [- - - -] (*a–A*) *yellow*

murasaki [-'- -] (*a–D*) *purple*

momoiro [- - - -] (*a–D*) *pink*. This is made up of **momo**, *a peach* and

---

* (*a–B*) is used for quasi-adjectives and (*a–D*) for nouns used for modifying nouns with **no**.

iro, *color.*

kusa [-'] *grass*, *herb*, pronounced as [k'sa]

ki [-] *a tree; plant*

ha [-] *a leaf; blade; foliage*

midoriiro [- - - - -] *(a-D) green*

de [-] a particle denoting an instrument or language used. (See Grammar 37.)

to [-] a particle corresponding to quotation marks in direct discourse. (See Grammar 38.)

iimasu [- - - -] *from* **iu**, *to say; call*

nezumiiro [- - - - -] *gray.* This is made up of **nezumi**, *rat* and **iro**, *color.*

Grammar

"Donna" and "Nan no"

32.   **Donna iro desu ka?** } *What color is it?*
      Nan no iro desu ka? }

Since both **donna** and **nan no** may be rendered into English with *what*, confusion may arise. **Donna** asks for a description of a thing while **nan no** refers to the identity of a thing in question.

Donna iro means *what (sort of) color*, asking whether it is red, blue or any other color while **nan no iro** asks if it is the color of the wall, sky, or any other thing.

        donna hon   *what sort of book*
        donna hako   *what sort of box*
        nan no hon   *what book* (on what subject)
        nan no hako   *what box* (the purpose or the use)

Quasi-Adjectives

33. In addition to true adjectives there are other words which may be used as adjectives. They are called *quasi-adjectives*.

Qusai-adjectives are practically the same as abstract nouns except that they are never used as subjects of sentences. When modifying nouns they take **na** after them, but when used predicatively nothing is added.

Kore wa rippa na kabin desu. *This is a splendid flower vase.*

Kabin no naka ni kirei na hana ga arimasu.

There are pretty flowers in the vase.

Kono e wa kirei desu. *This picture is beautiful.*

[Noun] x " no " Construction as Modifiers

34. In addition to the quasi-adjectives which take **na** when coming before a noun, there is another group which takes **no**. Generally speaking, the quasi-adjectives (which take **na**) are from abstract nouns and the modifiers with **no** are from concrete nouns.

chairo no	*brown* (**chairo**, *tea color* and **no**, *of*)
shikaku no	*square* (**shikaku**, *four angles* and **no**, *of*)
iroiro no	*various* (**iroiro**, *variety* and **no**, *of*)

Some nouns may take either **na** or **no**. **Na** seems to give a strong feeling of the word being a full-fledged adjective while **no** shows that it is a modifier formed by the [noun] x **no** construction.

35. **Shikaku** is an example of transition from a noun into an adjective. **Shikaku no** is orthodox, but we hear **shikaku na** just as frequently, and further, **shikakui** in the conversation of women and the younger generation. Similarly, **chairoi** as a true adjective is also used.

the Particle " Ya "

36. This is similar in use and meaning to **to**, but the difference lies in the fact that when two or more nouns are connected by **ya**, the speaker implies he has mentioned only a few out of the complete series. Like the **to** in the sense of *and*, **ya** is used only between nouns, but not between verbs or clauses. When more than two nouns are given, **ya** is used after each noun except the last.

> **kore ya sore ya are**   *this, that, that over there and others*
>
> **akai no ya, aoi no ya, kiiroi no**
>
> *red ones, blue ones, yellow ones and others*

"De "—a Particle denoting a Language Used

37. In Japanese **de** is used to express the idea suggested by *in, with* or *by* in English. This is a variety of **de** denoting a means or instrument which will be explained in Lesson 6, Grammar 40.

"To" in Direct Discourse

38.   **"Gray" wa Nippongo de nan to iimasu ka?**
        What do we call "gray" in Japanese?
       "Nezumiiro" to iimasu.   *We call it "nezumiiro".*

To more or less corresponds to quotation marks in direct discourse in which a quoted part is given as it is actually said or written.

Mijikai Kaiwa

jōzu [– – –] (a–B) *good at; skilful*

heta [–′] (a–B) *unskilful; poor*

kore de ii literally means *It is good with this; this is sufficient.*

machigai [– – – –] *a mistake.* This comes from a verb **machigau**, *to make a mistake.*

naoshite [–′– –] from **naosu**, *to correct a mistake* or *to repair something which is broken or out of order*

shōchi shimashita means *all right; O. K.* This is the polite past of **shōchi suru**, *to consent; agree.*

Exercises

A. Read aloud the following sentences. Then turn them into the negative. Be sure you understand the meaning.

1. Kono hana wa momoiro desu.
2. Watakushi no nekutai wa kiiroi desu.
3. Dai no ue ni kabin ga arimasu.
4. Anata no zubon wa nezumiiro desu.
5. Ano chairo no empitsu wa ano kata no desu.

B. *Fill in each blank with an appropriate word.*

1. Murasaki _____ hana mo arimasu ka ?
2. Anata no wa rippa _____ gaitō desu nē.
3. Hako no naka _____ iroiro _____ iro no empitsu ga arimasu.
4. Kono heya _____ tsukue _____ isu ga arimasu.
5. "Midoriiro" wa Eigo _____ nan _____ iimasu ka ?

C. *What is the Japanese equivalent of each of the following sentences?*

1. What is on that round table ?
2. There is a pretty vase on it.
3. Are there flowers of various colors in it ?
4. No, all of them are of the same color.
5. There are thin green books on this desk.
6. There are brown ones, pink ones, and purple ones.
7. What color are the leaves of this tree ?
8. They are yellow.
9. What is the Japanese word for " grass " ?
10. It is " kusa ". (We call it " kusa ".)
11. Give me that thick dictionary.
12. Shall I give you some paper, too ?

Roku

(Main Text)

A : Kao niwa me ya hana ga arimasu. Kuchi ya mimi mo arimasu.

Watakushitachi wa me de mimasu. Hon ya zasshi o yomimasu.

Kuchi de gohan ya iroiro no mono o tabemasu. Mizu ya ocha ya kōhii mo nomimasu.

Sono hoka kuchi de nani o shimasu ka ?

B : Kuchi de hanashimasu.

A : Watakushitachi wa mimi ya hana de nani o shimasu ka ?

B : Mimi de oto o kikimasu. Hana de nioi o kagimasu.

A : Te ya ashi de nani o shimasu ka ?

B : Te de iroiro no mono o torimasu. Ashi de arukimasu.

A : Inu ya neko nimo ashi wa arimasu. Keredomo te wa arimasen.

Sakana niwa te mo ashi mo arimasen.

(A Short Conversation)

A : Oyu ga arimasu ka ?

B : Hai, arimasu. Takusan irimasu ka ?

A : Sukoshi kudasai.

(For Memorizing)

1. Watakushitachi wa [me] de [mimasu].
1. We [see] with our [eyes].

2. [Te] ya [ashi] de nani o shimasu ka ?
2. What do you do with your [hands] and [feet] ?

3. Te de iroiro no mono o torimasu.
3. We take various things with our hands.

4. Ashi de arukimasu.
4. We walk with our legs and feet.

5. Inu ya neko nimo [ashi] wa arimasu.
5. Dogs and cats also have [paws].

6. Keredomo te wa arimasen.
6. But they have no hands.

7. Sakana niwa te mo ashi mo arimasen.
7. Fish have neither hands nor feet.

Roku — Lesson 6

Hombun

Glossary

kao [--] *a face*
niwa [--] *on; in* (See Grammar 39.)

me ['] *an eye*

hana [--] *a nose*

kuchi [--] *a mouth*

mimi [-'] *an ear*

watakushitachi [------] *we*

-tachi [--] a plural suffix for persons

de [-] *with* (See Grammar 40.)

mimasu [-'-] *see*

zasshi [---] *a magazine*

yomimasu [--'-] *read*

gohan ['--] *cooked rice ; meal*

mono [-'] *a thing* (concrete)

tabemasu [--'-] *eat*

mizu [--] *water* (cold). Hot water is **(o)yu.**

ocha [--] **o,** honorific and **cha,** *tea*

kōhii [----] *coffee*

nomimasu [--'-] *drink*

sono hoka [----] *besides*

shimasu [-'-] *do*

hanashimasu [---'-] *speak*

oto [-'] *a sound ; noise*

kikimasu [--'-] *hear ; listen*

nioi [-'-] *smell ; odor ; scent*

kagimasu [--'-] *smell*

te ['] *a hand*

ashi [-'] *a foot ; leg.* **Ashi** means the whole leg and foot, so whether
legs or feet or both are to be used in translating depends on circumstances.

torimasu [--'-] *take up*

arukimasu [---'-] *walk*

inu [-'] *a dog*

neko ['-] *a cat*

nimo ['-] combination of the particles **ni** and **mo** (See Grammar 45.)

keredomo ['---] *but ; however*

sakana [---] *a fish*

Grammar

"Niwa"

39.   **Kao niwa me ya hana ga arimasu.**

We have eyes and a nose on our face.

This **niwa** is the combination of **ni** (See Lesson 4, Grammar 25.), and **wa** (See Lesson 1, Grammar 4.).

"De"— a Particle denoting Means or Instrument

40. Most commonly **de** denotes means or instrument. In translating it, *with* or *by* may be used.

> **Anata wa me de nani o shimasu ka?**
>
> *What do you do with (your) eyes?*
>
> **Me de mimasu.**   *I see with (my) eyes.*

"O"— an Objective Particle

41. O chiefly serves to denote the direct object. It is generally safe to consider that the noun preceding **o** except when it is followed by a verb of motion is in the objective case.

> **Te de nani o shimasu ka?** *What do you do with (your) hands?*
>
> **Iroiro no mono o torimasu.** *I take various things.*

Regular Verbs

42. In Japanese, as in almost all languages, there are regular and irregular verbs. Irregular verbs in Japanese are very few in number — only two basic verbs in all. All the rest of the verbs are regular with the exception of a few which are slightly irregular in some respects.

The Japanese regular verbs are of two kinds — **Yodan** verbs and **Ichidan** verbs.

The **Yodan** verbs, literally *four-row verbs*, are so called because they have four different bases of conjugation. They are sometimes called strong verbs or consonant verbs.

The **Ichidan** verbs, literally *one-row verbs*, are so called because they have been thought, though erroneously, to have only one base of conjugation. They are sometimes called weak verbs or vowel verbs.

— *43* —

The names of **Yodan** and **Ichidan** were fairly appropriate when dealing with the classical grammar as well as the written grammar of spoken Japanese according to the classical spelling. However, this nomenclature does not apply when dealing with the grammar of spoken Japanese in Roman letters spelled according to the present-day pronunciation. Since there is no particular harm in using these terms as long as one is aware of the above warning, we shall continue to use these terms.

The forms of verbs appearing in dictionaries are their conclusive (the 3rd) bases which always end in **u**. The dictionary forms of **Yodan** verbs end in **ku**, **su**, **tsu**, **nu**, **mu**, **ru**, **bu**, **gu**, and **u**, but all **Ichidan** verbs end in either **iru** or **eru**.

43. If a verb you have looked up in a dictionary does not end in either **iru** or **eru**, you may take it for granted that it is a **Yodan** verb. The exceptions to this rule are the two irregular verbs which will be dealt with later and the following **Yodan** verbs that end in **iru** or **eru**. (All the following verbs will come out later in the text-book except **kiru**.)

hairu	*to enter ; go in*	**iru**	*to need ; require*
kaeru	*to return ; go back*	**kiru** (′-)	*to cut*
mairu	*to come ; go* (humble)	**shiru**	*to know*

There are more **Yodan** verbs of this category, but since they are not very common let it suffice for the present.

The Present Tense

44. The present tense of Japanese verbs in the ordinary polite speech ends in **masu** as:

yomi-masu	(*I*) *read*		**kiki-masu**	(*I*) *hear*
hanashi-masu	(*I*) *speak*		**mi-masu**	(*I*) *see*
aruki-masu	(*I*) *walk*		**tabe-masu**	(*I*) *eat*
tori-masu	(*I*) *take*		**shi-masu**	(*I*) *do*
ari-masu	(*It*) *exists ; there is*			

Actually they are the combinations of verbs and an auxiliary **masu** which makes the sentence polite. (Remember we have been studying the polite speech. Plain or non-polite speech will be dealt with later.)

In English, the present tense serves to express (1) an act which is taking place now or (2) a habitual action or (3) a general truth. For instance:

I read. (present action)

I speak English. (habitual action)

He comes here every day. (habitual action)

A fish has no feet. (general truth)

The earth is round. (general truth)

This is also true of Japanese.

"Nimo"

45.   **Inu ya neko nimo ashi wa arimasu.**

Dogs and cats also have legs and paws.

In Grammar 14, Lesson 2 we have learned that **mo** can be used instead of **wa** and adds the meaning of *also*. The same can be said in the case of **niwa** and **nimo**.

"Mo .... Mo"

46. These are correlative and express the following ideas:

(1)   Affirmative sentences

Anata mo watakushi mo seito desu.

Both you and I are students.

(2)   Negative sentences

Sakana niwa te mo ashi mo arimasen.

A fish has neither hands nor feet.

Mijikai Kaiwa

oyu [- -]   **o**, honorific and **yu**, *hot water*

takusan [- - - -] *plentiful; sufficient; much; many* (See Lesson 16, Grammar 130.)

irimasu [- -'-] *is needed; necessary*. Unlike the English verb *to need*, this is an intransitive verb and cannot take an object. Therefore it is more like *is needed* or *is necessary* and comes after **wa** or **ga** instead of **o**.

sukoshi [-'-] *a little bit; slightly*

Exercises

A. Read the following questions and give your answers.

1. Kao niwa nani ga arimasu ka ?
2. Me de mimasu ka ?
3. Kuchi de oto o kikimasu ka ?
4. Dewa kuchi de nani o shimasu ka ?
5. Nan de nioi o kagimasu ka ?
6. Te de arukimasu ka, iroiro no mono o torimasu ka ?
7. Dewa nan de arukimasu ka ?
8. Inu ya neko niwa te ya ashi ga arimasu ka ?
9. Sakana nimo te ya ashi ga arimasu ka ?
10. Anata wa kyō kōhii o nomimasu ka ?

B. *Fill in each blank with an appropriate particle.*
1. Te ____ iroiro ____ mono ____ torimasu.
2. Sakana niwa te ____ ashi ____ arimasen.
3. Inu ya neko ____ te ____ arimasen. Keredomo ashi ____ arimasu.
4. Kuchi de mizu ____ ocha ____ nomimasu.
5. Watakushitachi ____ me de hon ____ zasshi ____ yomimasu.

C. *Make questions for the following answers.*
1. Mimi de kikimasu.
2. Kono hana wa akai desu.
3. Sakana niwa te mo ashi mo arimasen.
4. Iie, sore wa watakushi no ja arimasen.
5. Watakushi no kaban wa tsukue no shita ni arimasu.
6. Hai, (watakushi no uwagi wa) aoi desu.
7. (Ringo wa) mittsu arimasu.
8. (Ringo o) futatsu kudasai.
9. " Momoiro " to iimasu.
10. Watakushi koso.

D. *What is the Japanese equivalent of each of the following sentences?*
1. Where are my socks ?
2. They are under the white coat.
3. What do you do with this pen ?
4. I correct mistakes with it.
5. What do you eat with ?

6. We eat with chopsticks (=*hashi*).
7. There is neither a book nor a magazine on the table.
8. We drink various things with our mouths.
9. Besides, we speak with our mouths.
10. Your English newspaper is over there.
11. Are there any mistakes?
12. No, there isn't any.

E. *What would you say when,*
   1. you want someone to speak more clearly?
   2. you want to ask someone how many there are?
   3. someone thanks you?
   4. you want to ask if it is good?
   5. you want to ask your teacher to correct your mistakes?

Shichi

(Main Text)

A · Watakushi wa ima Nippongo o hanashite imasu.

Anata wa Nippongo o kiite imasu.

Watakushi wa anata ni Nippongo o oshiete imasu ga, anata wa Nippongo o naratte imasu.

Nippongo ga yoku wakarimasu ka ?

B : Iie, mada yoku wakarimasen.

A : Nippongo wa muzukashii desu ka ?

B : Iie, muzukashiku wa arimasen. Keredomo yasashiku mo arimasen.

A : Kono e o goran nasai.

Migi no hō no hito wa hataraite imasu ga, mannaka no hito wa yasunde imasu.

Kono hito wa tatte imasu ka ?

B : Iie, benchi ni koshikakete imasu.

A : Hidari no michi o otokonohito to onnano-hito ga aruite imasu.

Kono hitotachi wa kodomo o tsurete sampo shite imasu.

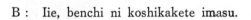

Otokonohito wa yōfuku o kite bōshi o kabutte imasu.

Onnanohito wa kimono o kite imasu.

Zōri o haite iru rashii desu, keredomo yoku wakarimasen.

Ki no ue o tori ga tonde imasu.

Hikōki mo sora o tonde imasu.

(A Short Conversation)

A : Gomen nasai.

B : Donata desu ka ?

A : Yamada desu.

B : Ohairi nasai.

— 50 —

1. Watakushi wa ima [Nippongo] o [hanashite] imasu.	1. I'm [speaking] [Japanese] now.
2. Anata ni [Nippongo] o oshiete imasu.	2. I'm teaching you [Japanese].
3. [Migi] no hō no [hito] wa [hataraite] imasu.	3. The [man] on the [right] is [working].
4. [Benchi] ni koshikakete imasu.	4. He is sitting on a [bench].
5. [Otokonohito] ga michi o aruite imasu.	5. A [man] is walking along the road.
6. Kono hitotachi wa [kodomo] o tsurete sampo shite imasu.	6. These people are taking a walk with their [child].

Shichi — Lesson 7

Hombun

Glossary

ima ['-] *now*

hanashite imasu [-'-----] *am (is, are) speaking*, **imasu** from **iru**, *to be* (See Grammar 49.)

kiite [---] *hearing*, from **kiku**, *to hear*

ni [-] a particle indicating an indirect object (See Grammar 50.)

oshiete [----] *teaching*, from **oshieru**, *to teach*. This word covers all situations from giving lessons to telling or informing. When a passer-by asks you the way, this word may be used.

ga [-] *but* (See Grammar 51.)

naratte [-'--] *learning*, from **narau**, *to learn*

yoku ['-] *well*, the adverbial form of **yoi** (ii), *good*

wakarimasu [-----] *understand* (See Grammar 52.)

mada ['-] *(not)...yet ; still*

muzukashii [-----] *(a-A) difficult, hard*, sometimes pronounced as [mutsukashii].

yasashii [----] (*a-A*) *easy*

e ['] *a picture . painting*

migi [-'] *right ; right-hand side*

hō ['-] *a side ; direction*

hito [-'] *a person ; human being*

hataraite [-----] *working*, from **hataraku**, *to work*

mannaka [----] *middle ; exact center*

yasunde [-'--] *resting*, from **yasumu**, *to rest*

tatte ['--] *standing*, from **tatsu**, *to stand*

benchi ['--] *a bench*

koshikakete [--'--] *sitting*, from **koshikakeru**, *to sit*

hidari [---] *left ; left-hand side*

michi [--] *a road ; way*

otokonohito [------] *a man ; male person*. **Otoko** means *male sex* and the word means literally *a person of male sex*.

onnanohito [------] *a woman ; female person*. **Onna** means *female sex* and the word means literally *a person of female sex*.

aruite [-'--] *walking*, from **aruku**, *to walk*

kodomo [---] *a child*

tsurete [---] *taking along*, from **tsureru**, *to take along*

sampo shite [-----] *taking a walk*, from **sampo suru**, *to take a walk*

yōfuku [----] *a western-style suit*

kite [--] *wearing ; putting on*, from **kiru**, *to wear ; put on*

kabutte [-'--] *wearing* (on a head), from **kaburu**, *to wear* (on a head)

kimono [---] *a kimono*

zōri [---] *Japanese sandals*

haite [---] *wearing* (a footgear), from **haku**, *to wear shoes, socks, trousers*, etc.

iru [--] the dictionary form of **imasu**, *to be*

rashii [-'-] *seem ; appear*. Details of this word will be dealt with in Lesson 16, Grammar 130.

tori [--] *a bird*

tonde [---] *flying*, from **tobu**, *to fly*

hikōki [-'--] *an airplane*

sora ['-] *sky*

Grammar

Te-form (Also Called the Gerund)

47. The form of a verb ending in **-te** or **-de** such as **kiite, totte, yonde,** etc. is sometimes called the gerund, as *-ing* (e.g., *going*) is in English. But since the functions of the gerunds in Japanese and English are so different, the term is misleading. English gerunds are noun substitutes, such as in *Seeing is believing.*

But Japanese gerunds are never used for such a purpose. Therefore, we shall call this the **te**-form in the future, since this form always ends in **-te,** or its euphonic changes **-tte** or **-de**.

Originally, this **te** was attached to the second base, e.g., **kiki-te.** This is still the case in the written language, and the conjugation is regular. However, in time euphonic changes took place and in spoken Japanese the formation appears irregular.

One very important thing to remember is that the irregular **te**-forms appear only in the case of **Yodan** verbs.

The following table should be carefully studied since the formation of the **te**-form of any **Yodan** verb is possible by analogy.

Dictionary Form (Conclusive Base)	2nd Base (Continuative)	Te-form
kaku* (*to write*)	**kaki**-masu	**kaite**
hanasu (to speak)	**hanashi**-masu	**hanashite**
motsu* (*to hold*)	**mochi**-masu	**motte**
shinu* (*to die*)	**shini**-masu	**shinde**
yomu (to read)	**yomi**-masu	**yonde**
toru (*to take*)	**tori**-masu	**totte**
kau* (*to buy*)	**kai**-*masu*	**katte**
nugu* (*to undress*)	**nugi**-masu	**nuide**
tobu (*to fly*)	**tobi**-masu	**tonde**

You may find the **te**-form of any **Yodan** verb by looking at the last syllable of its dictionary form. Take, for instance, such **Yodan** verbs as **hataraku** (*to work*) and **yasumu** (*to rest*). The **te**-form of **hataraku** is **hataraite** by analogy of **kaite** in the above table, and that of **yasumu** is **yasunde** by

---

* These words have not appeared in the text yet.

analogy of **yonde**.

Thus, it is not very difficult to find the **te**-form from the dictionary form, but to trace the dictionary form from its **te**-from is not easy,　since the same **te**-form may come from two or three different sources.

The **te**-form of **yobu*** (*to call*) and **yomu** (*to read*) are the same **yonde**, and those of **katsu*** (*to win*), **karu*** (*to reap*) and **kau*** (*to buy*) are all **katte**.　In actual speech, however, the difference in tone helps in distinguishing the meaning, and no serious difficulty is felt.

The only exception to the above rule is the **te**-form of **iku*** (*to go*), which is **itte** instead of **iite**.　For this reason **iku** is listed by some grammarians as an irregular verb.

The Te-form of "Ichidan" and Irregular Verbs

48. The **te**-form of **Ichidan** verbs is regular and simple.　It is merely to add **te** to the second base, that is, the final **ru** of its dictionary form replaced by **te**, e. g., **tabete** from **tabe-ru**, **akete** from **ake-ru**,* **mite** from **mi-ru**, **karite** from **kari-ru*** (*to borrow*), etc.

The **te**-forms of the **Irregular** verbs which are basically only two in number — **kuru** and **suru** — are **kite** and **shite** respectively.

Perhaps the simplest rule to remember is that the **te**-forms of both **Ichidan** and **Irregular** verbs are formed by replacing **masu** of the present tense by **te**, e. g., **ki-te** from **ki-masu**.

Nani o shimasu ka?	*What do you do?*
Nani o shite imasu ka?	*What are you doing?*
Hon o yomimasu.	*I read the book.*
Hon o yonde kudasai.	*Please read the book.*

Te-form followed by "Iru"

49. When **imasu** is used by itself as a principal verb it means that a self-propelling body exists in a particular place.　(See Lesson 12, Grammar 92.) But when **imasu** is used after the **te**-form of a principal verb, it is used more or less like a helping verb and denotes an action in progress or a state of being. In this meaning it can be used for both living beings and inanimate objects, but because of the fact that inanimate objects are seldom involved in a progressive

---

* These words have not appeared in the text yet.

— 54 —

action they are less frequently used in this connection.

Watakushi wa tatte imasu. *I am standing.* (state)

Nippongo o hanashite imasu. *I am speaking Japanese.* (progressive)

Indirect Object

50. In the previous lesson we noted that a direct object is shown by the particle **o**. Likewise an indirect object is expressed by the use of **ni**.

Watakushi wa anata ni Nippongo o oshiete imasu.

I'm teaching you Japanese.

As you see in the above example, it is usual to follow the order of [indirect object] x **ni** x [direct object] x **o** x [verb], although it is possible to place a direct object before an indirect object.

"Ga" at the End of a Clause

51. When **ga** connects two or more clauses, it generally means *but*. Sometimes this meaning is very vague and may be better rendered into English with *and*.

Murasaki no wa arimasen ga, momoiro no ga arimasu.

There are no purple ones, but there are pink ones.

Kore wa isu desu ga, sore wa tsukue desu.

This is a chair, whereas that is a desk.

Transitive and Intransitive Verbs

52. It is needless to explain to an English-speaking person that there are transitive and intransitive verbs in English and that transitive verbs take an object. In Japanese also there is this distinction, and Japanese transitive verbs take the objective particle **o** as explained above.

This much is very easy to understand. There is, however, one difficulty which baffles an English-speaking beginner. It is the difference in the nature of Japanese and English verbs.

In English the verb *to understand* is a transitive verb whereas the Japanese verb **wakaru** is an intransitive verb. There is no corresponding English intransitive verb. The English adjective *comprehensible* or *understandable* or *clear* is more like it, but they are not verbs. Remember that the verb **wakaru** is intransitive and should follow the particle **ga** or **wa** instead of **o**.

Nippongo ga wakarimasu. *I understand Japanese.*

Kore wa wakarimasen. *I do not understand this.*

Adverbs and Adverbial Forms of Adjectives

53.   **Watakushi wa ima Nippongo o hanashite imasu.**

I'm speaking Japanese now.

Watakushi wa Nippongo ga mada wakarimasen.

I don't understand Japanese yet.

Besides these genuine adverbs, the adverbial form of true adjectives may be used as modifiers. It is formed by changing the final **i** of a true adjective into **ku**.

Dictionary Form		Adverbial Form	
yoi	*good*	**yoku**	*well*
yasashii	*easy*	**yasashiku**	*easily*

Yoku wakarimasen.

I don't understand it well.

"Wa" after the Adverbial Form

54. In Lesson 2 we had the negative form of true adjectives as being **-ku wa arimasen** — such as **akaku wa arimasen, ōkiku wa arimasen**, etc. These **akaku** and **ōkiku** are none other than the adverbial form of the true adjectives **akai** and **ōkii**.

In Lesson 4 we studied that negative sentences usually take **wa** because the emphasis generally falls on the negative word. For the same reason **wa** is often inserted after an adverb or the adverbial form of a true adjective.

Muzukashiku wa arimasen.   *It is not difficult.*

Mada yoku wa wakarimasen.   *I don't understand it well yet.*

It is quite possible to leave out these **wa**'s, but their existence have a bearing on the meaning.

(1)   **Mada yoku wakarimasen.**

(2)   **Mada yoku wa wakarimasen.**

In these two sentences (1) is a straightforward statement to the effect that one does not understand something yet, whereas (2) implies that one understands some, but not quite well yet. Similarly, **Sukoshi wa wakarimasu** means *I can't say I understand all, but I can say that I understand some all right.*

"O" with Places of Motion

55. **Kono michi o hito ga aruite imasu.**

Some people are walking along this road.

Ki no ue o tori ga tonde imasu.

Some birds are flying over the trees.

In the above sentences despite the fact that both the verbs **aruku** (*to walk*) and **tobu** (*to fly*) are intransitive, the particle **o** is used as though the nouns preceding it, i.e. **michi** (*road*) and **ki no ue** (*space over the trees*) were in the objective case.

This is peculiar in Japanese. But the fact remains that a place in which or through which a motion such as *walking, running, flying, swimming, passing, turning,* etc. takes place, is expressed by the use of **o** following it.

Irregular Verb "Suru"

56. (a) **Kuchi de nani o shimasu ka?**

What do you do with (your) mouth?

(b) **Shōchi shimashita.** *I have consented; All right.*

(c) **Yoshida San wa sampo shite imasu.**

Mr. Yoshida is taking a walk.

In sentence (a), **shimasu** is used singly, but in sentences (b) and (c), it is used together with an abstract noun. In fact one of the important functions of the irregular verb **suru** is to convert an abstract noun into its corresponding verb. Thus, the nouns **shōchi** and **sampo** are made into the verbs **shōchi suru,** *to consent* and **sampo suru,** *to take a walk.*

When one wants to use a foreign word — usually a foreign verb — in a Japanese sentence as a verb, this is the form one should use.

If, for instance, one wants to use the word *print* as a verb in Japanese, one may say *print* **suru,** e.g.,

Dōzo *print* **shite kudasai.** *Please print it.*

Copy **shimashō ka?** *Shall I copy it?*

The Conjunctive Use of the Te-form

57. **Kono hitotachi wa kodomo o tsurete sampo shite imasu.**

These people are taking the child along and are taking a walk.

When two or more verbs run together, the verbs except the last take their te-forms.

Okusan wa kimono o kite aruite imasu.

The wife is wearing a kimono and is walking.

Te-form at the End of a Clause

58.　　**Yoshida San wa yōfuku o kite bōshi o kabutte imasu.**

Mr. Yoshida wears a western-style suit and has a hat on.

When a sentence has a compound predicate ending with verbs, all the verbs except the final one end in the **te**-form. This is another case of the conjunctive use of the **te**-form.

Mijikai Kaiwa

gomen [– – –]　*a pardon; excuse*

ohairi [– – – –]　from **hairu**, *to enter*

To express a polite command corresponding to *please do* or *please go*, etc., the construction pattern **o** x [verb] x **nasai** is used. The base of the verb used is the same as the base which **masu** follows. This base is called the second base, or the continuative base, or the indefinite base.

　　　　Ohairi nasai.　　*Please come in.*

　　　　Oyasumi nasai.　　(Lit.) *Please rest;* hence, *Good night.*

　　　　Oaruki nasai.　　*Please walk.*

Exercises

A. Practise converting from one form to the other rapidly and fluently.

Conversion Table 3

Present	Present Progressive	Meaning
kikimasu	kiite imasu	*hear*
hatarakimasu	hataraite imasu	*work*
arukimasu	aruite imasu	*walk*
hanashimasu	hanashite imasu	*speak*
tachimasu	tatte imasu	*stand*
yasumimasu	yasunde imasu	*rest*
torimasu	totte imasu	*take*
koshikakemasu	koshikakete imasu	*sit*
kimasu	kite imasu	*wear*
shimasu	shite imasu	*do*

B. Change the following into the progressive form, noting the difference in the meaning.

> *Example:* Anata wa Nippongo o **oshiemasu**. (*You teach Japanese.*)
>
> Anata wa Nippongo o **oshiete imasu**.
>
> (*You are teaching Japanese.*)

1. Anata wa nani o naraimasu ka ?
2. Watakushi wa Eigo o hanashimasu.
3. Anata wa nani o shimasu ka ?
4. Nani mo shimasen.
5. Ano otokonohito wa shimbun o yomimasu.
6. Watakushi wa tachimasu.

C. Fill in each blank with an appropriate word.

1. Ano kodomo wa yōfuku o ____ imasu ga, bōshi o ____ imasen.
2. Ano hito wa okusan to kodomo o ____ sampo ____ imasu.
3. Kono hitotachi wa michi ____ aruite imasu.
4. Sono kata wa benchi ____ koshikakete yasunde ____.
5. Eigo wa yasashiku wa ____. Keredomo ____ mo arimasen.

D. What is the Japanese equivalent of each of the following sentences?

1. I'm reading a Japanese magazine.
2. Are you teaching Japanese to the Americans ?
3. No, I am not teaching, but learning English.

4. Do you understand German well?
5. No, I don't understand German well yet.
6. Mr. Suzuki is working now.
7. But Mr. Tanaka is sitting on a chair and is resting.
8. A child is walking along the road.
9. The child is wearing a foreign suit and brown shoes, but not a hat.

E. What would you say when,
1. you want to praise your friend's fluency?
2. you want to say you are not fluent yet?
3. you enter your friend's house?
4. you want to know who the man is?
5. you want to tell who you are?

F. Here is a short conversation between Mr. Tanaka and Mr. Brown. They are acquaintances. Take the part of Mr. Brown and express the ideas indicated.

Tanaka: Konnichi wa.
Brown: (*Good afternoon.*)
Tanaka: Ii otenki desu nē.
Brown: (*Yes, it is.*)
Tanaka: Ogenki desu ka?
Brown: (*Yes, thank you.*)
Tanaka: Anata wa Nippongo o naratte imasu ka?
Brown: (*Yes, I am.*)
Tanaka: Ojōzu desu nē.
Brown: (*No, I am poor yet.*)
Tanaka: Nippongo wa muzukashii desu ka?
Brown: (*No, it is not difficult. But it is not easy, either.*)
Tanaka: Anata no sensei wa donata desu ka?
Brown: (*He is Mr. Suzuki. He is a Japanese.*)
Tanaka: Ii sensei desu ka?
Brown: (*Yes, he is a good teacher. I teach him English.*)
Tanaka: Sō desu ka?
Brown: (*Look! Mr. Suzuki is there; he's taking a walk with his children. Excuse me, Mr. Tanaka. See you again tomorrow.*)
Tanaka: Sayōnara.

Hachi

(Main Text)

A : Buraun San, anata wa ima nani o shite imasu ka ?

B : Nippongo o benkyō shite imasu.

A : Dōzo tatte kudasai.

Koko e kite kudasai.

Anata wa doko e kimashita ka ?

B : Koko e kimashita.

A : Sō desu. Dewa, doa no tokoro e itte kudasai.

Doa o akete soto e dete kudasai.

Heya no naka e haitte doa o shimete kudasai.

Watakushi no tsukue no tokoro e kite kudasai.

Tsukue no ue no hon o totte kudasai.

Sono hon o tsukue no ue ni oite kudasai.

Anata wa sakki doko e ikimashita ka ?

B : Doa no tokoro e ikimashita.

A : Anata wa ima doko e kimashita ka ?

B : Anata no tsukue no tokoro e kimashita.

A : Nani o torimashita ka ?

B : Hon o torimashita.

A : Sono hon o doko ni okimashita ka ?

B : Tsukue no ue ni okimashita.

A : Sō desu. Yoku dekimashita.

Dewa, anata no seki e modotte kudasai.

Koshikakete kudasai.

Chōmen o dashite anata no namae o kaite kudasai.

Anata wa ima nani o shimashita ka ?

B : Watakushi no namae o kakimashita.

A : Nani ni kakimashita ka ?

B : Chōmen ni kakimashita.

A : Mannenhitsu de kakimashita ka ?

B : Iie, mannenhitsu de kakimasen deshita.

A : Nani o tsukaimashita ka ?

B : Empitsu o tsukaimashita.

(A Short Conversation)

A : Chotto kite kudasai.

B : Nan desu ka ?

A : Tēburu o katazukete kudasai.

B : Chotto matte kudasai.

A : Mizu o koboshimashita.

Hayaku fuite kudasai.

(For Memorizing)

1.	Dōzo [tatte] kudasai.	1.	Please [stand up].
2.	[Koko] e kite kudasai.	2.	Please come [here].
3.	[Doa] no tokoro e itte kudasai.	3.	Please go to the [door].
4.	Doa o akete soto e dete kudasai.	4.	Please open the door and go out.

5. [Tsukue] no ue no [hon] o totte kudasai.

5. Please take the [book] on the [desk].

6. [Doa] no tokoro e ikimashita.

6. I went to the [door].

7. [Watakushi no] namae o kakimashita.

7. I wrote [my] name.

8. [Empitsu] de [chōmen] ni kakimashita.

8. I wrote it in the [notebook] with a [pencil].

9. [Mannenhitsu] de kakimasen deshita.

9. I didn't write it with a [fountain pen].

Hachi — Lesson 8

Hombun

Glossary

benkyō suru [------] *to study*

e [-] a particle showing direction   (See Grammar 60.)

kite [-'] from **kuru**, *to go ; come*

-mashita [---] the past form of **masu**   (See Grammar 61.)

kimashita [-'--] from **kuru**, *to come ; go*

tokoro [---] *a place*   (See Grammar 62.)

itte [---] from **iku**, *to go*

akete [---] from **akeru**, *to open*

soto ['-] *outside*

dete ['-] from **deru**, *to go out*

haitte ['---] from **hairu**, *to enter*

shimete ['--] from **shimeru**, *to close ; shut*

oite [---] from **oku**, *to put ; place*

sakki ['--] *a few minutes ago*

deki- [--] from **dekiru**, *to be completed ; be able to*

seki ['-] *a seat*

modotte [-'--] from **modoru**, *to go back ; return*

chōmen [--'-] *a notebook*

dashite ['--] from **dasu**, *to take out*
namae [---] *a name*
kaite ['--] from **kaku**, *to write*
mannenhitsu [--'---] *a fountain pen*
deshita [---] the past form of **desu**
tsukai- [---] from **tsukau**, *to use*

Grammar

" -te Kudasai "

59. We have already had the following sentences using **kudasai**.

      Motto yukkuri itte kudasai.   *Speak more slowly, please.*
      Motto hakkiri itte kudasai.   *Speak more clearly, please.*
      Naoshite kudasai.   *Please correct me.*

All these sentences carry the idea of a polite request. It is done by the use of **kudasai** after the **te**-form. **Kudasai** is the imperative form of **kudasaru** which means *to bestow* or *to condescend*. When it comes after the **te**-form, it has a function of a polite request meaning *please do me a favor of ...ing.*

If the word **dōzo** is added at the beginning of a sentence that ends with **kudasai**, it becomes very polite, but even when it is not used, the deferential nature of the word **kudasai** itself makes it advisable to add *please* or *will you* in the English translation.

" E "—a Particle showing Direction

60. The particle which denotes a direction in colloquial Japanese corresponding to the *to*, of *come to*, *go to*, etc., is **e**. Sometimes **ni** is used instead, but it is less common. Strictly speaking, **ni** expresses a point, and **e** direction. Therefore, **Anata no seki ni okaeri nasai** is more exact than **Anata no seki e okaeri nasai**, since the seat is a point of arrival rather than the direction in which one goes. But this distinction has been lost in spoken Japanese and with the exception of a few fastidious grammarians, the distinction is not strictly observed.

The Past Tense

61. The past tense of a verb is expressed by **mashita**, and that of **desu** by **deshita**. The past negative of a verb is expressed by the combination of **masen** and **deshita**.

> **Anata wa sakki doko e ikimashita ka?**
>
> *Where did you go a little while ago?*
>
> **Doko emo ikimasen deshita.**   *I didn't go anywhere.*

"Tokoro"—"the Place"

62.   **Doa no tokoro e itte kudasai.**

This sentence literally means *Please go to the place of the door.* In English one may go to the door or to a person, although one goes to the doctor's (office), the grocer's (shop), etc., but in Japanese one does not go to the door or to a person. Instead one goes to the place where the door is or to the place where someone is. Likewise one comes from the place of the door or from the place where someone is. One can go, however, to a seat, a room, a house, a station, etc., in which one can stay.

> **Tanaka San no tokoro e itte kudasai.** *Please go to Mr. Tanaka's.*
>
> **Mado no tokoro e ikimashita.**   *He went to the window.*
>
> **Anata no heya e modotte kudasai.**   *Go back to your room, please.*

The Present Perfect Tense

63. In English the difference between the present perfect tense and the past tense is marked. There is a distinct difference both in form and in meaning between *He went* and *He has gone*.

In Japanese this distinction is not shown in one definite form, but is expressed in various ways. Sometimes, however, it is rather difficult to distinguish between the two except by context.

The past form of Japanese verbs expresses the past as well as the present perfect tense. Thus, **Hon o akemashita** means *I opened the book*, or *I have opened the book*.

An affirmative sentence such as the above makes little difference whether one translates ι Japanese verb of **mashita** ending with an English verb in the past or the present perfect tense.

But with negative sentences the case is somewhat different. **Hon o ake-masen deshita** usually means *I did not open the book.* The idea of *I have not opened the book* is often expressed by the present negative form, **Hon o akemasen**. The reason for this is that in the case of a negative sentence an action has not yet taken place and therefore no such action is present.

In rendering an English sentence in the present perfect tense into Japanese, it is safe to translate an affirmative sentence with a verb of **mashita** ending, and a negative sentence in the present tense.

I have done (it).	**Shimashita.**
I have not done (it).	**Shimasen.**

Needless to say, **Shimasen** has another meaning of *I don't do (it).* or *I won't do (it).*

"Yoku Dekimashita"

64. Since **dekiru** here means *to be completed,* the sentence literally means *It has been well done (by you).*

Mijikai Kaiwa

chotto ['--] *a short while; slightly*
katazukete [--'--] from **katazukeru**, *to tidy up; straighten up*
matte ['--] from **matsu**, *to wait*
koboshi- [---] from **kobosu**, *to spill; slop*
hayaku ['--] *early; quickly*, from **hayai** (*a-A*), *fast; quick*
fuite [---] from **fuku**, *to wipe*

Exercises

A. *Practise converting from one form to another rapidly and fluently.*

— 68 —

Conversion Table 4

Present	Past	Request	Meaning
tsukaimasu	tsukaimashita	tsukatte kudasai	*use*
kakimasu	kakimashita	kaite kudasai	*write*
dashimasu	dashimashita	dashite kudasai	*take out*
tachimasu	tachimashita	tatte kudasai	*stand up*
tobimasu	tobimashita	tonde kudasai	*fly ; jump*
yasumimasu	yasumimashita	yasunde kudasai	*rest*
hairimasu	hairimashita	haitte kudasai	*enter*
ikimasu	ikimashita	itte kudasai	*go*
akemasu	akemashita	akete kudasai	*open*
mimasu	mimashita	mite kudasai	*see*
benkyō shimasu	benkyō shimashita	benkyō shite kudasai	*study*
kimasu	kimashita	kite kudasai	*come*

B. Turn the following sentences first into the past and then into the polite request.

> *Example :* Hon o **akemasu.**
>
> Past : Hon o **akemashita.**
>
> Polite reguest : Hon o **akete kudasai.**

1. Eigo o benkyō shimasu.
2. Doa no tokoro e ikimasu.
3. Heya no naka e hairimasu.
4. Doa o shimemasu.
5. Watakushi no tokoro e kimasu.
6. Zasshi o tsukue no ue ni okimasu.
7. Anata no seki e modorimasu.
8. Isu ni koshikakemasu.
9. Chōmen ni kakimasu.
10. Hon o yomimasu.

C. Fill in each blank with an appropriate word.

1. Uchi no naka ____ haitte kudasai.
2. Anata wa doko ____ ikimashita ____ ?
3. Watakushi wa mado no ____ e ikimashita.

4. Heya no ____ e hairimashita.
5. Mado ____ tokoro e ____ kudasai.
6. Tsukue no ue ____ hon o totte kudasai.
7. Empitsu ____ dashite anata no namae o ____ kudasai.
8. Anata wa nan ____ namae o kakimashita ka?
9. Anata wa chōmen ____ kakimashita ka?
10. Onamae ____ mannenhitsu ____ kaite kudasai.

D. *What is the Japanese equivalent of each of the following sentences?*
1. Where did you go?
2. I went to the door.
3. Please shut the window.
4. Please go to your seat and sit down.
5. Please come here.
6. Mr. Suzuki has (just) come here.
7. Where did you put your bag?
8. I put it on the table.
9. Please take out your fountain pen and write your name here.
10. I haven't written my name here yet.

Ku

(Main Text)

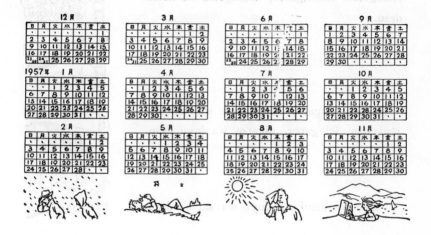

A : Goran nasai. Kore we karendā desu.

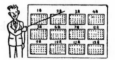

Ichigatsu kara jūnigatsu made arimasu.

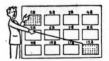

Ichigatsu wa hajime no tsuki de, jūnigatsu wa owari no tsuki desu.

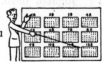

Ichigatsu to nigatsu wa samukute yuki ga furimasu.

Sangatsu, shigatsu, gogatsu wa haru de,
rokugatsu, shichigatsu, hachigatsu wa natsu
desu.

Kugatsu, jūgatsu, jūichigatsu wa aki de,
jūnigatsu, ichigatsu, nigatsu wa fuyu desu.

Natsu wa atsukute, fuyu wa samui desu.

Haru wa attakakute, aki wa suzushii desu.

Kongetsu wa nangatsu desu ka?

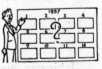

B : Jūgatsu desu.

A : Dewa, raigetsu wa jūichigatsu desu ne.

B : Sō desu.

A : Sengetsu wa nangatsu deshita ka ?

B : Kugatsu deshita.

A : Ichinen niwa nankagetsu arimasu ka ?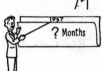

B : Jūnikagetsu arimasu.

A : Dōzo ichi kara jūni made kazoete kudasai.

B : Ichi, ni, san, shi, go, roku, shichi, hachi, ku, jū, jūichi, jūni.

A : Sō desu. Yoku dekimashita.

Dewa, ichi to ni de ikutsu ni narimasu ka ?

B : San ni narimasu.

A : Shi to go to dotchi ga ōkii desu ka ?

B : Go no hō ga ōkii desu.

A : Roku wa shichi yori ōkii desu ka, chiisai desu ka ?

B : Roku wa shichi yori chiisai desu.

A : Hachigatsu to kugatsu to dotchi ga haya-ku kimasu ka ?

B : Hachigatsu no hō ga hayaku kimasu.

A : Jūgatsu wa jūichigatsu yori samui desu ka, attakai desu ka ?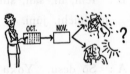

B : Attakai desu.

(A Short Conversation)

A : Shitte imasu ka ?

B : Shirimasen.

A : Oboete imasu ka ?

B : Oboete imasen.

(For Memorizing)

1. Ichigatsu to nigatsu wa samu-kute, yuki ga furimasu.
2. Kongetsu wa nangatsu desu ka ?
3. Raigetsu wa [jūichigatsu] desu ne.
4. Sengetsu wa nangatsu deshita ka ?
5. Dōzo [ichi] kara [jū] made kazoete kudasai.
6. [Shi] to [go] to dotchi ga ōkii desu ka ?
7. [Go] no hō ga ōkii desu.
8. [Jūgatsu] wa [jūichigatsu] yori attakai desu.

1. It's cold in January and February, and snow falls.
2. What month is this month ?
3. Next month is [November], isn't it ?
4. What month was last month ?
5. Please count from [one] to [ten].
6. Which is larger, [four] or [five] ?
7. [Five] is larger.
8. [October] is warmer than November.

Ku — Lesson 9

Hombun

Glossary

karendā [-'---] *a calendar*
ichigatsu [----] *January*
kara [--] *from*
jūnigatsu [-----] *December*

— 75 —

hajime [- - -] *beginning; first*

tsuki [-′] *a month; moon*

owari [- - -] *end; last*

nigatsu [- - -] *February*

samukute [′- - -] from **samui** (*a-A*), *cold*

yuki [-′] *snow*

furi- [- -] from **furu**, *to fall*

sangatsu [′- - -] *March*

shigatsu [- - -] *April*

gogatsu [′- -] *May*

haru [′-] *spring*

rokugatsu [- - - -] *June*

shichigatsu [- - - -] *July*

hachigatsu [- - - -] *August*

natsu [-′] *summer*

kugatsu [′- -] *September*

jūgatsu [- - - -] *October*

jūichigatsu [- - - - - -] *November*

aki [′-] *autumn; fall*

fuyu [-′] *winter*

atsukute- [′- - -] from **atsui** (*a-A*), *hot*

attakakute [- -′- - -] from **attakai** (*a-A*), *warm*

suzushii [- -′-] (*a-A*) *cool* (of weather)

kongetsu [- - - -] *this month*

nangatsu [′- - -] *what month*

raigetsu [′- - -] *next month*

ne [′] a particle used for making sure

sengetsu [′- - -] *last month*

ichinen [-′- -] *one year*

nankagetsu [- -′- -] *how many months*

-kagetsu [′- -] (*so many*) *months*

jūni [- - -] *twelve*

kazoete [-′- -] from **kazoeru**, *to count*

jū [- -] *ten*

jūichi [- - - -] *eleven*

nari- [- -] from **naru**, *to become*
dotchi ['- -] *which ; which one* (of the two)
yori ['-] *than*

Grammar

Two Sets of Numerals

65. We have already had a set of numerals up to ten. There is another set of numerals.

	1st set	2nd set
1	hitotsu	ichi
2	futatsu	ni
3	mittsu	san
4	yottsu	shi or yon
5	itsutsu	go
6	muttsu	roku
7	nanatsu	shichi or nana
8	yattsu	hachi
9	kokonotsu	ku or kyū
10	tō	jū

Above ten the second set of numerals must be used. Eleven is **jūichi** which is the combination of **jū**, *ten* and **ichi**, *one*, and twelve, **jūni** which is made up of **jū**, *ten* and **ni**, *two*. Thirteen, fourteen, etc. are **jūsan**, **jūshi**, etc. up to twenty which is **nijū**, *two tens*. Thirty is likewise **sanjū**, *three tens*, and forty, **shijū** or **yonjū**, *four tens*.

50	gojū	*fifty*
60	rokujū	*sixty*
70	shichijū or nanajū	*seventy*
80	hachijū	*eighty*
90	kujū or kyūjū	*ninety*
100	hyaku	*one hundred*

In the case of 4, 7 and 9, alternatives are often used, particularly when counting money or when exactness is required, largely due to a possible confusion between **shi** (4) and **shichi** (7), and **roku** (6) and **ku** (9). The superstition about **shi** (4) and its homonym **shi** meaning *death* plays little in this case.

Months

66. **Gatsu** is used with the second set of numerals in naming months, e.g.,

ichigatsu, nigatsu, sangatsu, shigatsu, gogatsu, etc.

July is **shichigatsu**. **Nanagatsu** is seldom used.

In counting the number of months, **-kagetsu** is used with the second set of numerals. Thus,

ikkagetsu	*one month*
nikagetsu	*two months*
sankagetsu	*three months*
shikagetsu or **yonkagetsu**	*four months*
gokagetsu	*five months*
rokkagetsu	*six months*
shichikagetsu or **nanakagetsu**	*seven months*
hachikagetsu or **hakkagetsu**	*eight months*
kukagetsu or **kyūkagetsu**	*nine months*
jikkagetsu	*ten months*

The Te-form of a True Adjective

67. The **te**-form of an adjective is formed by replacing the final **i** by **kute**, e.g.,

samui	**samukute**	*cold*
atsui	**atsukute**	*hot*
attakai	**attakakute**	*warm*

When a non-final clause ends with an adjective, the **te**-form of an adjective is used.

Ichigatsu wa samukute yuki ga furimasu.

It's cold in January and snow falls.

In this use, the **te**-form of an adjective is exactly parallel to the **te**-form of a verb.

"Nē" and "Ne"—English Disjunctive Questions

68. **Atsui desu nē.** *It's hot, isn't it?*

Samui desu nē.	*It's cold, isn't it?*
Ii otenki desu nē.	*It's fine weather, isn't it?*
Ojōzu desu nē.	*You are good at it, aren't you?*

In English disjunctive questions, e.g., *isn't it, aren't you, is it, are you,* etc. are used at the end of a sentence when the speaker assumes the agreement of the listener. When one says, *It's a beautiful day, isn't it?*, one presupposes that the listener is of the same opinion. In Japanese **nē** is used to express the same idea.

But when there is a certain amount of interrogation in a disjunctive question, **nē** may be replaced by **ne** which is used for making sure.

If, in the above sentence, the speaker wants to put a straight question, he will say,

Ii otenki desu ka?   *Is it fine weather?*

But when he thinks it is fine weather and wants to make sure it is so, he will say,

Ii otenki desu ne?   *It's fine weather, is it?*

And when he knows perfectly well it is fine weather and uses the sentence as a social conversational expression, he will say,

Ii otenki desu nē.   *It's fine weather, isn't it?*

So, **Raigetsu wa jūichigatsu desu ne** is used when the speaker is pretty certain that next month is November and wants to make sure it is so.

Raigetsu wa jūichigatsu desu nē is used when he knows perfectly next month is November and uses this sentence with the feeling *How time flies!*

Omission of "Ga" and "O" after Numerals

69. Compare the following sentences.

Kao niwa me ya hana ga arimasu.

Lit. *There are eyes and nose in our face.*

Ichinen niwa jūnikagetsu arimasu.

There are twelve months in one year.

There is the particle **ga** indicating the nominative case after the subject "**me ya hana**" in the former sentence, while there is no particle after **jūnikagetsu** in the latter sentence. **Jūnikagetsu** is a numeral. After numerals which are used adverbially, no particles are used. The same can be said of the objective particle **o**.

— 79 —

70. **Naru** from which **narimasu** comes means *to become, turn into, change into,* etc. It takes the particle **ni** when it follows a noun or a numeral.

> **Ichi to ni de ikutsu ni narimasu ka?**
>
> *What do one and two make?*
>
> **Shi to go de ku ni narimasu.**
>
> *Four and five make nine.*

De here has a similar meaning of instrument or material as in the cases of **de** in **me de mimasu.** Therefore, the above Japanese sentences literally mean,

> *With one and two what number does it become?*
>
> *With four and five it becomes nine.*

In this construction **de** is not generally replaced by either **wa** or **ga**. If we are to use **wa** (or **ga** in some rare cases), the following construction is generally used.

> **Ichi to ni wa ikutsu desu ka?**
>
> **Shi to go wa ku desu.**

The Comparison

71. The comparison in Japanese may be expressed by various ways since it is a question of words rather than a fixed grammatical form.

> **Roku to shichi to dotchi ga ōkii desu ka?**
>
> *Which is larger, six or seven?*

There is no fixed grammatical form for the comparative degree. The adjective does not undergo any change in form. **Dotchi ga ōkii** literally means *which is large*, but by the use of **dotchi** which implies in itself the idea of comparison, the meaning is very clear without having any special form to show it.

For the same reason one may say in answer to the above sentence **Shichi ga ōkii desu** which literally means *Seven is large*. The situation helps to make clear what is meant.

But by the use of **no hō ga** after nouns the idea of comparison can be very definitely expressed.

> **Kore no hō ga ōkii desu.** *This is larger.*

Hō is a form noun whose basic meaning is *a side*. **Kore no hō** means *the side of this* or *this side*. Thus, **Kore no hō ga ōkii desu** literally means *this side is large*.

A form noun is a noun which remains a noun in form but is used more to express a grammatical function.

When the standard of comparison is to be indicated, **yori** which means *than* is used.

Tōkyō wa Kyōto yori ōkii desu. *Tokyo is larger than Kyoto.*

It is possible to add **no hō ga** to the above.

Tōkyō no hō ga Kyōto yori ōkii desu.
Tokyo is larger than Kyoto.

Mijikai Kaiwa

shitte [- - -] from **shiru**, *to know*. **Shitte imasu** literally means *I have knowledge of it* and *I am in that state*. The negative form **Shirimasen** means *I have no knowledge of it*.

oboete [-'- -] from **oboeru**, *to learn*. **Oboete imasu** means *I have learned it* and *I am in that state*. The negative form is **Oboete imasen**, *I am not in the state of having learned it*, hence *I don't remember*.

Exercises

A. Make appropriate questions for the following answers.

1. Hajime no tsuki wa ichigatsu desu.
2. Sangatsu to shigatsu to gogatsu desu.
3. Kongetsu wa nigatsu desu.
4. Natsu no hō ga hayaku kimasu.
5. Shichigatsu no hō ga atsui desu.

B. Answer the following questions.

1. Ima aki desu ka ?
2. Sengetsu wa nangatsu deshita ka ?
3. Raigetsu wa jūichigatsu desu ka ?
4. Jūichigatsu wa samui desu ka ?

5. Ichinen niwa nankagetsu arimasu ka ?
6. San to shi de ikutsu ni narimasu ka ?
7. Tōkyō to Yokohama to dotchi ga ōkii desu ka ?
8. Shigatsu wa sangatsu yori attakai desu ka, samui desu ka ?
9. Anata wa ichinen no tsuki no namae o shitte imasu ka ?
10. Anata wa ichi kara jūni made oboete imasu ka ?

C. *What is the Japanese equivalent of each of the following sentences?*
1. Is November the last month of the year ?
2. No, it isn't. December is the last.
3. Spring is warm whereas autumn is cool.
4. This month is February. It's cold.
5. Do you know the name of that man ?
6. No, I don't know.
7. This basket is larger than that one.
8. Which are more expensive, black shoes or brown ones ?
9. What do two and three make ?
10. They make five.
11. Please count these desks.
12. Do you remember me ?
13. Come into the room and sit down.
14. Clean up the room, please.

Jū

(Main Text)

A : Ikkagetsu niwa yaku yonshūkan arimasu.

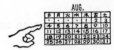

Nichiyōbi wa isshūkan no hajime no hi de, doyōbi wa owari no hi desu.

Nibamme no hi wa getsuyōbi de, sambamme no hi wa kayōbi desu.

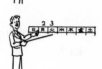

Isshūkan no mannaka no hi wa naniyōbi desu ka ?

B : Suiyōbi desu.

A : Mokuyōbi wa kin'yōbi no mae desu ka ato desu ka ?

B : Mae desu.

A : Kyō wa naniyōbi desu ka ?

B : Kin'yōbi desu.

A : Kinō wa mokuyōbi de, ototoɪ wa suiyōbi deshita.

Ashita to asatte wa naniyō desu ka ?

B : Ashita wa doyō de, asatte wa nichiyō desu.

A : Naze nichiyōbi niwa seito wa gakkō e ikimasen ka ?

B : Yasumi da kara desu.

A : Fuyu wa yuki ga furimasu. Naze desu ka ?

B : Samui kara desu.

(A Short Conversation)

A : Kinō kimasen deshita ne.

B : Dōmo sumimasen. Wasuremashita.

Itsu kimashō ka ?

A : Kayōbi ni kite kudasai.

(For Memorizing)

1. [Nibamme] no hi wa [getsu-yōbi] de, [sambamme] no hi wa [kayōbi] desu.

2. Kyō wa naniyōbi desu ka ?

3. Ashita wa [suiyōbi] de, asatte wa [mokuyōbi] desu.

4. Naze [gakkō] e ikimasen ka ?
5. [Yasumi] da kara desu.
6. [Samui] kara desu.

1. The [second] day is [Monday], and the [third] day is [Tuesday].

2. What day of the week is it today ?

3. Tomorrow will be [Wednesday], and the day after will be [Thursday].

4. Why don't they go to [school]?
5. Because it's a [holiday].
6. Because it is [cold].

Jū — Lesson 10

Hombun

Glossary

yaku ['-] *about ; roughly*
shūkan ['- - - or - - - -] *week(s)*
nichiyōbi [- -'- -] *Sunday*
issūkan [- -'- - -] *one week*
hi ['] *a day*
doyōbi [-'- -] *Saturday*
nibamme [- - - -] *second* (See Grammar 72.)
getsuyōbi [- -'- -] *Monday*

kayōbi [-'- -] *Tuesday*

naniyōbi [- -'- -] *what day of the week*

suiyōbi [- -'- -] *Wednesday*

mokuyōbi [- -'- -] *Thursday*

kin'yōbi [- -'- -] *Friday*

mae ['-] *before*

ato ['-] *after; behind*

kinō [-'-] *yesterday*

ototoi [- -'-] *the day before yesterday*

asatte [-'- -] *the day after tomorrow*

naniyō [- - - -] abbreviation of **naniyōbi**

doyō [-'-] abbreviation of **doyōbi**

nichiyō [- - - -] abbreviation of **nichiyōbi**

naze ['-] *why*

gakkō [- - - -] *a school*

yasumi [- - -] *a holiday*

da [-] the plain form of **desu**, *is, am* or *are*

kara [- -] *because*

Grammar

Ordinal Numbers

72.   Ordinal numbers are expressed in various ways, but the commonest is to add **bamme** after the second set of numerals.

ichibamme	*1st*
nibamme	*2nd*
sambamme	*3rd*
yobamme or **yombamme**	*4th*
gobamme	*5th*

Instead of **ichibamme**, **hajime no** meaning *the beginning* or **saisho no** meaning *the very beginning* is often used. **Ban** means *number*, and so **ichiban** means *No. 1*, and **niban**, *No. 2*. **Me** is a suffix which has the function of changing a cardinal number into an ordinal number. Thus **futatsume** means *the second*, **mittsume** means *the third*.

The Present Tense for Future Sense

73. **Ashita wa yasumi desu ka?** *Will tomorrow be a holiday?*

Asatte wa yasumi desu. *The day after tomorrow will be a holiday.*

Desu in these sentences refers to the future. There is no definite future tense in Japanese, but the present tense form has future meanings just like the English sentence *I'm going there tomorrow* expresses a future meaning in the present progressive form.

"Ni(wa)"—a Particle referring to the Time of Action

74. The particle **ni** (or **niwa** which is the combination of **ni** and **wa** (See Lesson 6, Grammar 39.) is used when the time of action is to be expressed.

Nichiyō niwa gakkō e ikimasen.

I don't go to school on Sunday.

Nigatsu ni yuki ga takusan furimasu.

It snows a lot in February.

Kayōbi ni kite kudasai. *Please come on Tuesday.*

"Naze" and "Kara"

75. **Naze** is an interrogative word meaning why. The answer is **kara desu** or simply **kara** put after the sentence showing the reason.

Naze ikimasen ka? *Why don't they go?*

Yasumi da kara (desu). *Because it is a holiday.*

In ordinary polite conversation **dōshite** is often used instead of **naze**, because **dōshite**, meaning *how come*, is less direct and is softer in the tone of questioning.

The Use of the Plain or Non-Polite Form

76. In Japanese there is the plain or non-polite style which is used in daily conversation among relatives or close friends and in writing. Remember that the plain forms are grammatical mechanisms. They are used in many cases when there is no actual rudeness involved.

Even in polite style, it is correct and usual to use the plain form in the middle of a sentence as long as the polite style is used at the end.

"Da"—a Copula in the Plain Style

77. **Yasumi da kara desu.** *It's because it is a holiday.*

Da is the same as **desu** in meaning, but is used in the plain style. In the above example **desu kara desu** can be used, but it sounds rather awkward.

The Plain Form of True Adjectives

78.   **Samui kara desu.**   *Because it is cold.*

In this sentence you can say **Samui desu kara desu**. But **samui** has the same meaning as **samui desu**, that is, it means not only *cold*, but also *is cold*. Among close friends, this plain form may be used more often than the polite form.

      Samui desu nē.   (polite)

      Samui nē.   (familiar)

Mijikai Kaiwa

kimasen deshita [----'--] *didn't come*

dōmo ['--] *indeed, really, very much*, etc. This is used at the beginning of a sentence.

sumimasen [---'-] *I am sorry; excuse me.*

wasure- [---] from **wasureru**, *to forget*

itsu ['-] *when; what time*

-mashō [---] *probably...is; maybe; shall.* This will be dealt with more in detail later.

Exercises

A. Answer the following questions.

  1. Kyō wa naniyōbi desu ka ?

  2. Kinō wa yasumi deshita ka ?

  3. Ashita wa nichiyōbi desu ka ?

  4. Nichiyōbi wa isshūkan no hajime no hi desu ka, owari no hi desu ka ?

  5. Isshūkan no mannaka no hi wa naniyōbi desu ka ?

  6. Isshūkan no nibamme no hi wa naniyōbi desu ka ?

  7. Asatte anata wa gakkō e ikimasu ka ?

  8. Anata wa naniyōbi ni Nippongo o naraimasu ka ?

  9. Anata wa doyōbi ni hatarakimasu ka ?

 10. Kayōbi wa getsuyōbi no mae desu ka, ato desu ka ?

B. Fill in each blank with an appropriate word.

1. Ikkagetsu ___ yaku ___ shūkan arimasu.
2. Hajime ___ hi wa nichiyōbi ___, nibamme ___ hi wa ___ desu.
3. Isshūkan no ___ no hi wa suiyōbi desu.
4. Watakushi wa getsuyōbi ___ kin'yōbi ___ hataraite, doyōbi to nichiyōbi ___ yasumimasu.
5. Naze gakkō ___ ikimasen ka? Yasumi ___ kara desu.

C. What is the Japanese equivalent of each of the following sentences?

1. The first desk is Mr. Tanaka's and the second one is mine.
2. There are ten chairs in this room.
3. Is the last day of the week Saturday or Sunday?
4. Saturday is not a holiday, but Wednesday is.
5. Will you go to school tomorrow?
6. It was fine yesterday, but it is snowing today.
7. Where is Friday's paper?
8. I don't know (where it is). But Sunday's is on the table.
9. Look at the calendar. There are many holidays in November.
10. "Why don't you wear a coat?" "Because it is hot today."
11. Please come to my house on Saturday.
12. I went to Mr. Suzuki's on Monday with my wife (=*kanai*) and children.

D. Here is a short conversation between X and Y. Take the part of Y and answer along the lines indicated.

X: Kyō wa kin'yō desu ka, doyō desu ka?
Y: (*It's Saturday today.*)
X: Anata wa kyō gakkō e ikimashita ka?
Y: (*No, I didn't go.*)
X: Naze desu ka?
Y: (*Our school is from Monday to Friday, and Saturday and Sunday are holidays.*)
X: Sō desu ka? Dewa doyōbi to nichiyōbi niwa benkyō shimasen ne?
Y: (*Oh Yes, I do. I don't go to school on Saturday and Sunday, but I study at home.*)

Jūichi

(Main Text)

A : Kore wa tokei desu.

Tokei wa jikan o shiru no ni tsukaimasu.

Tokei niwa nihon no hari ga arimasu.

Ryōhō no hari ga jūni o sasu to chōdo jūniji
desu.

Ichijikan wa rokujippun desu. Nagai hari wa
ichijikan ni hitomawari shimasu.

Jūni kara ichi made wa gofun de, ichi kara ni
made mo gofun desu.

Jūni kara san made wa jūgofun de, shi made
wa nijippun desu.

— 90 —

Mijikai hari wa hitomawari suru no ni jūnijikan kakarimasu.

Ima mijikai hari wa san to shi no aida o sashite imasu.   Nagai hari wa roku o sashite imasu.   Nanji desu ka ?

B :   Sanjihan desu.

A :   Nagai hari ga ku o sasu to nanji ni narimasu ka ?

B :   Yoji jūgofun mae ni narimasu.

A :   Ichinichi wa nijū-yojikan de, sore o gozen to gogo ni wakemasu.

Desukara, ichinichi niwa onaji jikan ga nido arimasu.   Tatoeba rokuji wa gozen nimo gogo nimo arimasu.

Gozen no rokuji wa asa de gogo no rokuji wa yūgata desu.

Asa kara yūgata made ga hiruma de, yūgata kara asa made ga yoru desu.

Hi wa higashi kara dete nishi ni hairimasu.

Hi ga deru to akaruku narimasu.

Hi ga hairu to kuraku narimasu.

(A Short Conversation)

A : Ima nanji desu ka ?

B : Niji jūgofun sugi desu.

A : Anata no tokei wa tadashii desu ka ?

B : Sō omoimasu. Ima isogashii desu ka ?

A : Ima jikan ga arimasen. Ato ni shite kudasai.

Gozenchū wa hima desu.

(For Memorizing)

1. Ryōhō no hari ga jūni o sasu to chōdo jūniji desu.

1. When both hands point to twelve, it's just twelve o'clock.

2. Nagai hari wa ichijikan ni hitomawari shimasu.

2. The long hand makes one round in an hour.

3. Ichinichi wa nijū-yojikan de, sore o gozen to gogo ni wake-masu.

3. There are twenty-four hours in a day, and we divide them into forenoon and afternoon.

4. Hi ga [deru] to [akaruku] narimasu.

4. When the sun [rises], it becomes [light].

5. Ima nanji desu ka ?

5. What time is it now ?

6.
ippun	nifun
sampun	yompun
gofun	roppun
shichifun	hachifun
kyūfun	jippun
jūgofun	
...nijippun mae	

6.
one minute	two minutes
three miuntes	four minutes
five minutes	six minutes
seven miuntes	eight minutes
nine minutes	ten minutes
fifteen minutes	
twenty-minutes to...	

Hombun

Glossary

jikan [---]   *the hour; time*
...no ni [--]   *in order to*   (See Grammar 79.)
nihon ['--]   *two long pieces*   (See Grammar 81.)
hari ['-]   *a needle; hand* (of a watch)
ryōhō [----]   *both*
sasu ['-]   *to point*
to [-]   a particle meaning *when* or *if*   (See Grammar 83.)
chōdo [---]   *just; exactly*
-ji [-]   *o'clock*
ichijikan [-----]   *one hour*

rokujippun [- -′- - -] *sixty minutes*

nagai [-′-] (*a-A*) *long*

hitomawari [-′- - -] *one round*

-fun [′-] *minutes*

mijikai [- -′-] (*a-A*) *short*

kakari- [- - -] from **kakaru**, *to require; cost*

aida [- - -] *between*

nanji [′- -] *what time...*

sanjihan [- - - - -] *half past three*

ichinichi [- - - -] *one day*

nijū-yojikan [′- - - - - -] *twenty-four hours*

gozen [′- - or - - -] *forenoon; a. m.*

gogo [′-] *afternoon; p. m.*

wake- [- -] from **wakeru**, *to divide*

desukara [′- - -] *therefore*

nido [-′] *twice* (See Grammar 86.)

tatoeba [-′- -] *for instance*

asa [′-] *morning*

yūgata [- - - -] *evening; dusk; twilight* (time between daylight and night)

hiruma [- - -] *daytime*

yoru [′-] *night*

hi [-] *the sun*

higashi [- - -] *east*

nishi [- -] *west*

akaruku [- - - -] from **akarui** (*a-A*), *light* (not dark)

kuraku [- - -] from **kurai** (*a-A*), dark

Grammar

"... no ni "—" in Order to "

79. ...**no ni** indicates purpose or aim and corresponds roughly to *for the purpose of* or *in order to* or merely *for*.

Tokei wa jikan o shiru no ni tsukaimasu.

We use a watch to tell the time.

Numeral Classifiers

80. When counting the quantity of material nouns such as *water*, *paper*, *metal*, *cattle*, etc., such words as *glass*, *sheet*, *pound*, *head*, etc. are used in English, but in counting common nouns such as *desks*, *books*, *pencils*, no special words are needed except such cases as *a set of tools*, *a pair of shoes*, etc.

In Japanese as well as in Chinese the so-called *numeral classifiers* are used together with the second set of numerals when counting various objects.

Which classifier is to be used depends on the shape of an object. When it is difficult to determine the proper classifier the first set of numerals is used.

> **Kao niwa me ga futatsu, hana ga hitotsu, kuchi ga hitotsu arimasu.**
>
> *On the face are two eyes, one nose and one mouth.*

"Hon"—a Classifier for Long Objects

81. **Hon** is a numeral classifier used for long and thin objects such as *pencils*, *matches*, *cigarettes*, *fingers*, *arms*, *legs*, *pillars*, *poles*, etc.

Note the euphonic changes in counting 1, 3, 6 and 10.

> **ippon, nihon, sambon, shihon** (or **yonhon**), **gohon, roppon, shichihon** (or **nanahon**), **hachihon** (or **happon**), **kuhon** (or **kyūhon**), **jippon, jūippon, jūnihon, jūsambon**; **ikuhon** (*how many...*), etc.

[Numeral] x "no" x [Noun]

82. (a) **Tokei niwa nihon no hari ga arimasu.**

    (b) **Tokei niwa hari ga nihon arimasu.**

Both of these sentences may be rendered into English as *A clock has two hands*. Then, what is the difference between the two?

(a) is more specific about the number in the speaker's mind than (b), in which the number is incidental. (a) means that a clock is two-handed, while (b) means that a clock has some hands which, in this case, happen to be two in number.

In the following two sentences,

    (a) **Sono nihon no empitsu o kudasai.**

(b) **Sono empitsu o nihon kudasai.**

(a) means that there are only two pencils and you want somebody to give you both of them. (b) means that there are many pencils and you want any two out of the lot as in the case of a customer buying some pencils, hence,

(a) *Please give me those two pencils.*

(b) *Please give me two of those pencils.*

"To" meaning "When" or "If"

83. **Ryōhō no hari ga jūni o sasu to chōdo jūniji desu** means *Both hands point to 12, (and) it's just twelve o'clock.* **To** used at the end of a non-final clause means *whenever.* It often corresponds to *when* or *if.*

To in this sense is always used after a present tense form regardless of whether the verb of the final clause is in the present or past.

Method of Counting Time

84. In telling the time, the second set of numerals is used with the classifiers **ji** (*o'clock*) for hours, and **fun** for minutes.

ippun	*1 minute*	**roppun**	*6 minutes*
nifun	*2 minutes*	**shichifun**	*7 minutes*
		(or **nanafun**)	
sampun	*3 minutes*	**hachifun**	*8 minutes*
		(sometimes **happun**)	
yompun	*4 minutes*	**kyūfun**	*9 minutes*
(or **shifun**)		(or **kufun**)	
gofun	*5 minutes*	**jippun**	*10 minutes*

For counting the number of hours, **jikan** is used, e. g., **ichijikan**, *an hour*, **nijikan**, *two hours*, **sanjikan**, *three hours*, **yojikan**, *four hours*, **gojikan**, five hours, etc.

In telling the time **sugi** is used after the minutes, in the sense of *past* or *after* and **mae** after the minutes in the sense of *before* or *to*.

Sugi is often omitted especially in reading from a time-table or talking about schedules.

Han is used for *half* but *a quarter* is always **jūgofun**.

1:10 **ichiji jippun (sugi)**

2:15	niji jūgofun (sugi)
3:30	sanjihan
4:45	yoji yonjū-gofun (sugi) or **goji jūgofun mae**

"Onaji"—"the Same"

85. **Onaji** is a noun that came from a true adjective.

> **Gogo no rokuji wa jūhachiji to onaji desu.**
>
> *Six o'clock in the afternoon is the same as eighteen o'clock.*

Onaji is also used as a modifier of a noun. It comes directly before a noun without any connecting particle.

> **Ichinichi niwa onaji jikan ga nido arimasu.**
>
> *There is the same time twice in a day.*

Onaji is sometimes pronounced as **onnaji**.

"-Do" meaning "....Times"

86. **Do** is a classifier for *...times*. **Ichido** means *once*; **nido**, *twice*; **sando**, *three times*; **yodo**, *four times*, etc. Don't use **do** in the meaning of *"times"* (3 times 3) as in multiplication. (cf. Lesson 14, Grammar 104.)

"Naru" (Become) with a True Adjective

87. In Lesson 9 we had a case of **ni naru** used with a noun in the sense of *become* or *turn into*. (See Lesson 9, Grammar 70.)

In English the verb *become* is an incomplete intransitive verb and its complement is an adjective instead of an adverb, e. g.,

> *to become light*   (instead of *lightly*)
>
> *to become wide*   (instead of *widely*)

In Japanese this is not the case. When an adjective comes before **naru**, its adverbial form, i. e. the form ending with **ku** is used.

> **Hi ga deru to akaruku narimasu.**
>
> *When the sun rises, it becomes light.*

> **Hi ga hairu to kuraku narimasu.**
>
> *When the sun sets, it becomes dark.*

Mijikai Kaiwa

-sugi [- -] *past*
tadashii [- -'-] (*a-A*) *correct*
omoi- [- - -] from **omou**, *to think*
isogashii [- - -'-] (*a-A*) *busy*
ato ['-] *later; afterwards:* **ato ni suru** means *to postpone; do... later.*
-chū [- -] *during*
hima [- -] *leisure; time to spare*

Exercises

A. Answer the following questions.

1. Ima nanji desu ka?
2. Ima tokei no mijikai hari to nagai hari wa nani o sashite imasu ka?
3. Ryōhō no hari ga jūni o sasu to nanji desu ka?
4. Mijikai hari wa ichinichi ni hitomawari shimasu ka, futamawari (=two rounds) shimasu ka?
5. Nagai hari wa hitomawari suru no ni nampun kakarimasu ka?
6. Hi wa doko kara dete doko ni hairimasu ka?
7. Hiruma wa akarui desu ka, kurai desu ka?
8. Itsu kuraku narimasu ka?
9. Ichinichi niwa onaji jikan ga ichido dake arimasu ka?
10. Anata wa gozen ni benkyō shimasu ka?

B. Fill in each blank with an appropriate word.

1. Hi ga deru ___ akaruku ___.
2. Ichinichi no hajime ___ jūnijikan wa ___ de, sono tsugi no (=next) jūnijikan wa ___ desu.
3. Ima sanjihan desu. Mijikai hari wa san ___ shi ___ aida o sashite, nagai hari wa ___ o sashite imasu.
4. ___ wa akarukute yoru wa ___ desu.
5. Mijikai hari wa hitomawari suru no ___ jūnijikan kakarimasu ga, nagai hari wa ___ dake kakarimasu.

C. Express in Japanese the following points of time.

1. 5 : 30 a. m.
2. 7 : 10 a. m.
3. 8 : 50 p. m.
4. 10 : 45 a. m.
5. 11 : 12 p. m.
6. 12 : 00 (noon)
7. 1 : 20 p. m.
8. 3 : 55 p. m.
9. 6 : 17 a. m.
10. 10 : 35 a. m.

D. What is the Japanese equivalent of each of the following sentences?

1. Where did you put your watch?
2. What time is it now?
3. It's just ten o'clock.
4. What is the long hand pointing to?
5. It is pointing (at the place) between five and six.
6. It takes an hour to walk to his house.
7. It takes twenty minutes from here.
8. Please divide this into two.
9. I worked from morning till evening.
10. When it becomes light, it is after (=past) six a.m.
11. It snowed twice this winter.
12. We are studying in the same school.
13. My watch has three hands.
14. There are six pencils in this bag.
15. Wait a moment, please, as I am busy now.
16. This watch is not correct.
17. I am free on Sundays.

Jūni

(Main Text)

A : Ikkagetsu niwa sanjūnichi arimasu.

Maigetsu sanjūnichi arimasu ka ?

B : Iie, sanjū-ichinichi no tsuki mo arimasu shi, nijū-hachinichi no tsuki mo arimasu.

A : Tsuki no hajime no hi wa nan to iimasu ka ?

B : Ichijitsu to iimasu.　Mata tsuitachi to mo iimasu.

A : Ichijitsu kara sanjū-ichinichi made jun ni itte kudasai.

B : Ichijitsu, futsuka, mikka, yokka, itsuka, muika, nanuka......

A : Chotto matte kudasai.　"Nanuka" to mo iimasu ga futsū "nanoka" desu.

Dōzo tsuzukete kudasai.

B : Yōka, kokonoka, tōka, jūichinichi, jūninichi, jūsannichi, jūyokka, jūgonichi, jūrokunichi, jūshi- chinichi, jūhachinichi, jūkunichi, hatsuka, nijū-ichi- nichi, nijū-ninichi, nijū-sannichi, nijū-yokka, nijū- gonichi, nijū-rokunichi, nijū-shichinichi, nijū-hachi- nichi, nijū-kunichi, sanjūnichi, sanjū-ichinichi.

A : Kyō wa nannichi desu ka ?

B : Yokka desu.

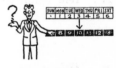

A : Raishū no getsuyōbi wa nannichi ni narimasu ka ?

B : Yōka ni narimasu.

A : Anata wa senshū no doyōbi ni doko e ikimashita ka ?

B : Doko emo ikimasen deshita. Ichinichijū uchi ni imashita. Byōki datta kara desu.

A : Sakuban mo uchi ni imashita ka ?

B : Iie, dekakemashita.

A : Komban mo dekakemasu ka ?

B : Iie, keredomo myōban wa dekakemasu.

(A Short Conversation)

A : Itsu dekimasu ka ?

B : Hatsuka ni dekimasu.

A : Isoide kudasai.

B : Yoroshū gozaimasu.

(For Memorizing)

1. Senshū no [doyōbi] ni doko e   1. Where did you go last
   ikimashita ka ?   [Saturday] ?

2. Doko emo ikimasen deshita.   2. I didn't go anywhere.

3. Ichinichijū [uchi] ni imashita.   3. I was at [home] all day.

Hombun

Glossary

sanjū ['---] *thirty*

-nichi [--] a clasifier for *day(s)* (See Grammar 88.)

maigetsu [----] *every month*

sanjū-ichi ['-----] *thirty-one*

shi [-] a sign of frequentatives (See Grammar 90.)

nijū-hachi ['----] *twenty-eight*

ichijitsu [---- or -'--] *the first day of the month*

mata [--] *also*

tsuitachi [----] *the first day of the month*

sanjū-ichinichi ['-------] *the 31st; thirty-one days*

jun ni [---] *consecutively*

futsuka [---] *the 2nd; two days*

mikka [---] *the 3rd; three days*

yokka [---] *the 4th; four days*

itsuka [---] *the 5th; five days*

muika [---] *the 6th; six days*

nanuka [---] *the 7th; seven days*

futsū [---] *usually; normally*

nanoka [---] *the 7th; seven days*

tsuzukete [----] from **tsuzukeru**, *to continue; go on*

yōka [---] *the 8th; eight days*

kokonoka [----] *the 9th; nine days*

tōka [---] *the 10th; ten days*

jūsan ['---] *thirteen*

jūyokka ['----] *the 14th; fourteen days*

jūgo ['--] *fifteen*

jūroku [----] *sixteen*

jūshichi [----] *seventeen*

jūhachi [----] *eighteen*

jūku ['--] *nineteen*

hatsuka [---] *the 20th; twenty days*

nijū-ichi ['----] *twenty-one*

nijū-ni ['---] *twenty-two*

nijū-san ['----] *twenty-three*

nijū-yokka ['-----] *the 24th; twenty-four days*

nijū-go ['---] *twenty-five*

nijū-roku ['----] *twenty-six*

nijū-shichi ['----] *twenty-seven*

nijū-ku ['---] *twenty-nine*

nannichi ['---] *what day of the month*

raishū [----] *next week*

senshū [----] *last week*

ichinichijū [------] *all day long:* **-jū** is a suffix meaning *all through; whole*

i- [-] from **iru**, *to be; stay*

byōki [---] *sickness; illness*

datta ['--] the plain form of **deshita** (See Grammar 93.)

sakuban [-'--] *last night*

dekake- [---] from **dekakeru**, *to go out*

myōban ['---] *tomorrow evening*

Grammar

Days of the Month

88. The names of the days of the month are irregular up to the 10th. After that **n'chi** (or **nichi**, when it is a little formal) is added to the second set of numerals with the exception of the 14th, 20th and 24th.

Nanoka is sometimes pronounced as **nanuka**, but in Tokyo the former is used.

These words may be used to tell the date as well as for telling the number of days with the exception of **tsuitachi**.

> **Futsuka ni kite kudasai.** *Please come on the 2nd.*
>
> **Futsuka kakarimasu.** *It takes two days.*

Among the four words **tsuitachi**, **ichijitsu**, **ichinichi** and **ichinchi** for *the first day of the month*, **ichijitsu** is officially adopted for broadcasting, but

tsuitachi seems to be most popular while **ichinichi** and **ichinchi** are seldom used for the date and exclusively used for the number of days.

> Tsuitachi ni ikimasu.   *I'll go on the 1st.*
>
> Ichinichi yasumimashita.   *I took a day off.*

"Mai"—a Prefix meaning "Every"

89. **Mai** is a prefix meaning *every* and forms the following compounds.

mai-asa	*every morning*	**mai-shū**	*every week*
mai-ban	*every evening*	**mai-getsu**	*every month*
mai-nichi	*every day*	**mai-nen**	*every year*

"Shi"—a Connective Particle

90. The particle **shi** used at the end of a non-final clause has a force of a connective and is often rendered into English by *and* or *some..., and some....*

> **Sanjū-ichinichi no tsuki mo arimasu shi, nijū-hachinichi no tsuki mo arimasu.**
>
> *There are some months which have thirty-one days, and there is a month which has twenty-eight days.*
>
> **Tanaka San mo sō iimashita shi, Suzuki San mo sō iimashita.**
>
> *Mr. Tanaka said so, and Mr. Suzuki said so, too.*

More than one **shi** may be used in one sentence to denote two or more events.

Interrogative Word plus "Mo" means "No...."

91. **Nani** (or **nan**), *what,* **ikutsu**, *how many,* **doko**, *where,* **itsu**, *when,* etc. are words used solely for questions. These interrogative words followed by **mo** mean *no...* with a negative.

> Doko emo ikimasen deshita.   *I went nowhere.*
>
> Nani mo arimasen.   *There is nothing.*
>
> Bōshi wa doko nimo arimasen.   *My hat is nowhere to be seen.*

"Arimasu" and "Imasu"

92. Both **aru** and **iru** mean *to be, to exist, to lie, there is (are),* etc. A common explanation given is that **aru** is used with reference to lifeless inanimate objects such as desks, chairs, buildings, etc. while **iru** is used for living things such as human beings, animals, fish, insects, etc.

While the above explanation is not incorrect, it is better to say that the criterion is whether an object is able to change its location by its own strength. Trees and plants cannot change their positions, so that **aru** is to be used with them. Ships and motorcars have self-propelling power, so that it is usual to use **iru** with them. However, when a speaker feels that a ship or a motorcar is going to stay in one position for a long time such as a ship under repair or a motorcar which had a breakdown, he will naturally use **aru**.

> **Asuko ni tsukue ga arimasu.** *There is a desk there.*
>
> **Tsukue no mae ni hito ga imasu.**
>
> *There is a man in front of the desk.*

"Datta" and "Deshita"

93. **Datta** is the contraction of **de atta** in the plain style and corresponds to **deshita** in the polite style, i. e. **datta** is the past form of **da**. (See Lesson 10, Grammar 77.)

> **Byōki datta kara desu.**   It was because I was sick.
>
> (=**Byōki deshita kara desu.**)

Mijikai Kaiwa

deki- [--] from **dekiru**, *to be made; be finished; be possible; be able* (See Lesson 8, Grammar 64.)

isoide [-'--] from **isogu**, *to hurry*

yoroshū [----] from **yoroshii** (*a-A*), *good; all right*

Exercises

A. Answer the following questions.

1. Sanjū-ichinichi no tsuki wa nangatsu de, sanjūnichi no tsuki wa nangatsu desu ka ?

2. Nigatsu niwa nannichi arimasu ka ?

3. Kyō wa nannichi desu ka ?

4. Ototoi wa nannichi deshita ka ?

5. Tsuki no hajime no hi wa nan to iimasu ka ?

6. Kono tsugi no nichiyōbi wa nannichi ni narimasu ka?
7. Anata wa senshū no nichiyōbi ni doko e ikimashita ka?
8. Komban wa uchi ni imasu ka?
9. Anata wa myōban isogashii desu ka?
10. Anata wa raishū yasumimasu ka?

B. *What is the Japanese equivalent of each of the following sentences?*
1. What day of the month is it today?
2. Some months have thirty days.
3. Is today the second or the third?
4. Today is the eighth.
5. Please tell me the names of the days of the week (=one week) in order.
6. I work from the first to the fourteenth and rest on the fifteenth.
7. Please come the day after tomorrow.
8. My shoes will be ready on the twenty-fifth.
9. I was out last night, but I will stay at home and study this evening.
10. Tomorrow is the thirteenth and is Friday.

C. *Here is a conversation between Mr. Tanaka and Mr. Brown. See if you understand and then try to carry on a similar conversation.*

Mr. Tanaka : Kyō wa sanjūnichi desu **ne**.

Mr. Brown : Sō desu.

Mr. Tanaka : Dewa ashita wa rokugatsu tsuitachi desu ne.

Mr. Brown : Iie, ashita wa sanjū-ichinichi desu.

Mr. Tanaka : Sō desu ka. Gogatsu niwa sanjū-ichinichi arimasu nē. Wasuremashita.

Mr. Brown : Anata wa natsu ni Karuizawa e ikimasu ka?

Mr. Tanaka : Shichigatsu ni naru to ikimasu. Anata wa?

Mr. Brown : Watakushi wa Karuizawa ni uchi ga mada arimasen. Anata wa arimasu ka?

Mr. Tanaka : Hai, arimasu. Chiisai no desu keredomo....

Mr. Brown : Sō desu ka? Kyō wa atsui desu nē.

Mr. Tanaka : Sō desu nē. Yūgata ni naru to motto suzushiku narimashō.

Mr. Brown ; Shichigatsu ni naru to motto atsuku narimashō ne.

Review (Lessons 1—12)

A. Vocabulary Check-up

Complete the following diagram by filling up each blank space with an appropriate word.

Color	akai ( )	aoi ( )	( ) *white*	( ) *yellow*	( ) *black*	
	nezumiiro ( )	( ) *brown*	( ) *pink*	midoriiro ( )	murasaki ( )	
Things in a room	tsukue ( )	kabe ( )	( ) *chair*	( ) *table*	( ) *window*	( ) *door*
Location	ue ( )	shita ( )	( ) *in*	( ) *by*	doko ( )	( ) *here*
	( ) *there*	hidari ( )	( ) *right*	asuko ( )	soto ( )	
Bodily organs	kuchi ( )	hana ( )	( ) *ears*	( ) *eyes*	te ( )	( ) *legs, feet*
Activity	tabemasu ( )	( ) *to smell*	( ) *to hear*	( ) *to see*	( ) *to take up*	arukimasu ( )
People	watakushi ( )	( ) *you*	( ) *he, she*	( ) *we*	( ) *these people*	
	sensei ( )	seito ( )	kodomo ( )	( ) *man*	( ) *woman*	
Nationals	Nipponjin ( )	( ) *American*	( ) *Britisher*	( ) *French*	( ) *German*	( ) *Russian*
Languages	( ) *Japanese*	Eigo ( )	( ) *French*	( ) *German*	( ) *Russian*	
True adjectives	ōkii ( )	( ) *small*	ii ( )	( ) *bad*	samui ( )	( ) *hot*
Adverbial	ōkiku ( )	chiisaku ( )	yoku ( )	( ) *badly*	( ) *coldly*	atsuku ( )
Quasi-adjectives	kekkō ( )	( ) *splendid*	jōzu ( )	( ) *unskilful*	kirei ( )	genki ( )

Stationery, Reading materials	empitsu ( )	( ) *paper*	chōmen ( )	( ) *book*	shimbun ( )	( ) *magazine*
Activity	kaku ( )			yomu ( )		
Things to wear	uwagi ( )	( ) *vest*	waishatsu ( )	kutsu ( )	( ) *trousers*	( ) *hat, cap*
Activity	kiru ( )			haku ( )		kaburu ( )
Names of Months	Ichigatsu ( )	( ) *February*	sangatsu ( )	( ) *April*	gogatsu ( )	( ) *June*
Seasons	fuyu ( )		( ) *spring*			natsu ( )
Names of Months	shichigatsu ( )	( ) *August*	kugatsu ( )	( ) *October*	jūichigatsu ( )	( ) *December*
Seasons	natsu ( )		( ) *fall*			fuyu ( )
Days of the week	( ) *Sunday*	( ) *Monday*	( ) *Tuesday*	( ) *Wednesday*		
Activity	yasumu ( )	hataraku ( )				
Days of the week	( ) *Thursday*	( ) *Friday*	( ) *Saturday*			
Activity	hataraku ( )		dekakeru ( )			

Counting	hitotsu ( )	( )	( )	( )	( )
	ichi	ni	( )	( )	( )	( )
	nanatsu ( )	( )	tō		
	shichi ( )	( )	( )	jūichi	( )

Days of the Month	tsuitachi (ichijitsu)	futsuka	( )	( )	( )	( )
	nanoka	yōka	( )	( )	( )	( )

Days of the Month	( )	jūyokka	( )	( )	( )	( )
	( )	hatsuka	( )	( )	( )	( )
	( )	( )	( )	( )	( )	( )
	( )					

V	Present	akemasu ( )	shimemasu ( )	( )	( )	hanashimasu ( )	( )
e	Past	akemashita	( )	ikimashita	( )	( )	( )
r	te-form	akete	( )	( )	kite	( )	kiite
b	Present	yomimasu ( )	( )	( )	katazukemasu ( )	( )	( )
s	Past	( )	kakimashita	( )	( )	mimashita	( )
	te-form	( )	( )	totte	( )	( )	benkyō shite

B. *Fill in each blank with an appropriate word.*

1. Tsukue ＿＿ ue ＿＿ nani ＿＿ arimasu ＿＿ ?
2. Sono ringo ＿＿ kudasai.
3. "Green" wa Nippongo ＿＿ nan ＿＿ iimasu ＿＿ ?
4. Watakushitachi ＿＿ mimi ＿＿ oto ＿＿ kikimasu.
5. Sakana ＿＿ te ＿＿ ashi ＿＿ arimasen.
6. Watakushi ＿＿ anata ＿＿ Nippongo ＿＿ oshiete ＿＿.
7. Nippongo ＿＿ muzukashiku ＿＿ arimasen. Keredomo yasashiku ＿＿ arimasen.
8. Michi ＿＿ otokonohito ＿＿ onnanohito ＿＿ aruite imasu.
9. Kodomo ＿＿ yōfuku ＿＿ ＿＿, zōri ＿＿ ＿＿ iru rashii desu.
10. Tsukue ＿＿ ue ＿＿ hon o ＿＿ kudasai.
11. Ichinen ＿＿ ichigatsu ＿＿ jūnigatsu ＿＿ arimasu.
12. Go ＿＿ roku ＿＿ dotchi ＿＿ ōkii desu ＿＿ ?

13. Roku no ___ ga ōkii desu.
14. Jūichigatsu ___ jūgatsu ___ samui desu.
15. Naze nichiyōbi ___ seito ___ gakkō ___ ikimasen ka ?
16. Yasumi ___ kara desu.
17. Tokei ___ jikan ___ shiru ___ ni tsukaimasu.
18. Ima mijikai hari ___ shi ___ go ___ aida ___ sashite imasu.
19. Ichinichi ___ gozen ___ gogo ___ wakemasu.
20. Hi ___ deru ___ akaruku narimasu.
21. Senshū ___ nichiyōbi ___ doko ___ ikimasen deshita. Byōki ___ kara desu.

C. *All the words and construction patterns used in the following conversation are supposed to be known to you. Read the conversation and see if you can understand all of it.*

Tanaka : Ohayō gozaimasu.
Brown : Ohayō gozaimasu. Warui otenki desu nē.
Tanaka : Sō desu nē. Samui desu nē.
Brown : Ogenki desu ka ?
Tanaka : Ee, genki desu.
Brown : Sore wa kekkō desu.
Tanaka : Anata wa ?
Brown : Watakushi mo.
Tanaka : Sō desu ka ? Sore wa kekkō desu.
Brown : Ano kata wa donata desu ka ?
Tanaka : Yamada San no okusan desu. Ano kata wa sensei desu.
Brown : Sō desu ka ? Nan no sensei desu ka ?
Tanaka : Eigo no sensei desu.
Brown : Kono gakkō no sensei desu ka ?
Tanaka : Ee, sō desu.
Brown : Kono gakkō wa ōkii desu nē.
Tanaka : Ee, ōkii desu.
Brown : Anata mo Eigo o oshiemasu ka ?
Tanaka : Iie, watakushi wa Furansugo o oshiemasu. Anata wa Furansugo ga wakarimasu ka ?
Brown : Iie, wakarimasen. Keredomo Doitsugo o sukoshi shitte imasu.

Tanaka: Sō desu ka? Sore wa ii desu nē.

Brown: Anata wa doyōbi nimo oshiemasu ka?

Tanaka: Iie, doyōbi niwa oshiemasen; yasumi desu kara. Keredomo getsuyō kara kin'yō made mainichi kono gakkō e kimasu.

Brown: Sō desu ka? Isshūkan ni nanjikan oshiemasu ka?

Tanaka: Hachijikan oshiemasu. Getsuyōbi to suiyōbi niwa ichijikan desu ga, kayō, mokuyō, kin'yō niwa nijikan desu.

Brown: Sō desu ka? Asa hayaku gakkō e kimasu ka?

Tanaka: Gozen kuji ni kimasu.

Brown: Seito wa yoku benkyō shimasu ka?

Tanaka: Ee, yoku benkyō shimasu kara jōzu desu.

Brown: Sore wa ii desu nē. Otokonohito ga kodomo o tsurete asuko o aruite imasu ne.

Tanaka: Yōfuku o kite bōshi o kabutte imasu nē.

Brown: Ano kata wa watakushi no tomodachi rashii desu. Dewa mata ashita. Sayōnara.

Tanaka: Sayōnara.

D. All the sentences you have in "For Memorizing" and in "A Short Conversation" are to be learned thoroughly. But above all, the following sentences are so important that they should be given special attention to, so that they may be reproduced rapidly and fluently. See if you can do so.

1. Sore wa pen desu ka, empitsu desu ka?	1. Is that a pen or a pencil?
2. Kono tokei wa chiisaku wa arimasen.	2. This watch isn't small.
3. Kago no naka ni ringo ga arimasu.	3. There are some apples in the basket.
4. Donna iro desu ka?	4. What color is it?
5. Marui, rippa na kabin desu.	5. It's a round, splendid vase.
6. Shiroi no ya momoiro no mo arimasu.	6. There are white ones and pink ones, too.
7. 'Gray' wa Nippongo de nan to iimasu ka?	7. What's the Japanese for 'gray'?
8. Te de iroiro no mono o tori-	8. We take various things with our

masu.

9. Inu ya neko nimo ashi wa arimasu.

10. Watakushi wa anata ni Nippongo o oshiete imasu.

11. Otokonohito ga michi o aruite imasu.

12. Doa no tokoro e itte kudasai.

13. Doa o akete soto e dete kudasai.

14. Empitsu de chōmen ni kakimashita.

15. Mannenhitsu de kakimasen deshita.

16. Ichigatsu to nigatsu wa samukute yuki ga furimasu.

17. Shi to go to dotchi ga ōkii desu ka?

18. Go no hō ga ōkii desu.

19. Jūgatsu wa jūichigatsu yori attakai desu.

20. Nibamme no hi wa getsuyōbi de sambamme no hi wa kayōbi desu.

21. Yasumi da kara desu.

22. Hi ga deru to akaruku narimasu.

23. Senshū no doyōbi ni doko e ikimashita ka?

24. Doko emo ikimasen deshita.

25. Ichinichijū uchi ni imashita.

26. Shitte imasu ka?

27. Oboete imasu.

hands.

9. Dogs and cats also have legs and paws.

10. I'm teaching you Japanese.

11. A man is walking along the road.

12. Please go to the door.

13. Please open the door and go out.

14. I wrote it in the notebook with a pencil.

15. I didn't write it with a fountain pen.

16. It's cold in January and February and snow falls.

17. Which is larger, four or five?

18. Five is larger.

19. October is warmer than November.

20. The second day is Monday and the third day is Tuesday.

21. Because it's a holiday.

22. When the sun rises, it becomes light.

23. Where did you go last Saturday?

24. I didn't go anywhere.

25. I was at home all day.

26. Do you know?

27. I remember.

Jūsan

(Main Text)

A : Kore wa kippu desu. Nan no kippu desu ka ?

B : Kisha no kippu to basu no kippu desu.

A : Densha no kippu mo arimasu ka ?

B : Iie, densha no kippu wa arimasen.

A : Minna de ikumai arimasu ka ?

B : Jūmai arimasu.

A : Tsukue no ue ni hon ga nisatsu to empitsu ga nihon arimasu.

Hidari no hon wa atsukute kuroi desu ga, migi no wa usukute aoi desu.

Atsui no wa jibiki de, usui no wa kaiwa no hon desu.

Kono jibiki wa haba ga semai desu ga, kaiwa no hon wa haba ga hiroi desu.

Kono empitsu wa onaji nagasa desu ka ?

B : Iie, ippon wa nagakute, mō ippon wa mijikai desu.

A : Kiiroi empitsu to chairo no empitsu to dotchi ga nagai desu ka ?

B : Kiiroi empitsu no hō ga nagai desu.

(A Short Conversation)

A : Yokohama nitō ichimai.

B : Katamichi desu ka ?

A : Ōfuku o kudasai.

(For Memorizing)

1	ichimai	nimai		1.	one (ticket, paper, etc.) two		
	sammai	yomai	gomai		three	four	five
2.	issatsu	nisatsu		2.	one (book, notebook, etc.) two		
	sansatsu	shisatsu	gosatsu		three	four	five
	rokusatsu	shichisatsu	hassatsu		six	seven	eight
	kyūsatsu	jissatsu			nine	ten	
3	ippon			3.	one (pencil, fountain pen, etc.)		
	nihon	sambon	shihon		two	three	four
	gohon	roppon	shichihon		five	six	seven
	hachihon	kyūhon	jippon		eight	nine	ten

4. Hidari no [hon] wa [atsukute] [kuroi] desu.

4. The [book] on the left is [thick] and [black].

5. Kono [jibiki] wa haba ga [semai] desu.

5. This [dictionary] is [narrow].

6. Kono [empitsu] wa onaji [nagasa] desu ka ?

6. Are these [pencils] of the same [length] ?

7. Ippon wa [nagakute], mō ippon wa [mijikai] desu.

7. One is [long], and the other is [short].

Hombun

Glossary

kippu [---] *a ticket*

nan no ['--] *what* (See Lesson 5, Grammar 32.)

kisha [--] *a steam train; train drawn by a locomotive* (either steam or eletric)

basu ['-] *a bus*

densha ['--] *an electric car; streetcar; electric train* (without locomotive)

minna de [--'-] *in all*

ikumai ['---] *how many sheets*

-mai [--] a classifier for counting flat and thin objects

-satsu [--] a classifier for counting books, magazines, etc.

kaiwa [---] *conversation*

haba [--] *width*

semai [-'-] *narrow*

hiroi [-'-] *wide; broad*

nagasa [---] *length* (See Grammar 98.)

mō [--] *more; the other; additional*

"Mai"—a Classifier for Thin Objects

94. **Mai** is a numeral classifier used for thin, flat objects such as sheets of paper, rugs, carpets, boards, plates, kimonos.

> **ichimai, nimai, sammai, yomai** (or **yommai, shimai**), **gomai, rokumai, shichimai** (or **nanamai**), **hachimai, kumai** (or **kyūmai**), **jūmai,** etc.

Over ten, **mai** is likewise to be added to numerals.

> **jūichimai, jūnimai, jūsammai, jūyomai** (or **jūyommai**), **jūgomai,** etc.

"Satsu"—a Classifier for Books, etc.

95. **Satsu** is a numeral classifier used for volumes of books, magazines, notebooks, etc.

> **issatsu, nisatsu, sansatsu, shisatsu** (or **yonsatsu**), **gosatsu, rokusatsu, shichisatsu** (or **nanasatsu**), **hassatsu** (or **hachisatsu**), **kusatsu** (or **kyūsatsu**), **jissatsu,** etc.

"Iku-"—an Interrogative Prefix

96. **Iku-** which is related to **ikutsu** (how many) and **ikura** (how much) is used to form a compound meaning *how many.*

> **ikumai**   *how many sheets*
>
> **ikunen**   *how many years*
>
> **ikujikan**   *how many hours*

Two Nominative Particles in One Sentence

97.   **Kono hon wa haba ga hiroi desu.**   *This book is wide.*

The literal translation of the above sentence is *As for this book, the width is wide.* The particle **wa** denotes the subject of the whole sentence and the particle **ga** is the subject of the predicate clause **haba ga hiroi.**

The above is the orthodox explanation of the construction pattern [Noun] x **wa** x [noun] x **ga** x [predicate]. However, it may be simpler and easier to understand to say that **wa** is the subject of the sentence and [noun] x **ga** is merely added to clarify the ambiguity of the predicate.

> **Kono hon wa hiroi desu.**   *This book is wide.*

This is not clear enough.   A reader cannot tell whether the book is wide in width or length, so that, **haba**, *the width* is added to make it clear.

Similarly, **Ano hito wa ōkii desu** (*He is large*) is not clear enough. He may be large in body, head, mouth, eyes, age, etc.   Therefore, a specific indication is necessary.   Thus,

> **Ano hito wa atama ga ōkii desu.**   *He has a large head.*
> **Ano hito wa me ga ōkii desu.**   *He has large eyes.*
> **Ano hito wa hana ga ōkii desu.**   *He has a large nose.*

"Sa"—a Noun-forming Suffix

98. **Sa** is a suffix which has the function of changing an adjective into its corresponding noun.   It is added to the stem of a true adjective, i. e. the form without the final **i.**

ōkii	(*large*)	**ōkisa**	(*size ; bigness*)
nagai	(*long*)	**nagasa**	(*length*)
atsui	(*thick*)	**atsusa**	(*thickness*)
hayai	(*quick*)	**hayasa**	(*speed*)
omoi	(*heavy*)	**omosa**	(*weight*)
takai	(*high*)	**takasa**	(*height*)
yoi	(*good*)	**yosa**	(*goodness*)
nai	(*non-existent*)	**nasa**	(*non-existence*)

Quasi-adjectives are originally nouns, but some of them form abstract nouns in the same way.

kirei na	(*pretty*)	**kireisa**	(*beauty*)
rippa na	(*fine*)	**rippasa**	(*fineness*)

Mijikai Kaiwa

nitō [- - -] *second class:* **tō** is used for counting classes, grades, etc.
katamichi [- - - -] *one way*
ōfuku [- - - -] *round trip*

Exercises

A. Fill in each blank with a numeral with an appropriate classifier.

Example: Basu no kippu ga __(3)__ arimasu.   *Answer:* sammai.

1. Shiroi kami ga __(2)__ arimasu.
2. __(1)__ wa haba ga hiroi keredomo hoka no wa haba ga semai desu.
3. Empitsu ga __(6)__ arimasu.
4. Tēburu no ue ni jibiki ga __(2)__ arimasu.
5. Akai mannenhitsu ga __(1)__ to aoi no ga __(2)__ arimasu.

B. As you know, you can turn a true adjective into a noun by changing the final -i into -sa. Turn the following adjectives into their corresponding nouns, and see what they mean.

Example: nagai ⟶ nagasa (length)

ōkii ⟶   (   )

samui ⟶   (   )

attakai ⟶   (   )

omoi ⟶   (   )

atarashii ⟶   (   )

C. What is the Japanese equivalent of each of the following sentences?

1. He has one dictionary here, two at school, and one at home.
2. How many dictionaries in all does he have?
3. Are they all Japanese dictionaries?
4. That blue, thick one is a conversation book.
5. Whose is this wide and thin magazine?
6. The black shoes and the brown ones are of the same size.
7. I have two fountain pens.
8. One is red and the other is blue.
9. Which is longer, the red one or the blue one?
10. The blue one is longer.
11. Give me two round-trip tickets to Kōbe.
12. The blue ticket is for the second class (coach) and the white one for the first class.
13. How many bus tickets are there?
14. There is one bus ticket, but five streetcar tickets.

Jūshi

(Main Text)

A : Kore wa watakushi no saifu desu.

Kawa de koshiraete arimasu.

Kono naka ni okane ga haitte imasu.

Ikura haitte iru deshō ?

B : Shirimasen.

A : Soredewa akete mimashō.

Goran nasai. Kore wa jūen de kore wa
hyakuen desu.

Hyakuen no jūbai wa sen'en de, sen'en
no jūbai wa ichiman'en desu.

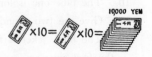

Ichiman'en no hambun wa ikura desu
ka ?

B : Gosen'en desu.

A : Dewa, sen'en no shibun-no-ichi wa
ikura desu ka ?

B : Nihyaku gojūen desu.

A : Kore wa hyakuen-satsu de, kore wa
jūen no dōka desu.

Saifu no naka ni hyakuen-satsu ga
sammai, jūen wa yottsu irete arimasu.

Minna de ikura desu ka ?

B : Sambyaku yonjūen desu.

A : Goen to jūen to gojūen no naka de
dore ga ichiban ōkii desu ka ?

B : Gojūen ga ichiban ōkii desu.

A : Satsu wa kami de koshiraemasu ga, dōka wa dō de koshiraemasu.

Kinka wa kin de, ginka wa gin de koshiraemasu.

Kin ya gin wa kane desu. Dō ya tetsu mo kane desu.

Gin wa kin gurai takai desu ka ?

B : Iie, gin wa kin hodo takaku wa arimasen.

A : Bin ya koppu wa nan de koshiraemasu ka ?

B : Garasu de koshiraemasu.

A : Kono bin niwa nani ga irete arimasu ka ?

B : Inki ga irete arimasu.

A : Bin no omote ni nani ga hatte arimasu ka ?

B : Kami ga hatte arimasu.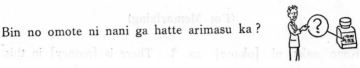

(A Short Conversation)

A : Kore wa ikura desu ka ?

B : Hitotsu hyaku nanajūen desu.

A : Takasugimasu. Motto yasui no wa arimasen ka ?

B : Kore wa ikaga desu ka ? Hachijūen desu.

A : Dewa sore o itadakimasu.

B : Arigatō gozaimasu. Nijūen no otsuri desu.

— 123 —

(For Memorizing)

1. Kono naka ni [okane] ga haitte imasu.
1. There is [money] in this.

2. [Ikura] haitte iru deshō?
2. Do you know [how much] there is?

3. Soredewa [akete] mimashō.
3. Then, let's [open] it and see.

4. Saifu no naka ni [hyakuen-satsu] ga irete arimasu.
4. There are [one-hundred-yen bills] in the purse.

5. [Ichien] to [goen] to [jūen] no naka de dore ga [ichiban ōkii] desu ka?
5. Which is the [largest], a [one-yen piece], a [five-yen piece], or a [ten-yen piece]?

6. [Satsu] wa kami de koshi-raemasu.
6. [Bills] are made of paper.

7. [Gin] wa [kin] gurai takai desu ka?
7. Is [silver] as expensive as [gold]?

8. [Gin] wa [kin] hodo takaku wa arimasen.
8. [Silver] is not as expensive as [gold].

Hombun

Glossary

saifu [- - -] *a purse; pocket-book; wallet.* A small purse to keep small change in is called **gamaguchi**.

kawa [-′] *skin; hide; leather*

koshiraete [- - - - -] from **koshiraeru**, *to make; manufacture*

okane [- - -] *money*

ikura [′- -] *how much*

deshō [- - -] the conjectural form of **desu**, *I suppose; probably*

soredewa [- -′-] *then*

mi- [-] from **miru**, *to see*

mimashō [- - - -] *I'll see* (See Lesson 16, Grammar 128.)

jūen [- - - -] *10 yen* (See Grammar 103.)

— *124* —

hyaku [-′]   *one hundred*

-bai [- -]   ...*times*: **jūbai**, *ten times*   (See Grammar 104.)

ichiman [- -′-]   *ten thousand*

hambun [- -′-]   *half*

sen [′-]   *thousand*: **gosen**, *five thousand*

shibun-no-ichi [- - - - - -]   *a quarter*; *one fourth*   (See Grammar 105.)

gojū [-′-]   *fifty*

satsu [- -]   *paper money*; *bank note*

dōka [′- -]   *a copper coin*

irete [- - -]   from **ireru**, *to put in*

sambyaku [′- - -]   *three hundred*

yonjū [′- - -]   *forty*   (See Lesson 9, Grammar 65.)

dore [′-]   *which one* (of the three or more)   (See Grammar 108.)

ichiban [- - - -]   *No. 1*; *most* (a sign of the superlative degree)

dō [′-]   *copper*

kinka [′- -]   *a gold coin*

kin [′-]   *gold*

ginka [′- -]   *a silver coin*

gin [′-]   *silver*

kane [- -]   *metal*

tetsu [- -]   *iron*

-gurai [- - -] or -kurai [- - -]   *as...as*; *about*

hodo [- -]   *not so...as*; *not to the extent*

bin [′-]   *a bottle*

koppu [- - -]   *a drinking glass*.   This word is most likely derived from the
   Spanish word *copa* meaning a tumbler.   Because of the similarity of the
   sound, many people imagine that it came from the English word *cup*.   But
   a cup is **chawan** in Japanese.

garasu [- - -]   *glass* (material)

inki [′- - or - - -]   *ink*

omote [- - -]   *surface*; *front* (but not *in front*)

hatte [- - -]   from **haru**, *to paste*

Grammar

"Aru" and "Iru" after the Te-form

99.   **Ano kata wa tatte imasu.**   *He is standing.*

But,   **Anata wa shitte imasu ka?**   *Do you know?*

Iru after the **te**-form describes either an action in progress or a state. In the case of intransitive verbs, context alone decides whether an action in progress or a state of being is meant.

    Kono naka ni okane ga haitte imasu.   *There is money in it.*

However, in the case of transitive verbs the distinction is made by the use of different terminal verbs, i. e. **iru** and **aru**.

When **iru** is used after the **te**-form of a transitive verb, it means an action in progress.

    Inki o irete imasu.   *He is putting ink in.*

    Doa o shimete imasu.   *He is shutting the door.*

When a state is to be expressed by a transitive verb, **aru** is used after its **te**-form with the nominative particle **ga** or **wa** instead of **o**.

    Kami ga hatte arimasu.   *Paper is pasted on.*

    Mado wa shimete arimasu.   *The window is shut.*

    To wa akete arimasu.   *The door is open.*

    Inki ga irete arimasu.   *Ink is in it.*

"Deshō"

100.   **Ikura haitte iru deshō?**   *Do you know how much is in it?*

Deshō is the conjectural form of **desu**. It is less positive, more doubtful than **desu**. It denotes the idea of *perhaps*, *may be*, *probably*, *I guess*, etc. (See Lesson 16, Grammar 127.)

Deshō with a rising tone expresses the idea of *Don't you think that......?* or *What......do you think......?*

Terminal Verbs

101.   A certain number of verbs, which are called terminal verbs, have special meanings when they come after the **te**-form of other verbs.

We have so far had the following terminal verbs.

kudasai : **Sore o totte kudasai.** *Please take it.*

Koko e kite kudasai. *Please come here.*

imasu : **Ano kata wa shimbun o yonde imasu.**

He is reading a newspaper.

arimasu : **Bin niwa inki ga irete arimasn.**

In the bottle is some ink.

Remember that the terminal verbs have their special meanings <u>only when</u> they come after the **te**-form of other verbs.

Sono hon o kudasai. *Give me that book.*

Dare mo imasen. *Nobody is here.*

Inki ga arimasu ka? *Is there any ink?*

" Miru "—a Terminal Verb

102. **Miru** as a terminal verb always comes after the **te**-form of a verb and means *to see to find out*, or *try to do such-and-such and see how it will turn out*.

Chotto itte mite kudasai. *Just go and see (who it is).*

Kite mi nasai. *Try it on (and see how it fits).*

Classifiers for Money

103. The *yen* is the unit of Japanese currency. When Japan was on the gold standard, one *yen* corresponded to approximately 50 cents or a little more than 2 shillings. The **sen** is a hundredth of a *yen*.

1 yen	**ichien**	10 sen	**jissen**	
2 yen	**nien**	20 sen	**nijissen**	
3 yen	**san'en**	30 sen	**sanjissen**	
4 yen	**yoen**	40 sen	**yonjissen**	
5 yen	**goen**	50 sen	**gojissen**	
6 yen	**rokuen**	60 sen	**rokujissen**	
7 yen	**shichien** (or **nanaen**)	70 sen	**shichijissen** (or **nanajissen**)	
8 yen	**hachien**	80 sen	**hachijissen**	
9 yen	**kuen** (or **kyūen**)	90 sen	**kujissen** (or **kyūjissen**)	
10 yen	**jūen**			

11 yen	**jūichien**	50 yen	**gojūen**
14 yen	**jūyoen**	60 yen	**rokujūen**
20 yen	**nijūen**	70 yen	**shichijūen** (or **nanajūen**)
21 yen	**nijū-ichien**	80 yen	**hachijūen**
24 yen	**nijū-yoen**	90 yen	**kujūen** (or **kyūjūen**)
40 yen	**yonjūen**	100 yen	**hyakuen**

Pay special attention to the pronunciation of 4-**en**, 7-**en**, 9-**en**, 14-**en**, 10-**sen**, etc. In Tokyo nowadays 10-**sen** is pronounced **jussen** by many people, especially by the young generation, but **jissen** is still considered to be preferrable.

Multiples and Fractions

104. Multiples such as *twice, three times, four times,* etc. are expressed by a number with the numeral classifier **bai.** Thus, **nibai** means *twice,* **sambai** means *three times,* etc.

yombai (or **shibai**)	*four times*	**hachibai**	*eight times*
gobai	*five times*	**kyūbai** (or **kubai**)	*nine times*
rokubai	*six times*	**jūbai**	*ten times*
shichibai	*seven times*		
(or **nanabai**)			

> **Watakushi no heya wa kono heya no nibai arimasu.**
>
> *My room is twice as large as this room.*

105. A fraction is expressed by the construction pattern of [denominator] **x bun-no-** x [numerator]. Thus $\frac{1}{2}$ is **nibun-no-ichi** and $\frac{1}{3}$ is **sambun-no-ichi.**

$\frac{1}{4}$ **shibun-no-ichi** (or **yombun-no-ichi**)

$\frac{2}{3}$ **sambun-no-ni**

$\frac{3}{4}$ **shibun-no-san** (or **yombun-no-san**)

$\frac{1}{10}$ **jūbun-no-ichi**

For *half* the word **hambun** is more commonly used except in arithmetic lessons.

More Numerals

106. *One hundred* is almost always **hyaku** and,

200	nihyaku			
300	sambyaku			
400	yonhyaku (sometimes **shihyaku**)			
500	gohyaku			
600	roppyaku			
700	shichihyaku (or **nanahyaku**)			
800	happyaku			
900	kyūhyaku (sometimes **kuhyaku**)			

One thousand may be **issen** or just merely **sen**, but ten thousand is nearly always **ichiman**.   Thus,

1,000	**sen** (or **issen**)		10,000	**ichiman**
2,000	**nisen**		20,000	**niman**
3,000	**sanzen**		30,000	**samman**
4,000	**yonsen** (sometimes **shisen**)		40,000	**yoman** (or **yomman**, sometimes **shiman**)
5,000	**gosen**		50,000	**goman**
6,000	**rokusen**		60,000	**rokuman**
7,000	**nanasen** (or **shichisen**)		70,000	**nanaman** (or **shichiman**)
8,000	**hassen**		80,000	**hachiman**
9,000	**kyūsen** (sometimes **kusen**)		90,000	**kyūman** (or **kuman**)
			10,000	**jūman**

The Superlative Degree

107.   The superlative degree is expressed by the use of **ichiban** which means *No. 1* before an adjective or an adverb.

> **Goen to jūen to gojūen no naka de dore ga ichiban ōkii desu ka?**
>> *Which is the largest, a five-yen piece, a ten-yen piece, or a fifty-yen piece?*
>
> **Gojūen ga ichiban ōkii desu.**   *A fifty-yen piece is the largest.*

"Dore" and "Dotchi"

108.   Both **dore** and **dotchi** mean *which*, but **dore** means the choice among three things or more, while **dotchi** is the choice between the two.   Hence,

dore is used for the superlative degree, while **dotchi** is for the comparison.

Dore ga ichiban ōkii desu ka?

Which is the largest (among three or more)?

Dotchi ga ōkii desu ka?   *Which is larger* (of the two)?

"Gurai" and "Hodo"

109.   The particle **gurai** (sometimes **kurai**) means *about*, or, *as much as*, and **hodo** means *to the extent of.* In comparing things, **gurai** is used in an affirmative sentence and **hodo** in a negative sentence, although there is a tendency for **hodo** to be used in both cases.

Akai empitsu wa aoi no gurai nagai desu ka?

Is the red pencil as long as the blue one?

Hai, akai empitsu wa aoi no gurai nagai desu.

Yes, the red pencil is as long as the blue one.

Iie, akai empitsu wa aoi no hodo nagaku wa arimasen.

No, the red pencil is not so long as the blue one.

Mijikai Kaiwa

-sugimasu [– – – –] *it's too......* ; *it's excessively.......* This is combined with the stem of true adjectives and quasi-adjectives, as well as with the 2nd base of verbs.

Kore wa rippasugimasu.   *This is too grand (for me).*

Kyō wa benkyō shisugimashita.   *I studied too much today.*

motto [′– –] *more.* **Mō** also means *more.* But number or quantity words come after **mō**, and other adjectives, adverbs, and verbs are used after **motto**.

Mō hitotsu kudasai.   *Please give me one more.*

Motto yukkuri itte kudasai.   *Please say it more slowly.*

Motto hanashimashō ka?   *Shall I speak more?*

itadaki- [– – – –] from **itadaku**, *to receive*

otsuri [– – –] *change.* **Otsuri** is the *balance* or *change* one receives when one pays. Thus, if a person buys eighty yen worth of something and pays with a hundred-yen coin, he gets twenty-yen **otsuri**. This word should never be used in the sense of small change. In case one wants to change a large note for small change, one should say **Dōzo kore o komakaku shite kudasai** (*Please make this smaller*), or **Kore o kuzushite kudasai** (*Please break this up*).

Exercises

*A. You know that the **te**-form of a transitive verb expresses an action in progress when it is followed by **imasu** and a state when it is followed by **arimasu**. Practise converting from one form to another rapidly and fluently.*

Conversion Table 5

Dictionary Form	Action in Progress	State	Meaning
kaku	kaite imasu	kaite arimasu	*write*
naosu	naoshite imasu	naoshite arimasu	*correct*
haru	hatte imasu	hatte arimasu	*paste*
toru	totte imasu	totte arimasu	*take*
akeru	akete imasu	akete arimasu	*open*
shimeru	shimete imasu	shimete arimasu	*close*
koshiraeru	koshiraete imasu	koshiraete arimasu	*make*
kazoeru	kazoete imasu	kazoete arimasu	*count*
yomu	yonde imasu	yonde arimasu	*read*
benkyō suru	benkyō shite imasu	benkyō shite arimasu	*study*

*B. To express a state, the **te**-form of a transitive verb followed by **arimasu** or the **te**-form of an intransitive verb followed by **imasu** is used. Fill in each blank with either **arimasu** or **imasu**. Be sure you understand the meaning.*

1. Kono tokei wa kin de koshiraete ___.
2. Watakushi no uwagi wa kawa de dekite ___.
3. Doa wa aite ___ ga, mado wa shimete ___.
4. Kono saifu no naka ni okane ga ikura haitte ___ ka?
5. Kami niwa nani mo kaite ___.

C. Fill in each blank with an appropriate word.

1. Kono tegami wa Nippongo de ___ arimasu kara yoku wakarimasen.
2. Chotto yonde ___ kudasai.

3. Okane o kazoete ____ kudasai. Ikura arimasu ka ?

4. Hyakuen-satsu ga ____ arimasu kara, sen'en arimasu.

5. Sen'en no ____ wa gohyakuen desu.

6. Sen'en no ____ wa ichiman'en desu.

7. Tōkyō to Yokohama to Ōsaka no ____ de ____ ga ichiban ōkii desu ka ?

8. Tōkyō ga ____ ōkii desu.

9. Soredewa Yokohama to Ōsaka to ____ ga ōkii desu ka ?

10. Ōsaka no ____ ga ōkii desu.

11. "Igirisu wa Amerika gurai ōkii desu ka ?" "Iie, Amerika ____ ōkiku wa arimasen."

12. Bin wa garasu ____ koshiraemasu.

D. *Answer the following questions.*

1. Anata no saifu wa kawa de koshiraete arimasu ka ?

2. Anata no saifu no naka ni okane ga haitte imasu ka ?

3. Satsu mo ginka mo irete arimasu ka ?

4. Ima anata wa dōka ga irimasu ka ?

5. Ichijikan no shibun-no-ichi wa jippun desu ka ?

6. Gin no tokei wa kin no gurai takai desu ka ?

7. Pen wa nan de koshiraemasu ka ?

8. Anata no mannenhitsu niwa inki ga haitte imasu ka ?

9. Inki no bin niwa kami ga hatte arimasu ka ?

10. Tōkyō kara Yokohama made iku no ni ikura kakaru deshō ?

E. *What is the Japanese equivalent of each of the following sentences?*

1. How much are these apples (each) ?

2. They are thirty-five yen each.

3. How many apples are there in that basket ?

4. There are ten in it.

5. How much is one-fourth of ten thousand yen ?

6. What is ten times ten thousand ?

7. This flower vase is made of silver.

8. But the stand is made of copper.

9. This desk is made of metal. It is light, though.

10. Your chair is not so large as mine.
11. But it is as high as mine.
12. All my pencils are kept in this desk.

F. What would you say when,
1. you want to hurry up ?
2. you are busy and want to make it later ?
3. you want a round-trip ticket ?
4. you want to know how much an article is ?
5. you want a little cheaper one ?

G. Here is a short conversation between Mr. Brown and a shopkeeper. Take Mr. Brown's role and express in Japanese the ideas suggested by the English sentences.

Mr. Brown : (*Have you got flower vases ?*)

Shopkeeper : Hai, takusan arimasu. (*Shopkeeper shows some.*)

Mr. Brown : (*How much is this purple one ?*)

Shopkeeper : Sore wa sanzen'en desu.

Mr. Brown : (*It's too expensive. Haven't you got cheaper ones ?*)

Shopkeeper : Kore wa ikaga desu ka ?

Mr. Brown : (*How much is it ? Is it cheaper than the purple one ?*)

Shopkeeper : Hai, yasui desu. Sen happyaku'en desu.

Mr. Brown : (*How much is that red one ?*)

Shopkeeper : Are wa kore yori takai desu. Nisen gohyakuen desu.

Mr. Brown : (*Then, give me that one.*)

Shopkeeper : Sō desu ka ? Arigatō gozaimasu.

Mr. Brown : (*Here are three one-thousand-yen bills.*)

Shopkeeper : Arigatō gozaimasu. Gohyakuen no otsuri desu.

Jūgo

(Main Text)

A : Kono e o goran nasai.

Migi no hō ni ikken no ie ga arimasu.

Nihon no ie desu ka ?

B : Iie, yōkan desu.

A : Entotsu kara kemuri ga dete imasu.

Ie no soba ni ki ga nihon arimasu.

Ie no chikaku de kodomo ga asonde imasu.

Ie no mae ni michi ga arimasu. Semai michi desu ka ?

B : Iie, kanari hiroi massugu na michi desu.

Keredomo ie no soba no michi wa magatte imasu.

A : Mukō kara ichidai no jidōsha ga kimasu.

Ima uchi no mae e kuru tokoro desu.

Dare ga unten shite imasu ka ?

B : Wakarimasen. Onnanohito no yō desu.

Gaikokujin kamo shiremasen.

A : Hidari no hō wa umi desu.

Shima no soba o fune ga issō tōtte imasu.

Kaigan ni hito ga imasu. Ikunin imasu
ka ?

B : Shichinin imasu.

A : Kono e no naka ni hito ga ikunin imasu
ka ?

B : Hitori, futari, sannin, yonin, gonin,
rokunin, shichinin, hachinin, kunin, jūnin,
jūichinin, — jūichinin imasu.

A : Jidōsha o unten shite iru hito o ireru
to ikunin desu ka ?

B : Jūninin desu.

A : Tōku no hō ni yama ga arimasu.

Hikui yama desu ka?

B : Iie, kanari takai yama desu.

(A Short Conversation)

B : Kono michi wa Ginza e ikimasu ka?

A : Ikimasu.

B : Koko wa doko desu ka?

A : Tamachi-eki no chikaku desu.

B : Ginza made dono gurai arimasu ka?

A : Nikiro gurai desu.

(For Memorizing)

1. [Ie] no chikaku de kodomo ga asonde imasu.

1. Some children are playing near the [house].

2. Mukō kara [ichidai no jidōsha] ga kimasu.

2. [A motor-car] is coming from the distance.

3. Ima [uchi] no [mae] e kuru tokoro desu.

3. Now it's coming [in front of] the [house].

4. [Onnanohito] no yō desu.

4. It seems to be a [woman].

5. [Gaikokujin] kamo shiremasen.

5. Maybe it's a [foreigner].

6. Shima no soba o [fune] ga tōtte imasu.

6. A [boat] is passing by the island.

7. [Jidōsha] o unten shite iru hito o ireru to ikunin desu ka?

7. How many people are there including the one who is driving the [car]?

Hombun

Glossary

-ken [--] or **-gen** [--] a classifier for houses (See Grammar 110.)

ie [-′] *a house*

Nihon [-′-] *Japan*

yōkan [----] *a foreign-style house*

entotsu [----] *a chimney*

kemuri [---] *smoke*

chikaku [-′-] *nearby ; vicinity*

asonde [----] from **asobu**, *to play ; enjoy oneself*

kanari [′--] *fairly ; pretty*

massugu [--′-] *(a-B) straight*

magatte [----] from **magaru**, *to bend ; turn*

mukō [---] *the other side ; the other person or party*

-dai [--] a classifier for counting vehicles

tokoro [---] *about to* (See Grammar 114.)

dare ['-] *who*

unten suru [------] *to drive*

yō (desu) ['-(--)] *(a-B) to seem; appear*

gaikokujin [------] *a foreigner.* **Gaijin,** an abbreviated form, is also used.

...kamo shiremasen ['------] *maybe......; perhaps; it could be; it is possible*

umi ['-] *the sea*

shima [-'] *an island*

fune ['-] *a boat; ship*

-sō [--] a classifier for boats

tōtte ['---] from **tōru,** *to pass through*

kaigan [----] *the seashore*

-nin [--] a classifier for persons

hitori [-'-] *one person*

futari [---] *two persons*

yonin [---] *four persons*

ireru [---] *to include*

tōku [---] *a distant place; distance*

yama [-'] *a mountain*

Grammar

"Ken"—a Classifier for Houses

110. **Ken** is used with the second set of numerals in counting the number of houses, shops, etc.

> **ikken, niken, sangen, yonken** (or **shiken**)**, goken, rokken, shichiken** (or **nanaken**)**, hachiken** (or **hakken**)**, kyūken** (or **kuken**)**, jikken,** etc.

"Ie no Chikaku de"

111. **Chikaku** here is a noun derived from the adverbial form of the adjective **chikai,** *near.* Similarly from **tōi,** *far* is derived the noun **tōku,** *distance.* **Tōku de,** therefore, means *in the distance.*

"De"—a Particle denoting a Place of Action

112. Besides the meanings given in the previous lesson, **de** refers to the place where an action is performed. It does not matter whether a place of action is a wide area or not. It may, therefore, be translated by *in* or *at.*

> **Gakkō de naraimasu.** *I learn (it) at school.*
> **Nippon de mimashita.** *I saw (it) in Japan.*
> **Ie no chikaku de asonde imasu.**
> *They are playing near the house.*

Since **ni** also has a locative sense and is often translated by *in* or *at*, confusion may arise. The difference is that **ni** refers to the place where a person or a thing exists whereas **de** denotes the place of action.

> **Koko ni hon ga arimasu.** *There is a book here.* (existence)
> **Koko de naraimasu.** *I learn (it) here.* (place of action)
> **Chikaku ni ie ga arimasu.** *There is a house nearby.* (existence)
> **Tōku de kiite imasu.** *He is listening in the distance.*
> (action)

"Dai"—a Classifier for Vehicles

113. **Dai** is a classifier for motorcars, carriages, bicycles, and motorcycles, etc. as well as machines.

> **ichidai, nidai, sandai, yodai** (or **yondai**), **godai, rokudai, shichidai** (or **nanadai**), **hachidai, kudai** (or **kyūdai**), **jūdai,** etc.

"Tokoro"—"About to"

114. This is a form noun meaning a place or a scene from which developed a derivative meaning of *about to*, *just*, etc. **Jidōsha ga tōru tokoro desu** literally means *It is the scene of a motorcar passing*, and actually means *A motorcar is about to pass.*

> **Ie no mae o tōru tokoro desu.**
> *It is about to pass in front of the house.*
> **Kore kara dekakeru tokoro desu**. *I am going out now.*
> **Doa o akeru tokoro desu.** *I am about to open the door.*

"Yō"—"Appearance"

115. **Yō** which means *appearance, manner, likeness,* etc., was originally a noun, and is, in fact, used as a ı oun in many instances. But it has now come to be a quasi-adjective-like partic.e.

Are wa onnanohito no yo desu.

That seems to be a woman. (That has an appearance of a woman.)

Kanari ōkii fune no yō desu. *It seems to be a fairly large boat.*

After an adjective and a verb it is tacked on to their 3rd (conclusive) base.

Ano yama wa takai yō desu.	*That mountain appears to be high.*
Okane ga aru yō desu.	*He seems to have money.*
Yuki ga futte iru yō desu.	*It seems to be snowing.*
Haru ga kuru yō desu.	*It seems that spring is coming.*

"Kamo shiremasen"—"May"

116. This is the equivalent of the English word *may* or *may be* in the sense of possibility but not when it expresses permission.

Kodomo kamo shiremasen.	*It may be a child.*
Sō ja nai kamo shiremasen.	*Maybe it isn't so.*
Kaku kamo shiremasen.	*He may write it.*

"Sō"—a Classifier for Vessels

117.   **issō, nisō, sansō** (or **sanzō**), **shisō** (or **yonsō**), **gosō, rokusō, shichisō** (or **nanasō**), **hassō** (or **hachisō**), **kusō** (or **kyūsō**), **jissō,** etc.

"Soba o Tōru"—"to Pass"

118. In Lesson 7, Grammar 55 we explained that verbs of motion in moving from one place to another such as walking, running, etc. take **o** even though they are intransitive verbs. The verb **tōru** is one of them, so you can say **michi o tōru** in the sense of *passing along a road.* But when you want to express the idea of passing an island or a house, trouble starts, because the Japanese verb **tōru** means *to go through*, and **shima o tōru** will mean *to pass through an island*, and **ie o tōru** will mean *to pass through a house.*

Therefore, we must specify the place where one passes through when we use tŏru.

ie no mae o tŏru	*to pass in front of the house*
gakkŏ no chikaku o tŏru	*to pass near the school*
shima no soba o tŏru	*to pass (by) an island*

Numeral Classifier for People

119. Counting of people is a little irregular. **Nin** may be called a classifier for people except one, two, and sometimes four persons, i. e.,

hitori, futari, sannin, yonin (or **yottari**), **gonin, rokunin, shichinin** (or **nananin**), **hachinin, kunin** (or **kyūnin**), **jūnin, jūichinin, jūninin,** etc.

Modifying Phrases or Clauses (1)

120.   **Jidŏsha o unten shite iru hito wa dare desu ka?**
Who is the person who is driving the car?
Kore wa watakushi ga itsumo tsukau jibiki desu.
This is the dictionary I always use.

As seen in the above examples, modifiers, regardless of whether they are single words, phrases or clauses, come before the nouns they modify. Since there are no relative pronouns in Japanese, sometimes a long string of modifying words may come before a noun.

Jidŏsha o unten shite iru hito literally means *the car-driving-person,* and **itsumo tsukau jibiki** literally means *the always-use-dictionary.*

When a verb comes at the end of a modifying phrase or clause, the conclusive base of the verb, i.e. the dictionary form, is used.

watakushi ga kaku hon	*the book I write*
ie e kaeru hito	*the person who goes home*

Since **masu** is in the conclusive base, such uses as the following are quite possible, but they are not usually used except in very polite sentences, because a sentence may be polite enough as long as it ends with **masu.**

watakushi ga kakimasu tegami	*the letter I write*
ie e kaerimasu hito	*the person who goes home*
jidŏsha o unten shite imasu hito	
	the person who is driving the car

The Plain Form of Verbs

121. (See Lesson 10, Grammar 76.)

Polite Present:	Jidōsha ga **kimasu.**
	Nippongo o **hanashimasu.**
	Kemuri ga **demasu.**
Plain Present:	Jidōsha ga **kuru.**
	Nippongo o **hanasu.**
	Kemuri ga **deru.**
Polite Past:	Jidōsha ga **kimashita.**
	Nippongo o **hanashimashita.**
	Kemuri ga **demashita.**
Plain Past:	Jidōsha ga **kita.**
	Nippongo o **hanashita.**
	Kemuri ga **deta.**

It will be seen from the above that the formation of the plain past is easily done by replacing the final **e** of the **te**-form of a verb by **a**.

Plain Present	Plain Past	Te-form	Meaning
kaku	**kaita**	**kaite**	*to write*
iku	**itta**	**itte**	*to go*
yomu	**yonda**	**yonde**	*to read*
taberu	**tabeta**	**tabete**	*to eat*
kiru	**kita**	**kite**	*to wear*
kuru	**kita**	**kite**	*to come*
suru	**shita**	**shite**	*to do*

When there are two or more verbs in one sentence, the sentence is polite as long as the final verb is in the polite form. Therefore, it is usual for a verb in a modifying phrase or a clause to be in the plain style.

Mijikai Kaiwa

eki ['–] *a station*

dono gurai [– – – – –] *about how much.* **Gurai** which is often pronounced as **kurai** corresponds in meaning to the English word *about* or *approximately* in denoting the approximate quantity. It comes *after* the number. It also forms such combinations as the following.

dono gurai (dono kurai)	*about how much*
kono gurai (kono kurai)	*about this much*
sono⎫ ano ⎭ gurai (sono⎫ ano ⎭ kurai)	*about that much*
ikutsu gurai (ikutsu kurai)	*about how many; about how old*
ikura gurai (ikura kurai)	*about how much (money)*
Dono gurai arimasu ka?	

> *About how much is there?; How far is it?*

Sanjū-gokiro gurai arimasu.

> *There are (=It is) about 35 kilometers.*

kiro ['-] *kilometer*

Exercises

A. Look at the picture on page 134 and fill in each blank with an appropriate word. As for the numbers in the blank, put appropriate classifiers after them and spell them out in Rōmaji.

1. Umi ＿＿＿ hito ga ＿(2)＿ haitte ＿＿＿.
2. Shima no ＿＿＿ o fune ga ＿(1)＿ tōtte imasu.
3. Mukō ＿＿＿ jidōsha ga ＿(1)＿ kimasu.
4. Jidōsha wa michi ＿＿＿ tatte iru hito no ＿＿＿ o tōrimashita.
5. E no naka ＿＿＿ yōkan ga ＿(1)＿ arimasu.
6. Kono ie wa gaikokujin no kamo ＿＿＿.
7. Yōkan no ＿＿＿ ni takai ki ga ＿(2)＿ arimasu.
8. Ie no chikaku ＿＿＿ kodomo ga ＿(2)＿ imasu.
9. Tōku no ＿＿＿ ni yama ga arimasu.
10. Sora ＿＿＿ hikōki ga tonde imasu ka?

B. Look at the same picture and answer the following questions.

1. Kono e no naka ni Nihon no ie ga arimasu ka?
2. Yōkan no entotsu kara nani ga dete imasu ka?
3. Jidōsha wa doko o tōru tokoro desu ka?
4. Anata wa jidōsha o unten shite iru hito o shitte imasu ka?
5. Umi niwa fune ga imasu ka?
6. Fune wa doko o tōtte imasu ka?
7. Fune wa ikusō tōtte imasu ka?

8. Kono e no naka ni iru hito wa minna hataraite imasu ka ?
9. Tōku no hō ni nani ga arimasu ka ?
10. Kore wa natsu no e desu ka, fuyu no e desu ka ?

C. *What is the Japanese equivalent of each of the following sentences?*
1. He has two cars. He uses one to go to school.
2. His wife uses the other car.
3. There is a foreign-style house on the seashore.
4. One boat is going to the island.
5. There seems to be one person in the car.
6. The road in front of the station is narrow but fairly straight.
7. The sea is in front of the house.
8. Two cars are passing by my house.
9. The people who are taking a walk may be foreigners.
10. In the distance a white bird is flying.
11. How far is it from your house to the school ?
12. I don't know exactly (=well), but it may be three kilometers.

Jūroku

(Main Text)

B : Sakura no hana wa sangatsu no sue goro sakimasu ka?

A : Tōkyō dewa mada sakanai deshō.

Taitei shigatsu no hajime ni sakimasu.

B : Sakura no hana wa taihen kirei da sō desu ne.

A : Sō desu.

B : Sakura no hana ga saku to hitobito wa dō shimasu ka?

A : Hanami ni dekakemasu.

B : Anata mo hanami ni ikimasu ka?

A : Tokidoki ikimasu. Keredomo kyonen wa ikimasen deshita.

B : Naze desu ka ?

A : Iku tsumori deshita ga byōki deshita.

B : Sō desu ka ? Sore wa ikemasen deshita nē.

Kotoshi wa issho ni ikimashō ka ?

A : Ikimashō. Doko ga ii deshō ?

B : Kamakura wa tōi desu ka ?

A : Densha de iku to ichijikan gurai de tsukimasu.

Eki kara wa aruku hō ga ii deshō.

B : Nihon dewa rokugatsu ni takusan ame ga furu sō desu ne.

A : Sō desu. Rokugatsu wa tenki ga warukute ame ga takusan furimasu.

Ame no furanai hi demo kumotte imasu.

B : Rokugatsu no owari niwa tenki ga yoku narimasu ka ?

A : Sono koro niwa mada yoku naranai deshō.

B : Nikkō wa itsu iku hō ga ii deshō ka ?

A : Jūgatsu no owari goro iku no ga ichiban ii rashii desu.

Shikashi gogatsu ka rokugatsu mo ii yō desu.

B : Atsuku naru to hitobito wa dō shimasu ka ?

A : Aru hito wa yama ya umi e ikimasu.

Tōkyō no hito wa Hakone ya Karuizawa e iku yō desu.

Soshite suzushiku natte kara kaerimasu.

B : Anata wa kotoshi wa yama e ikimasu ka ?

A : Ikitai desu ga isogashii desu kara iku koto ga dekiru ka dō ka wakarimasen.

(A Short Conversation)

B : Kisha ga arimasu ka ?

A : Arimasen. Keredomo basu ga arimasu.

B : Itsu demasu ka ?

A : Mō sugu demasu.

(For Memorizing)

1. [Tōkyō] dewa mada sakanai deshō.

1. In [Tokyo] they will probably not have bloomed yet.

2. [Iku] tsumori deshita ga byōki deshita.

2. I had intended to [go], but I was sick.

3. Sore wa ikemasen deshita nē.

3. I'm sorry to hear that.

4. [Densha] de iku to [ichijikan] gurai de tsukimasu.

4. We (can) get there in about [an hour] by [electric train].

5. [Eki] kara wa aruku hō ga ii deshō.

5. From the [station] it will be better to walk, I think.

6. [Jūgatsu] no [owari] ni iku no ga ichiban ii rashii desu.

6. It seems best to go there at the [end] of [October].

7. [Suzushiku] natte kara kaeri-masu.

7. They come back after it gets [cool].

8. [Iku] koto ga dekiru ka dō ka wakarimsen.

8. I'm not sure whether I can [go] or not.

Hombun

Glossary

sakura [- - -] *cherry*. This refers to the specie. Therefore, in expressing the tree, blossoms, fruit, definitely **sakura no ki** (*a cherry-tree*), **sakura no hana** (*cherry-blossoms*) and **sakura no mi** (*cherry fruit* which has another and usual name **sakurambō**) should be used.

sue [- -] *the end* (of the week, month, year, etc.)

goro ['-] *about* (approximate point of time)

saki- [- -] from **saku**, *to bloom; open* (flower)

dewa ['-] *in; at* (See Grammar 122.)

sakanai [- - - -] *do not bloom* (See Grammar 123.)

taitei [- - - -] *usually; generally*

taihen [- - - -] *very*

...sō desu [- - - -] *it is said; I hear* (See Grammar 124.)

hitobito [-'- -] *people*

dō ['-] *how ; in what way*

hanami [- - -] *flower-viewing*

tokidoki [- - - -] *occasionally ; once in a while*

kyonen ['- -] *last year*

tsumori [- - -] *intention* (See Grammar 127.)

ikemasen [- - - - -] *no good ; won't do*

kotoshi [- - -] *this year*

issho ni [- - - -] *together*

-mashō [- - -] probable form of **-masu** (See Grammar 128.)

tōi [- - -] *(a-A)* *distant ; far*

tsuki- [- -] from **tsuku**, *to reach*

ame ['-] *rain*

demo ['-] *even*

kumotte [-'- -] from **kumoru**, *to become cloudy*

sono koro [- -'-] *about that time ; around then*

shikashi [-'-] *but ; however*

ka [-] *or* (See Grammar 133.)

aru ['-] *some*

soshite [- - -] *and ; after that*

kara [- -] *after* (See Grammar 134.)

kaeri- [- - -] from **kaeru**, *to return*

-tai ['-] *desirous* (See Grammar 135.)

koto [- -] *a fact ; thing* (abstract) (See Grammar 136.)

ka dō ka [-'- -] *whether or not* (See Grammar 137.)

Grammar

" De (wa) "

122.　　**Tōkyō dewa mada sakanai deshō.**

　　　　In Tokyo they will probably not have bloomed yet.

　　Dewa is the combination of the particles **de** and **wa**. **Wa** is a particle denoting the topic of a sentence. **De** refers to the place where an action is performed as we learned in Lesson 15, Grammar 112.

The Negative Base

123. We know that the negative form of **masu** is **masen** and that of **desu** is **ja arimasen** There is, however, another way of forming the negative. It is to use an adjective-like auxiliary **nai** or its conjugation after the first base which is formed in the following way.

Mada saka-nai deshō.	(negative of **saku**)
Yoku nara-nai deshō.	(negative of **naru**)
Mada tabe-nai deshō.	(negative of **taberu**)
Koko e ko-naide kudasai.	(negative of **kuru**)

Nai has the same conjugation as a true adjective.

The **Yodan** *verbs :*

The negative form of **Yodan** verbs ends in **a**, that is, the final **u** of the dictionary form replaced by **a**.

Dictionary form	Negative form	Meaning
kaku	**kaka**-nai	*to write*
hairu	**haira**-nai	*to enter*
tatsu	**tata**-nai	*to stand*
shiru	**shira**-nai	*to know*
yomu	**yoma**-nai	*to read*
toru	**tora**-nai	*to take*
asobu	**asoba**-nai	*to play*
tobu	**toba**-nai	*to fly*
narau	**narawa**-nai	*to learn*

The **Ichidan** *verbs :*

The negative form of **Ichidan** verbs is quite simple.

It is the same as the second base, that is, the final syllable **ru** is taken off the dictionary form.

tabe-ru	**tabe**-nai	*to eat*
oshie-ru	**oshie**-nai	*to teach*
ki-ru	**ki**-nai	*to wear*
mi-ru	**mi**-nai	*to see*

The **irregular** *verbs :*

The negative forms of the two irregular verbs are irregular. In fact they get their name from the very fact that the formation of their negative form is irregular. In the case of other verbs the stem never changes. It is the ending that conjugates. But, these two verbs are exceptions.

kuru	**ko**-nai	*to come*
suru	**shi**-nai	*to do*

"Sō desu"—Given Information

124. When the speaker gives information received from another source in such forms as *I hear that, they say that, the story goes*, etc., the corresponding Japanese construction pattern is **sō desu** after the conclusive (i. e. the 3rd) base of a verb.

Sakura no hana wa taihen kirei da sō desu nē.

I hear that cherry-blossoms are very beautiful, aren't they?

Ueno no hana wa mō saita sō desu.

I hear the blossoms at Ueno have already bloomed.

"Dō," "Kō," "Sō," "Ā,"—"How," "This Way," "That Way"

125. **Dō** means how or what way. Hence, **Dō shimasu ka?** means *What will you do?*. Just as there is a group of words, **kore**, **sore**, **are**, **dore** (*which one*), there is a group of words, **kō** (*this way*), **sō** (*that way*), **ā** (*that way*), and **dō** (*what way*).

"Ni" followed by a Verb of Motion

126.   **Hanami ni ikimasu.**   *We go flower-viewing.*

Ni followed by a verb of motion such as **iku**, *to go*, **kuru**, *to come*, **kaeru**, *to return*, **dekakeru**, *to go out*, denotes the purpose. The verb form used before **ni** is the second base where **masu** is usually attached.

Mi ni ikimasu.	*I'll go to see it.*
Narai ni kimasu.	*He comes to study it.*
Hanami ni ikimashita.	*I went flower-viewing.*

"Tsumori"—"Intention"

127. **Tsumori** means *intention*. It is used as follows:

iku tsumori desu	*intend to go*
iku tsumori deshita	*intended to go*
iku tsumori ja arimasen	*don't intend to go*
iku tsumori deshō	*I suppose he intends to go*

Kyō iku tsumori deshita ga, ame ga futte imasu kara ikimasen.

> *I intended to go today, but as it is raining I won't go.*

Dō suru tsumori desu ka? *What do you intend to do?*
What is your intention?

"Mashō"—Probable Form of "Masu"

128. The English sentence in the future tense, *I will write*, may be rendered into Japanese in two ways.

(a) **Watakushi ga kakimasu.**

(b) **Watakushi ga kakimashō.**

From these you can see that both **masu** and **mashō** can describe an act of future occurrence.

The difference lies in the degree of certainty on the part of the speaker. **Masu** is much more positive than **mashō**. **Kakimasu**, therefore, means *I will write*, *I'm determined to write*, etc., while **kakimashō** means *I shall most likely write*, *I shall write (because you want me to)*, etc. **Mashō** is generally used in connection with future facts, not because it is the future form, but because future occurrences are usually uncertain.

Mashō referring to the first person may be rendered into English something like the following.

Itsu ikimashō ka? *When shall I go?*

Issho ni ikimashō. *Let's go together.*

Both **mashō** and **deshō** (See Lesson 14, Grammar 100.) denote probability. The difference is that **mashō** is always tacked on to the 2nd base of a verb whereas **deshō** is used after a noun or the dictionary form (3rd or conclusive base) of a verb or a true adjective.

Issho ni ikimashō ka? *Shall we go together?*

Nanji deshō? *What time is it, I wonder?*

Mada sakanai deshō. *Perhaps they are not out yet.*

Tsuki ga deru deshō. *The moon will rise, I suppose.*

"Hō ga Ii"—"Had Better"

129. Advice to the effect that it is the wiser course to do something is expressed by **hō ga ii** after the conclusive base. **Hō ga ii** literally means ......*side is good*. Thus, **aruku hō ga ii desu** means *Walking side is better* (*than taking an electric train*, etc.) which comes to mean *You had better walk*.

Hō ga ii has no sense of command or strong advice which the English *had better* sometimes implies.

"Takusan"—"a Lot," "Much"

130.   **Nippon dewa itsu ame ga takusan furimasu ka?**
        In Japan when does it rain a great deal?
        Takusan no hito ga yama ya umi e ikimasu.
        A lot of people go to the mountains or seashore.

Takusan is originally a noun, but since it expresses quantity, it is used like an adverb without any particle.

Numbers are treated in the same way, since they belong to the same category. (See Lesson 4, Grammar 28.)

"No" forming Noun Phrases or Clauses

131.   **Jūgatsu no owari goro iku no ga ichiban ii desu.**
        To go around the end of October is the best.

In order to make a phrase which ends with a verb (e.g. **jūgatsu no owari goro iku**) the subject of a sentence, that phrase must be made into a noun equivalent by adding **no** after it. **No** has the meaning of *an act of* ......*ing*.

        Nippon e iku no wa shigatsu no hajime desu.
        The fact of going to Japan is the beginning of April. (=*My trip to Japan will take place at the beginning of April.*)

"Rashii"—"Seem"

132. Rashii means *seem* or *appear* and can be placed after various parts of speech.

(a) *After a noun :*

Onnanohito rashii desu.   *It seems to be a woman.*

In a compound it sometimes corresponds to the termination -*sh* or -*ly* in English.

Ano hito wa kodomorashii hito desu. *He is a childish man.*

Otokorashii hito desu.   *He is a manly person.*

It is possible, however, that these compounds mean *seems to be a child* or *seems to be a man* respectively such as,

Are wa kodomo rashii desu.   *That seems to be a child.*

Aruite iru hito wa otoko rashii desu.

The person who is walking looks like a man.

The context, together with a variance in accentuation, i.e. (-'-) for *seem* and (- - -) for -*sh*, will usually, but not always, determine the meaning. In the former case there is the sensation of a pause before **rashii.**

(b) *After an adjective :*

Kanari chikai rashii desu.   *It seems fairly near.*

Me ni ii rashii desu.   *It seems to be good for the eyes.*

It forms a sort of compound adjective, such as **kitanarashii** (**kitanai**, *dirty* and *rashii*), **kawairashii** (**kawaii**, *lovely* and **rashii**), but in this case the final **i** of the adjective is left out.

(c) *After the present or the past form of a verb :*

Kyō iku rashii desu.   *He seems to be going today.*

Yonde iru rashii desu.   *He seems to be reading.*

Byōki datta rashii desu.   *He seems to have been sick.*

The meaning of **rashii** is very close to that of **yō** (See Lesson 15, Grammar 115.), and they are often interchangeable in meaning, but among the differences, one noteworthy point is that **rashii** seems to express a quality befitttng the noun in contrast to **yō** expressing the likeness or appearance rather than its intrinsic quality.

otokorashii hito   *manly person*

otoko no yō na hito   *mannish person*

The Particle " Ka " between Two Nouns

133. The particle **ka** between two nouns means *or* just as the particle **to** between two nouns means *and*.

Gogatsu ka rokugatsu mo ii yō desu.

May or June also seems to be a good time.

Anata wa pen ka empitsu ga arimasu ka?

Do you have a pen or a pencil?

"Kara" after the Te-form

134. **Kara** after the **te**-form means *after* or *subsequently*.

Suzushiku natte kara kaerimasu.

They return after it gets cool.

Shimbun o yonde kara dekakemasu.

I'll go out after I read newspapers.

Kara after a sentence (or a clause) means *because* as explained in Lesson 10, Grammar 75. **Kara** after a noun means *from* as in the case of **ichi kara** or **koko kara** as we learned in Lesson 9.

"Tai"—The Desiderative

135. A desire to do something which is expressed in English by *want to* or *I should like to* is expressed in Japanese by an adjective-like auxiliary **tai** attached to the second base.

Tai has the same conjugation as a true adjective.

> **Nani o kakitai desu ka?** *What do you want to write?*
>
> **Eki e ikitai desu.** *I'd like to go to the station.*
>
> **Nani mo shitaku wa arimasen.** *I don't want to do anything.*

Remember that **tai** is used when one wants to do something, but not when one wants an object. *I want a book* is expressed by a different word. It will be explained later.

"Koto ga dekiru"—"Can"

136. There are several ways of expressing the idea of *being able to do something*, but the easiest one is to put **koto ga dekiru** after the dictionary form (i.e. 3rd or conclusive base) of any verb.

> **Miru koto ga dekimasu.** *I can see.*
>
> **Kiku koto ga dekimasen.** *I cannot hear.*

Remember that this rule can be applied to any verb. Other ways of expressing the same idea are more troublesome because we have to choose verbs. This is the reason why we say this form is the easiest.

Koto ga dekiru literally means *a certain thing is possible*. Thus, **miru koto ga dekiru** means *a fact of seeing* (or simply *seeing*) *is possible*.

"Ka dō ka"—"Whether or not"

137. This is used after the conclusive form of a verb or adjective or clause and means *whether or not*.

> **Iku koto ga dekiru ka dō ka wakarimasen.**
>
> *I don't know whether I'll be able to go or not.*
>
> **Ii ka dō ka itte kudasai.**   *Please tell me whether it's good or not.*
>
> **Kuru ka dō ka kikimashō.**   *I'll ask him whether he'll come or not.*

Mijikai Kaiwa

de- [-] from **deru,** *to leave*
mō sugu [- -'-] *in a few minutes*

Exercises

A. Answer the following questions.

1. Sakura no hana wa Tōkyō dewa itsu goro sakimasu ka ?
2. Sakura no hana ga saku to anata wa hanami ni ikimasu ka ?
3. Tōkyō no chikaku dewa doko ga hanami ni ichiban ii deshō ka ?
4. Tōkyō kara Kamakura made densha to basu to dotchi de iku hō ga ii desu ka ?
5. Densha de iku to dono gurai kakarimasu ka ?
6. Nippon dewa nangatsu ni ame ga takusan furimasu ka ?
7. Shichigatsu no hajime niwa tenki ga yoku narimasu ka ?
8. Nippon dewa nangatsu ga ichiban atsui desu ka ?
9. Anata wa atsuku naru to doko e ikimasu ka ?
10. Anata no sensei wa natsu doko e iku rashii desu ka ?

B. Convert the following statements into their desiderative forms.

 Example: Yama e **ikimasu**.

    Yama e **ikitai desu**.

1. Ima soto e demasu.
2. Nippon ni motto imasu.
3. Gogo sampo ni dekakemasu.
4. Sukoshi yasumimasu ka ?
5. Yoku benkyō shimasu.
6. Uchi e kaerimasu.
7. Eki kara arukimasu.
8. Raishū mata kimasu.
9. Nichiyōbi ni asobimasu.
10. Nippongo o naraimasu ka ?

C. What is the Japanese equivalent of each of the following sentences?

1. Where did you go flower-viewing ?
2. I didn't go. I intended to go, but I was busy and could not go.
3. I am sorry to hear that.
4. Will you go to the seashore this year ?
5. No, I'll go to the mountains.
6. Will the weather improve this afternoon ?
7 No, it seems it will rain this afternoon.
8. When the weather becomes fine, it will become cold.
9. Will this yellow flower bloom in May ?
10. In Japan January and February are the coldest months.
11. I hear cherry-blossoms at Ueno are very beautiful.
12. Many people go there to see cherry-blossoms.
13. Because his house is pretty far from the station, you'd better go by bus.
14. When you go by bus, you get to his house in ten munutes.
15. Autumn is the best time to study.
16. The beginning of winter also seems to be a good time to study.
17. He came home after it became dark.
18. I'm not sure whether I shall be busy or not tomorrow.
19. I'd like to go to his house today, but I don't know whether he is at

home or not.

20. Let's hurry up. The bus will leave right away.

D. Carry on a conversation along the lines indicated.

X: (*It's fine weather, isn't it?*)

Y: Sō desu nē. Kinō wa warui otenki deshita ga, kyō wa ii otenki ni narimashita ne.

X: (*Have the cherry-blossoms bloomed?*)

Y: Iie, mada sakanai deshō. Keredomo asatte goro wa saku deshō.

X: (*Will you go flower-viewing?*)

Y: Isogashikute jikan ga nai kara iku koto ga dekiru ka dō ka wakari-masen.

X: (*I went to Kyōto last month.*)

Y: Sō desu ka? Kisha de ikimashita ka?

X: (*Yes, I went by train. I went with Mr. Thomas. Since we had no school, we left on Monday and returned on Friday.*)

Y: Kyōto dewa nani o mimashita ka?

X: (*We went to various places.*)

Y: Kinkakuji emo ikimashita ka?

X: (*What's the English for " Kinkakuji "?*)

Y: " Gold Temple " to iimasu.

X: (*Is that so? We went to the Gold Temple, too.*)

Jūshichi

(Main Text)

A : Watakushi wa maiasa rokuji ni okimasu.

Okiru to sugu ha o migaite kao o araimasu.
Hige mo sorimasu.

Sorekara sukoshi tatte asahan o tabemasu.

Hachiji sukoshi mae ni uchi o dete kaisha
e ikimasu.

Taitei aruite ikimasu ga osoi toki niwa basu
ka densha de ikimasu.

Basu ya densha ni noranaide takushii de iku
koto mo arimasu.

Kaisha dewa tegami o kaitari hito ni attari
shite, hiru made hatarakimasu.

Hiruhan wa jūniji to ichiji no aida desu.

Uchi kara obentō o motte ikimasen kara, taitei kinjo no shokudō de tabemasu.

Ichiji kara mō ichido kaisha de shigoto o shite, yūgata uchi e kaerimasu.

Tokidoki osoku made kaisha ni nokoru koto mo arimasu ga, taitei rokuji goro uchi e kaerimasu.

Shichiji goro yūhan o tabete, ofuro ni haitte kara, hon o yondari rajio o kiitari shimasu.

Doyōbi no gogo wa yasumi desu kara, kaimono o shitari eiga o mitari shimasu.

Ban niwa tomodachi ga asobi ni kimasu. Watakushi ga tazuneru toki mo arimasu.

Taitei jūji goro yasumimasu ga, doyōbi no ban wa osoku made okite imasu.

Shikashi tsukareta toki niwa osoku made okite inaide hayaku yasumimasu.

Watakushi wa karada ga jōbu desu shi, itsumo karada ni ki o tsukete imasu kara, hotondo byōki ni narimasen.

Keredomo tama ni atama ga itai koto
ya onaka no itai koto ga arimasu.

Sonna toki niwa kusuriya kara kusuri
o katte kite nomimasu.

Hidoi byōki no toki niwa isha e iku
ka isha o yobu ka shimasu ga, sonna
koto wa hotondo arimasen.

(A Short Conversation)

A : Doko ga warui desu ka ?

B : Onaka ga itai desu.

A : Netsu ga arimasu ka ?

B : Sukoshi arimasu. Taionkei o motte kite
kudasai.

A : Isha o yobimashō ka ?

B Iie. watakushi ga ikimasu. Takushii
o yonde kudasai.

A : Dōzo odaiji ni.

(For Memorizing)

1 Watakushi wa maiasa [rokuji] ni okimasu.

1. I get up at [six o'clock] every morning.

2. Okiru to sugu ha o migaite kao o araimasu.

2. Right after I get up, I clean my teeth and wash my face.

3. Osoi toki niwa [basu] ka [densha] de ikimasu.

3. When I am late, I go by [bus] or [streetcar].

4. Basu ya densha ni noranaide [takushii] de iku koto mo arimasu.

4. Instead of taking a bus or a streetcar, I sometimes go by [taxi].

5. Tegami o kaitari hito ni attari shite [hiru] made hataraki masu.

5. I work until [noon], writing letters and seeing visitors.

6. Hon o yondari rajio o kiitari shimasu.

6. I read books or listen to the radio.

7. Kaimono o shitari eiga o mitari shimasu.

7. I go shopping or see movies.

8. Itsumo karada ni ki o tsukete imasu.

8. I always pay attention to my health.

Hombun

Glossary

maiasa ['---] *every morning*
oki [--] from **okiru**, *to get up*
ha ['] *a tooth; teeth*
migaite [----] from **migaku**, *to polish; clean*
arai- [---] from **arau**, *to wash*
hige [--] *moustache; beard*

sori- [--] from **soru**, *to shave*. This is sometimes pronounced as [suru].

sorekara [----] *and then; after that*

tatte ['--] from **tatsu**, *to elapse; pass*

asahan [----] *breakfast*, from **asa**, *morning* and **han**, *meal*

kaisha [---] *a business firm; company*

osoi [---] *(a-A) late; slow*

toki [-'] *time; when*

nora- [--] from **noru**, *to ride*

-naide ['--] *without......; not......but* (See Grammar 140.)

takushii ['---] *a taxi*

tegami [---] *a letter*

-tari [--] *the frequentative* (See Grammar 142, 147.)

kaitari ['---] from **kaku**, *to write*

attari ['---] from **au**, *to meet; see*

hiru [-'] *noon*

hiruhan [----] *lunch*, from **hiru**, *noon* and **han**, *meal*

obentō [-----] **o**, honorific, and **bentō**, *luncheon; lunch*

motte ['--] from **motsu**, *to hold; have* (See Grammar 145.)

kinjo ['--] *neighborhood; vicinity*

shokudō [----] *a dining room; restaurant*

ichido [---] *once:* **mō ichido** means *once more.*

shigoto [---] *work; job; business*

osoku [---] from **osoi** *(a-A), late:* **osoku made** means *till late.*

nokoru [-'-] *to remain; stay behind*

yūhan [----] *dinner; supper; evening meal*, from **yū**, *evening* and **han**, *meal*

ofuro [-'-] an honorific **o**, and **furo**, *a bath.* **Ofuro ni hairu** means *to take a bath.*

rajio ['--] *radio*

kaimono [----] *shopping*

eiga ['-- or ---] *movies; cinema*

ban [--] *evening*

asobi [---] *play; pastime; pleasure.* **Asobi ni kuru** means *to visit without any special business.*

tazuneru [--'-] *to visit; call on*

tsukareta [-′--] *got tired*, from **tsukareru,** *to get tired*

karada [---] *a body*

jōbu [---] *(a-B) strong; robust*

itsumo [′--] *always*

ki [-] *mind*

ki o tsukeru [---′-] *to pay attention*. Usually used in the sense of the English *Be careful*.

hotondo [-′--] *almost*

tama ni [---] *once in a while; on rare occasions*

atama [---] *a head*

itai [-′-] *(a-A) painful; aching; sore*

onaka [---] *stomach; abdomen*

sonna [---] *such; like that*

kusuriya [----] *a druggist; drug store*

kusuri [---] *medicine*

katte [---] from **kau,** *to buy*

hidoi [-′-] *(a-A) terrible; hard; heavy* (of rain)

isha [--] *a doctor; physician*

yobu [--] *to call; invite*

Grammar

"to Sugu" — "As Soon As"

138.   **Okiru to sugu ha o migaite kao o araimasu.**

The literal translation of the above sentence is,

> *When I get up, I immediately brush my teeth and wash my face.*

Therefore, **...to sugu** means *immediately after* and such expressions as *as soon as, directly after, just after,* etc. may be used in expressing the same idea in English.

Uchi e kaeru to sugu dekakemashita.

> *As soon as he returned home, he went out.*
> *Directly after returning home, he went out.*

The Te-form denotes the Sequence

139.   As we have already seen, when two or more verbs run together, all the

verbs except the last take their **te**-form and usually denote the sequence of occurrences as,

> **Asa okite, ha o migaite, kao o aratte, asahan o tabete gakkō e ikimasu.**
>
> *I get up in the morning, brush my teeth, wash my face, eat breakfast and go to school.*

[Negative Base of a Verb] x " -naide " means " Without "

140.   **Densha ni noranaide takushii de ikimashita.**

>   *I went by taxi instead of taking a streetcar.*

Noranai is the plain negative form of **noru**, *to ride.* The negative verb followed by **de** means *without......, not......but.......*

> **Asobanaide benkyō shimashita.**
>
> *I did not enjoy myself, but studied.*

[Conclusive Base of a Verb] x " Koto (or Toki) mo Aru "

141.   When **koto** (or **toki**) **mo aru** follows the conclusive base, it means *one has the occasion to.*

> **Densha ni noranaide takushii de iku koto mo arimasu.**
>
> *Instead of taking a streetcar, I sometimes go by taxi.*
>
> **Tomodachi o tazuneru toki ga arimasu.**
>
> *I sometimes visit friends.*

Very often **koto** (or **toki**) **ga aru** is used instead of **koto** (or **toki**) **mo aru**. Both mean the same except that **koto** (or **toki**) **mo aru** suggests that the other case is usual. The first example means *I usually go by street-car, but sometimes I go by taxi.*

" Tari "—the Frequentative

142.   **Tegami o kaitari hito ni attari shimasu.**

>   *I sometimes write letters and sometimes see people.*

Hon o yondari rajio o kiitari shimasu.

>   *I sometimes read books and sometimes listen to the radio.*

The frequentative **tari** (or **dari**) is used after verbs when acts or states occur by turns. It is generally used in pairs, and the second member is frequently followed by the verb **suru** or its substitute. The frequentative is sometimes used when there is no repetition.

The forming of the frequentative is simple for anyone who knows the **te**-form of a verb, since it is nothing other than replacing the final **e** of the **te**-form with **ari**. Thus,

te-*form*	*frequentative*
kaite	**kaitari** (*writing*)
hanashite	**hanashitari** (*speaking*)
totte	**tottari** (*taking*)
yonde	**yondari** (*reading*)

Compare : **Sakuban tabete, nonde hanashimashita.**

Last night, we ate, then drank and finally talked.

Sakuban tabetari, nondari, hanashitari shimaishita.

Last night, we ate, drank and talked.

The **te**-form is used to indicate the sequence of action.

The **tari**-form indicates action during the specific period but does not indicate sequential order.

"Au" being Intransitive takes "Ni"

143. The English verb *meet*, being a transitive verb, takes a direct object as you *meet a person*. But in Japanese, the verb **au** is intransitive and must be preceded by the particle **ni**.

Tanaka San ni aimashita.   *I met Mr. Tanaka.*

Tomodachi ni aimashō.   *I shall meet a friend.*

"Obentō"—"a Lunch"

144. **Obentō** or **bentō** is any kind of food taken as a lunch to be eaten away from home. If it is for a picnic or some outing, it may range from mere rice-balls to elaborate food placed in a lacquered box. For everyday use such as the case of office workers, it is usually rice and side-dishes put in a box called **bentō-bako**.

"Motte" x [Verbs of Motion]

145. The combination of **motte**, *hold* and **kuru**, *come*, corresponds to the English word *bring something toward* the speaker and **motte**, *hold* and **iku**, *go*, corresponds to *take something away* from the speaker. Thus,

Motte kite kudasai. *Please bring it.*

Motte itte kudasai. *Please take it away.*

They are used in referring only to inanimate objects.

In bringing or taking a living thing, the combination with **tsurete** is used.

tsurete kuru	*to bring someone*
tsurete iku	*to take someone away*
Tsurete kite kudasai.	*Please bring him.*
Tsurete iki nasai.	*Take him away.*

"Dinner" and "Yūhan"

146. There is no special word that corresponds to *dinner*, the main meal. **Yūhan** merely means *an evening meal*, but since the evening meal is nearly always the main meal of the day, **yūhan** will generally serve the purpose.

"Shi," a Connective Particle and "Tari," the Frequentative

147. We have already learned about **shi** in Lesson 12, Grammar 90.

Because **shi** follows the conclusive base, when a noun or a quasi-adjective is to be used before it, **da** or **desu** comes between them.

> **Kyō wa nichiyō da shi tenki ga ii kara sampo ni ikimashō.**
>
> *Today is Sunday and the weather is fine; so I'll go out for a walk.*

> **Byōki desu shi isogashii kara dekakemasen.**
>
> *I'm indisposed and besides I'm busy; so I won't go out.*

The difference between **shi** and the frequentative **tari** is that **tari** suggests an alternate action or at least two actions not performed simultaneously, whereas **shi** merely describes two or more actions. Besides, **tari** is used only with the **te**-form of verbs (with its final **e** changed into **a**) and the plain past form of true adjectives.

kaite	kai**tari**	yon**de**	yon**dari**
nakatta	nakat**tari**	atsukatta	atsukat**tari**

The **te**-form at the end of a clause has also a force of a connective, but it is different from the function of **shi** or **tari**, in that the former describes a series of events in the order described, whereas the latter merely tells about a number of events without implying the order of occurence. Compare:

Ginza e itte kaimono o shite, tomodachi o tazunemashita.

I went to Ginza and did some shopping and visited a friend.

Ginza e itte kaimono o shitari tomodachi o tazunetari shimashita.

Ginza e itte kaimono mo shita shi, tomodachi mo tazunemashita.

I went to Ginza and did some shopping as well as visiting a friend.

"No" in a Modifying Clause

148.   Onaka no itai koto literally means *stomach's aching thing* or *a stomach-ache*.   **No** here means the same as **ga** does.   In a modifying clause, the subject is sometimes followed by **no** instead of **ga**.

Te-form plus "Kuru"—"Go and......"

149.   Kusuriya kara kusuri o katte kimashō.

I'll go to a pharmacy and get some medicine.

The sentence literally means *I'll buy some medicine and come from a pharmacy*.   When you go on an errand, it consists of three stages—going, doing the errand, and coming back.   In English you refer to the first two stages, while in Japanese, we refer to the second two stages.

Eiga o mite kimashita.   *I went and saw the movie.*

Tomodachi ni atte kimashita.   *I went and saw my friend.*

The Particle "Ka" after Clauses

150.   The particle **ka** which comes between clauses means *or*, just like **ka** between nouns means *or*.   (See Lesson 16, Grammar 133.)

Isha e iku ka isha o yobimasu.

I either go to the doctor's or call him.

Sometimes **ka** is added to the last clause, too.

Isha e iku ka isha o yobu ka shimasu.

I either go to the doctor's or call him.

Relative Frequency Chart of Adverbs of Time

151.

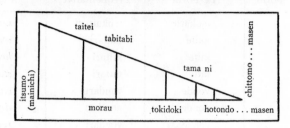

Mijikai Kaiwa

netsu [-'] *fever*

taionkei [--'---] *a clinical thermometer*

Odaiji ni. [-----] *Take care of yourself.* **O** is an honorific and **daiji ni** means *carefully*.

Exercises

A. Practise converting from one form to another rapidly and fluently.

Conversion Table 6.

Present Form	Desiderative	Negative **Te**-form	Meaning
kaimasu	kaitai desu	kawanaide	*buy*
tsukimasu	tsukitai desu	tsukanaide	*reach*
hanashimasu	hanashitai desu	hanasanaide	*speak*
machimasu	machitai desu	matanaide	*wait*
tachimasu	tachitai desu	tatanaide	*stand*
asobimasu	asobitai desu	asobanaide	*play*
nomimasu	nomitai desu	nomanaide	*drink*
yomimasu	yomitai desu	yomanaide	*read*
norimasu	noritai desu	noranaide	*ride*
narimasu	naritai desu	naranaide	*become*
ikimasu	ikitai desu	ikanaide	*go*
tazunemasu	tazunetai desu	tazunenaide	*visit*
imasu	itai desu	inaide	*stay*
shimasu	shitai desu	shinaide	*do*
kimasu	kitai desu	konaide	*come*

Conversion Table 7.

Dictionary Form	Te-Form	Frequentative	Meaning
tsukau	tsukatte	tsukattari	*use*
kaku	kaite	kaitari	*write*
kiku	kiite	kiitari	*hear*
tatsu	tatte	tattari	*stand*
yobu	yonde	yondari	*call*
nomu	nonde	nondari	*drink*
yomu	yonde	yondari	*read*
hairu	haitte	haittari	*enter*
iku	itte	ittari	*go*
tazuneru	tazunete	tazunetari	*visit*
taberu	tabete	tabetari	*eat*
miru	mite	mitari	*see*
suru	shite	shitari	*do*
kuru	kite	kitari	*come*

B. Answer the following questions.

1. Anata wa maiasa nanji ni okimasu ka ?
2. Okiru to sugu nani o shimasu ka ?
3. Nanji ni kaisha (gakkō, etc.) e ikimasu ka ?
4. Nan de ikimasu ka ?
5. Kaisha de nani o shimasu ka ?
6. Hiruhan wa nanji desu ka ?
7. Taitei nanji ni kaisha kara kaerimasu ka ?
8. Uchi e kaette kara nani o shimasu ka ?
9. Doyōbi mo yūgata made kaisha de hatarakimasu ka ?
10. Doyōbi no ban wa nanji goro yasumimasu ka ?
11. Anata wa hotondo byōki ni narimasen ka ?
12. Byōki ni naru to dō shimasu ka ?

C. Study the use of the frequentative "**-tari**" *from the following examples and then try to combine* (a) *and* (b) *using* "**-tari**."
Example: Non**dari** tabe**tari** shimashita.

> *We drank as well as ate.*

Hon o yon**dari** rajio o kii**tari** shimasu.

I sometimes read books and sometimes listen to the radio.

1. (a) demasu   (b) hairimasu
2. (a) asobimashita   (b) benkyō shimashita
3. (a) bōshi o kaburimasu   (b) kutsu o hakimasu
4. (a) mado o akemasu   (b) mado o shimemasu
5. (a) mimasu   (b) kikimasu

D. *Tell the class what you do every day.*

E. *What is the Japanese equivalent of each of the following sentences?*
1. Usually I go to the company by bus.
2. When I am late, I go by taxi.
3. Occasionally I walk from my house to the school.
4. On Sundays I go to church (=*kyōkai*) instead of going to school.
5. Please come to see me between 2 p.m. and 3 p.m. tomorrow.
6. After coming home in the evening, I sometimes read books and sometimes go to see movies.
7. I was very busy yesterday and stayed at the company till late.
8. It is a holiday and besides it is raining today, so I will stay at home and write letters to my friends.
9. When you get tired, don't study but go out for a walk.
10. As she always pays attention to her child's health, the child seldom becomes sick.
11. When I have a headache, I go to a drug store and get some medicine.
12. I had a stomach ache this morning, so I went to the doctor's.

F. *What would you say when,*
1. you want to ask if the road leads to Tokyo Station?
2. you want to know where you are?
3. you spilt some ink and want somebody to wipe it up quickly?
4. you want to know the price of an article?
5. you ask someone to call a taxi?
6. you hear that someone is sick?

Jūhachi

(Main Text)

B : Watakushi wa kinō kozutsumi o dashi ni yūbinkyoku e ikimashita.

A : Yūbinkyoku wa otaku kara tōi desu ka?

B : Iie, amari tōku wa arimasen. Kanari chikai desu.

Aruite jūni'sampun shika kakarimasen.
Jitensha nara go'roppun desu.

A : Hagaki ya tegami o dasu nimo yūbinkyoku made ikimasu ka ?

B : Aruite shi'gofun no tokoro ni posuto ga arimasu kara sore ni iremasu.

A : Yūbinkyoku wa doko desu ka?

B : Kyōkai no kado o migi e magatte massugu iku to byōin ga arimasu. Yūbinkyoku wa sono tonari desu.

(A Conversation at the Post Office)

A : Kono kozutsumi o dashitai no desu ga, ikura
kakarimasu ka ?

B : Kakitome desu ka ?

A : Iie, futsū de kekkō desu.

B : Futsū nara nanajū-goen desu.

A : Kono tegami wa jūen de ii desu ka ?

B : Omosugimasu kara kitte o mō ichimai
hatte kudasai.

A : Kono kōkūbin wa ikura desu ka ?

B : Hyaku yonjūen desu.

A : Beikoku made ikunichi kakarimasu ka ?

B : Isshūkan gurai kakarimasu.

(A Short Conversation)

A : Tegami ga arimasu ka ?

B : Kyō wa arimasen.

A : Kore o dashite kudasai.   Sokutatsu ni negaimasu.

(For Memorizing)

1. Kinō [kozutsumi] o dashi ni yūbinkyoku e ikimashita.
1. I went to the post office to send a [package] yesterday.

2. Aruite [jūni'sampun] shika kakarimasen.
2. It takes only [twelve or thirteen minutes] on foot.

3. Jitensha nara [go'roppun] desu.
3. If by bicycle, it's [five or six minutes'] ride.

4. [Yūbinkyoku] wa doko desu ka ?
4. Where is the [post office]?

5. [Kyōkai] no kado o [migi] e magatte massugu iku to [byōin] ga arimasu.

5. Go straight ahead and turn to the [right] at the corner of the [church], and you will come to a [hospital].

6. [Yūbinkyoku] wa sono tonari desu.

6. The [post office] is next door to that.

7. Kono [kozutsumi] o dashi-tai no desu ga ikura kakari-masu ka ?

7. I'd like to send this [package]; how much will it cost ?

8. Futsū de kekkō desu.

8. Ordinary mail will do.

9. Omosugimasu kara kitte o mō ichimai hatte kudasai.

9. Since it's too heavy, put an-other stamp on it, please.

10. [Beikoku] made ikunichi kakarimasu ka ?

10. How many days will it take to [the United States] ?

Hombun

Glossary

kozutsumi [-′- -] *a small package ; parcel post*
dashi- [- -] from **dasu**, *to send* (mail)
yūbinkyoku [- -′- - -] *a post office*
otaku [- - -] *your house :* **o** is an honorific and **taku** means *a house.*
amari [- - -] When used with a negative word it means *(not)......very.* With an affirmative word, it means *excessively ; too.......* **Ammari** is also used in familiar speech.
chikai [-′-] *(a-A) near ; close to*
jūni'sampun [- - -′- - -] *twelve or thirteen minutes*
shika (...**masen**) [- -] *only* (See Grammar 153.)
jitensha [- - - -] *a bicycle*
...nara [′-] *if it is......*
go'roppun [- - - - -] *five or six minutes*
shi'gofun [- - - -] *four or five minutes*
posuto [′- -] *a mailbox ; pillar box*

kyōkai [- - - -] *a church*

kado ['-] *a corner*

byōin [- - - -] *a hospital*

tonari [- - -] *next door*

kakitome [- - - -] *registered mail*

nanajū-goen [-'- -'- -] *seventy-five yen*

futsū [- - -] *ordinary; usual*

kitte [- -' or - - -] *a postage stamp*

kōkūbin [- - - - - -] *airmail*

Beikoku [- - - -] *U. S. A.* Literal translation is *a rice country*, but this has nothing to do with the fact. The word *American* was called **Meriken** in the early history of Japanese-American relations, and the Chinese character meaning rice happened to be used for the sound of **me** which is the first syllable of the word. Later this character which has a common reading **bei** followed by a character **koku** which means *a country* formed the word **Beikoku.**

ikunichi ['- - -] *how many days*

Grammar

[Number] x or x [Number]

152. When two numbers run together with *or* between them, the numbers may form compounds.

one or two hours	**ichi'nijikan**
two or three people	**ni'sannin**
three or four minutes	**san'shifun**
three of four hours	**san'yojikan**
four or five minutes	**shi'gofun**
five or six days	**go'rokunichi**
six or seven months	**roku'shichikagetsu**
seven or eight weeks	**shichi'hasshūkan**
eight or nine days	**hakkunichi**
nine or ten......	(not used)
twelve or thirteen minutes	**jūni'sampun**

Note that the numbers are consecutive and are in an ascending order.

"Shika" with a Negative Word

153. **Shika** meaning *only* is never used without a negative word coming after it.

Aruite jū'nisampun shika kakarimasen.

It takes only twelve or thirteen minutes on foot.

Nigatsu niwa nijūhachinichi shika arimasen.

There are only twenty-eight days in February.

In Lesson 1, we had **dake** meaning *only*.

Kyō wa sore dake desu.

(Lit.) *Today is that only.* (*That's all for today.*)

Isshūkan dake arimasu.   *We have only one week.*

Shika...masen and **dake** are very similar in meaning and both may be translated with *only*. The intrinsic difference is that the speaker is laying more emphasis on the positive side when he uses **dake**, while, when he uses **shika...masen**, he emphasizes the negative or non-existence.

Hyakuen dake arimasu.   *I have only 100 yen.*

(But it ought to be enough.)

Hyakuen shika arimasen.   *I have only 100 yen.*

(And I'm afraid that's not enough.)

An analogy may be found in the use of *a little* and *little*, and *a few* and *few*.

I have *a few* books.   (There are some.)

I have *few* books.   (There are not many.)

Nippongo dake hanashimasu.

I only speak Japanese. (=*Japanese is the only language I speak.*)

Nippongo shika hanashimasen.   *I speak nothing else but Japanese.*

The functional difference is twofold:

(1) **Dake** may be used in either an affirmative or negative sentence while **shika** is used only in a negative sentence.

Watakushi dake ikimasu.   *I alone go.*

Watakushi dake ikimasen.   *I'm the only one who doesn't go.*

Watakushi shika ikimasen.   *Nobody goes except me.*

(2) When used with another particle, **dake** may either precede or follow it, while **shika** always follows it.

Anata ni dake hanashimasu.   *I tell it to you only.*

Anata dake ni hanashimasu.   *I tell it to you only.*

Anata ni shika hanashimasen.

I don't tell it to anyone else but you.

"Nara"

154.   When **nara** is placed after a noun or a noun equivalent, it means *if it is.*

Jitensha nara go'roppun desu.

It takes five or six minutes by bicycle.

The literal meaning of the above sentence is *If it is (by) bicycle, it takes five or six minutes.* Similarly, **Hon nara arimasu** means *If it (what you are looking for) is a book, I've got one.*

"(no) nimo"

155.   In Lesson 11, Grammar 79 we had ...**no ni** meaning *in order to.*

Tokei wa jikan o shiru no ni tsukaimasu.

We use a watch in order to tell the time.

Mono o kau no ni okane ga irimasu.

We need money in order to buy things.

No of this **no ni** is sometimes omitted, particularly when **ni** is combined with **mo**.

Hagaki o dasu (no) nimo yūbinkyoku made ikimasu ka?

Do we go to the post office in order to mail a post card, too?

Kuchi wa hanasu (no) nimo tsukaimasu.

We also use the mouth in order to speak.

"...no desu"

156.   Historically speaking **desu** was to follow a noun or a noun substitute. It was considered wrong to use **desu** after a true adjective. **Kore wa ōkii desu** was considered a mistake by conservative grammarians thirty years ago and **no** which is a noun substitute to be placed before **desu**, e.g.,

Kore wa ōkii no (or n) desu.   *This is large.*

During the past thirty years or so the general tendency turned toward dropping this **no** or **n**, which is the corrupted form of **no**, altogether when **desu** is to be used after a true adjective.

It is, of course, proper to use **no** before **desu**, and one often hears this construction, but it adds a touch of emphasis in that case.

" ...de Kekkō (Ii) desu "—" Will do "

157. **Futsū de kekkō desu.** *Ordinary maill will do.*

Kono tegami wa jūen de ii desu ka?

Will ten yen do for this letter?

...**de kekkō (ii) desu** literally means *It is fine (good) with* ......, so ......*will do.*

" Goro " and " Gurai "

158. **Goro** means *approximate point of time* whereas **gurai** means *approximate amount.* Thus, **niji goro** means *about two o'clock* and **nijikan gurai** means *about two hours.* **Goro** is only used with words referring to time while **gurai** may be used with any word.

ikutsu gurai	*about how many*
isshūkan gurai	*about a week*
jūen gurai	*about ten yen*

Mijikai Kaiwa

sokutatsu [– – – –] *special delivery*

negaimasu [– – – – –] from **negau**, *to request*

Sokutatsu ni negaimasu may be regarded as a shortened form of **Sokutatsu ni suru yō ni negaimasu**, meaning literally *I request to make it special delivery.*

Exercises

A. Answer the following questions.

1. Kozutsumi o dashitai toki niwa doko e motte ikimasu ka?
2. Yūbinkyoku wa otaku kara aruite dono gurai kakarimasu ka?
3. Kitte o kaitai toki nimo yūbinkyoku e ikimasu ka?
4. Anata wa tokidoki kakitome no tegami o dashimasu ka?
5. Futsū no tegami to kōkūbin to dotchi ga hayai desu ka?

B. *What is the Japanese equivalent of each of the following sentences?*

1. I come to this school to study Japanese.
2. He went to a druggist in the neighborhood to buy some medicine.
3. How long will it take to go there on foot?
4. It takes 20 miuntes to the hospital, but by car, only 5 or 6 minutes.
5. Where do you go to buy postcards?
6. Since this package is too heavy, put another 10 yen stamp on it, please.
7. I want to send this by registered mail. How much will it cost?
8. It will take only about a week for airmail to reach New York, but by ordinary mail, it will take 20 days.
9. Since I sent a special delivery letter yesterday, he will come to see you this evening.
10. "Where is the hospital?"

   "Go straight on (=ahead) and turn to the left at the corner where there is a post office (=corner of a post office), and you will come to the hospital."

C. *The following is a conversation between Mr. Brown and a clerk at the post office. See if you understand all of it.*

Mr. Brown: Kono kozutsumi o dashitai no desu ga......

Clerk: Chotto matte kudasai. Kore wa nan desu ka?

Mr. Brown: Hon desu.

Clerk: Kakitome desu ka?

Mr. Brown: Iie, futsū de ii desu.

Clerk: Futsū nara kyūjū-goen desu.

Mr. Brown: Hawai (=*Hawaii*) made tegami wa ikunichi kakarimasu ka?

Clerk: Isshūkan ka tōka kakarimasu. Hikōbin nara futsuka ka mikka desu.

Mr. Brown: Hikōbin? Kōkūbin to onaji imi desu ne.

Clerk: Sō desu. Anata wa Nippongo ga ojōzu desu nē.

Mr. Brown: Dō itashimashite. Mada heta desu. Dewa Hawai made kōkūbin ni negaimasu.

Clerk: Nanajūen no kitte o hatte kudasai.

Mr. Brown: Hai, shōchi shimashita.

Jūku

(Main Text)

(ichi)

A : Suzuki San wa aru ginkō ni tsutomete ite, Aoyama ni sunde imasu.

Suzuki to iu no wa myōji de namae wa Haruo to iimasu.

Okusan wa Akiko San to iimasu.

Suzuki San wa kodomo ga sannin arimasu.

Otokonoko ga futari to onnanako ga hitori desu.

Chōnan no Tarō wa kotoshi nanatsu de, chōjo no Kinuko wa itsutsu desu.

Jirō wa kyonen umareta bakari de mada akambō desu.

Kono sannin wa kyōdai de, Tarō wa Kinuko to Jirō no ani de, Jirō wa Tarō to Kinuko no otōto desu.

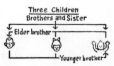

Kinuko wa Jirō no ane de, Tarō no imōto desu.

Suzuki San wa kodomotachi no chichi de, Akiko San wa haha desu.

Kono futari wa kodomotachi no oya desu.

Tarō to Jirō wa musuko de Kinuko wa musume desu.

Suzuki San no otōsan to okāsan wa kodomotachi no ojiisan to obāsan de, kodomotachi wa mago desu.

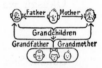

(ni)

A : Suzuki San wa sannin-kyōdai desu.

Niisan to imōtosan ga hitorizutsu arimasu.

Nēsan mo otōtosan mo arimasen.

Niisan wa Suzuki San yori toshi ga futatsu ue de, imōtosan wa mittsu shita desu.

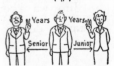

Niisan wa Takeo to itte imōtosan wa Michiko to iimasu.

Takeo San wa Tarō San-tachi no oji de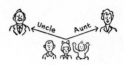
Michiko San wa oba desu.

Takeo San wa kodomo ga yonin arimasu.

Ichirō, Yukiko, Ginji, Saburō to iimasu.

Kono kodomotachi wa Tarō San-tachi no
itoko desu.

Ichirō San wa Suzuki San no oi de Yukiko
San wa mei desu.

Suzuki San no okāsan wa kotoshi shichijū
desu kara kanari toshiyori desu.

Takeo San no kazoku to issho ni inaka
ni sunde imasu.

Suzuki San no otōsan wa ototoshi nakunarimashita.

Michiko San wa mō kekkon shite chikaku
no machi ni sunde imasu.

(A Short Conversation)

(1)

A : Goshujin wa otaku desu ka ?

B : Hai, orimasu. Dōzo kochira e.

A : Shitsurei shimasu.

B : Dōzo okake kudasai.

(2)

B : Okusan wa oide desu ka ?

A : Kanai wa rusu desu.

B : (Dewa) mata mairimasu.

A : Dōzo goshujin ni yoroshiku.

1. Suzuki to iu no wa myōji de namae wa Haruo to iimasu.

   1. Suzuki is his surname and his first name is Haruo.

2. Chōnan no Tarō wa kotoshi [nanatsu] desu.

   2. Tarō, the eldest son is [seven years old] this year.

3. Jirō wa [kyonen] umareta bakari de mada akambō desu.

   3. Jirō was born only [last year] and he is still a baby.

4. Niisan wa Suzuki San yori toshi ga [futatsu] ue desu.

   4. His elder brother is his senior by [two] years.

5. Suzuki San no [otōsan] wa ototoshi nakunarimashita.

   5. Mr. Suzuki's [father] died the year before last.

6. Michiko San wa mō kekkon shite [chikaku no] machi ni sunde imasu.

   6. Michiko is already married and is living in a [nearby] town.

7.

otōsan	okāsan	father (honorific)	
		mother (honorific)	
chichi	haha	father	mother
ojiisan	obāsan	grandfather (honorific)	
		grandmother (honorific)	
mago		grandchild	
ojisan	obasan	uncle (honorific)	
		aunt (honorific)	
oi	mei	nephew	niece
niisan	nēsan	elder brother (honorific)	
		elder sister (honorific)	
ani	ane	elder brother	elder sister
otōto	imōto	younger brother	younger sister
kyōdai	itoko	brothers and sisters	cousin

(For Reference)

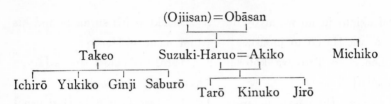

Hombun

(1)

Glossary

aru ['-]   *a certain*

ginkō [- - - -]   *a bank*

tsutomete [-'- -]   from **tsutomeru,** *to serve (at); work (in)*

sunde ['- -]   from **sumu,** *to live*

myōji ['- -]   *a surname*

otokonoko [- -'- -]   *a boy; child of male sex*

onnanoko [- -'- -]   *a girl; child of female sex*

chōnan ['- - - or - -'-]   *the eldest son*

chōjo ['- -]   *the eldest daughter*

umareta [- - - -]   from **umareru,** *to be born*

bakari ['- -]   *only ; just*

akambō [- - - - -]   *a baby; infant*

kyōdai ['- - -]   *brothers and sisters*

ani ['-]   *an elder brother*

otōto [- - - -]   *a younger brother*

ane [- -]   *an elder sister*

imōto [- - - -]   *a younger sister*

chichi [-']   *a father*

haha [-' or '-]   *a mother*

oya [-']   *parent(s)*

musuko [- - -]   *a son*

musume [- - -]   *a daughter*

otōsan [-'---] *a father* (honorific)
okāsan [-'---] *a mother* (honorific)
ojiisan [-'---] *a grandfather*
obāsan [-'---] *a grandmother*
mago [-'] *a grandchild*

Grammar

Japanese Names

159. In Japanese names the surname comes first and the given name last. Nobody has a middle name.

Family names came from various sources, but those which came from place names are greatest in number. Therefore, those which contain such characters as KI (tree), TA (field), HARA (moor), YAMA (mountain), KAWA (river), MIZU (water), MORI (woods), MURA (village), MACHI (town), etc. are numerous.

Kimura, Tanaka, Harada, Yamamoto, Kawashima, Shimizu, Morita, Yamamura, Machida, Suzuki, Yamada, etc.

The first male child in a family is often called **Tarō** or **Ichirō**, the second one **Jirō** or **-ji**, and the third one **Saburō** or **-zō**. Other common names end in **o**, **kichi**, **ichi**, **hei**, etc.

Female given names are usually of two or three syllables, and come from flowers, trees, seasons, etc., but those which end in **e** or **ko** are commonest among daughters of educated families.

Men's Given Names		Women's Given Names	
Tarō	Haruo	Haruko	Harue
Ichirō	Yoshio	Yoshiko	Yoshie
Jirō	Toshio	Toshiko	Toshie
Saburō	Shizuo	Shizuko	Shizue
Shirō	Masao	Masako	Masae
Gorō	Akira	Hanako	Matsu
Shichirō	Minoru	Akiko	Kiku
Hachirō	Hajime	Tsuruko	Hatsu

"Ni" x [Verbs of State]

160. In Lesson 15, Grammar 112 we have learned that **de** denotes the place where an action is performed. In Japanese, **sumu** (*to live*) and **tsutomeru** (*to serve*) are regarded as verbs denoting *state* just like **aru** and **iru**. Therefore, the place where one lives is followed by **ni**, and not by **de**, just like **aru** and **iru**.

> **Watakushi wa Tōkyō ni sunde imasu.** *I live in Tokyo.*
> **Suzuki San wa ginkō ni tsutomete imasu.**
> *Mr. Suzuki works in a bank.*
> **Ano kata wa ano heya ni imasu.** *He is in that room.*

Notice that **sumu** and **tsutomeru** are usually used in the **te**-form plus **iru** in the present tense.

"No" forming Noun Phrases or Clauses

161. The conclusive form of a verb can be made a noun equivalent by adding **no** after that. **Suzuki to iu no**...... literally means *that which we call Suzuki* or *what is called Suzuki*. For **to**, see Lesson 5, Grammar 38.

"Aru" with Human Relations

162. We have learned in Lesson 12, Grammar 92 that **iru** is usually used to express the location of a living creature, yet we often hear such a sentence as :

> **Anata wa tomodachi ga arimasu ka?** *Do you have a friend?*

in which **aru** is used with a living thing. This seems a direct contradiction to the above statement, but the case is quite different.

The above distinction between **aru** and **iru** is applicable *only* when they mean *to be in a place*. When **aru** is used with a term of human relationship such as a relative, a friend, a servant, etc., the expression means that one *has* such a relative, or that one is *born in such an environment*.

> **Okusan ga arimasu ka?**
> *Does he have a wife?; Is he married?*
> **Okusan wa imasu ka?**
> *Is the mistress here?; Is she at home?*

Niisan ga arimasu ka?   *Do you have an elder brother?*

Nēsan wa imasen.   *My elder sister is away.*

"No" between Two Equivalent Nouns—Apposition

163. When two nouns in apposition, that is, two nouns referring to one person such as **Tarō**, *the eldest son*, or **Kinuko**, *the eldest daughter* are to be expressed, the particle **no** is placed between the two nouns in the construction pattern [profession, rank, etc.] x **no** x [(proper) name]. Thus,

> **chōnan no Tarō**   *Tarō, the eldest son*
>
> **isha no Morita San**   *Mr. Morita, the doctor*
>
> **inu no Shiro**   *Shiro, the dog*

Counting Age

164. In counting the age of a person the first set of numerals is used.

> **Ano otokonoko wa ikutsu desu ka?**   *How old is that boy?*
>
> **Jūsan desu.**   *He's thirteen.*

In calculating one's age, the Japanese used to think of the calendar year rather than the exact number of years or months.

In 1950, however, it was decided by the Diet that the Western way of counting age be used even in non-official cases, so the old method is fast going out of use.

"Bakari"—"Just"

165. When **bakari** is used after the past form of a verb, it means that an action was performed a very short while ago.

> **Jirō wa kyonen umareta bakari desu.**
>
> *Jirō was born only last year.*
>
> **Konshū koko ni kita bakari desu.**
>
> *I just came here only this week.*

"Kyōdai"—"Brothers and/or Sisters"

166. **Kyōdai** means children of the same parents, and may mean either brothers only or sisters only, or both brothers and sisters. To express brothers specifically, **otoko no** is added. Likewise to mean sisters **onna no** is added.

Watakushi wa otoko no kyōdai wa sannin arimasu ga, onna no kyōdai wa arimasen. *I have three brothers, but no sisters.*

(2)

Glossary

niisan ['- - -] *an elder brother* (honorific)
-zutsu ['-] a suffix meaning *each*
nēsan ['- - -] *an elder sister* (honorific)
toshi [-'] *age; year*
ue [-'] *older*
shita [-'] *younger*
oji [-'] *an uncle*
oba [- -] *an aunt*
itoko [-'-] *a cousin*
oi [- -] *a nephew*
mei ['-] *a niece*
shichijū [- - - -] *seventy*
toshiyori [- - - -] *an old person*
kazoku ['- -] *a family*
inaka [- - -] *country; rural district*
ototoshi [-'- -] *the year before last*
nakunari- [- - - -] from **nakunaru**, *to die; be lost; disappear.* **Naku** is the adverbial form of **nai**, and **naru** is *to become*, so this word literally means *to become nil.* Referring to objects this means *lost* or *can't be found.*
kekkon suru [- - - - - -] *to marry*
machi [-'] *a town*

Grammar

Family Relations

167. The following are some common names for relatives:

	Plain	Humble	Honorific
father	**chichi**	**chichi; oyaji** (by men)	**otōsan**
mother	**haha**	**haha; ofukuro** (by men)	**okāsan**

grandfather	sofu	sofu	ojiisan
grandmother	sobo	sobo	obāsan
son	musuko	musuko; segare (by men)	musukosan
daughter	musume	musume	musumesan
elder brother	ani	ani	niisan
elder sister	ane	ane	nēsan
younger brother	otōto	otōto	otōtosan
younger sister	imōto	imōto	imōtosan
brother and/or sister	kyōdai	kyōdai	gokyōdai
uncle	oji	oji	ojisan
aunt	oba	oba	obasan
husband	shujin; otto	shujin; taku	goshujin; dannasama
wife	tsuma	kanai	okusan

" -zutsu "—a Suffix meaning " Each "

168. **Zutsu** is a suffix which is combined with a numeral or a quantity word, meaning *each*.

Niisan to nēsan ga hitorizutsu arimasu.

I have one elder brother and one elder sister.

Kore o sukoshizutsu tabe nasai.

Eat that a little bit each time.

Remember that **zutsu** is combined only with numbers or quantity words.

Seito ni hon o issatsuzutsu yarimashita.

I gave one book to each of the students.

(Wrong: Seito-zutsu ni hon o issatsu yarimashita.)

Heya niwa tsukue ga tōzutsu arimasu.

There are ten desks in each room.

(Wrong: Heya-zutsu niwa tsukue ga tō arimasu.)

Mijikai Kaiwa

(ichi)

goshujin [-'--] *a husband*: **go**, honorific and **shujin**, *master*

Goshujin wa otaku desu ka? We learned in Lesson 1, Grammar 5 that **desu** is used to connect two parts of a sentence as a kind of equal sign. When the subject is a person or a pronoun, this equal sign doesn't seem to apply. In sentences such as the following, in which the predicate noun is profession, rank, social position, etc., there is no difficulty.

Watakushi wa sensei desu.   *I am a teacher.*

Anata wa seito desu.   *You are a student.*

Tanaka San wa isha desu.   *Mr. Tanaka is a doctor.*

But, if one examines such sentences as the following with critical eyes, the logic appears shaky.

Goshujin wa otaku desu ka? (Lit.) *Is the master the house?*
(Actually) *Is the master at home?*

Byōin wa kinjo desu. (Lit.) *The hospital is neighborhood.*
(Actually) *The hospital is in the neighborhood.*

Anata wa gakkō desu ka? (Lit.) *Are you the school?*
(Actually) *Are you at school?*

The usual explanation offered is that the sentences are elliptical and that they should be more logically constructed as,

Goshujin wa otaku ni iru no desu ka?

Byōin wa kinjo ni aru no desu.

Anata wa gakkō ni iru no desu ka?

However, the fact remains that in reality, people usually don't use such sentences, and it is wrong to try to apply the criterion of one language to another. Therefore, we'd better accept such peculiarities as the above good-naturedly without making too much fuss about the logic.

ori- [– –] from **oru**, *to stay; be* (Used in place of *iru* in polite conversation.)

kochira [– – –] *this way; this side*

shitsurei [–'– –] *(a-B) rude; impolite.* **Shitsurei suru** literally means *to do rudeness.*

okake- [– – –] from **kakeru**, *to sit down:* **o** is an honorific.

(ni)

oide- [– – –] an honorific word meaning *to be, go,* or *come.* The situation decides which of the three the word means.

kanai ['– –] *(my) wife* (humble)

rusu ['–] *absent; out*

mairi- [- - -] from **mairu**, *to come* (polite)

Exercises

A. Make questions appropriate for the following answers.
1. Watakushi wa ani ga hitori arimasu.
2. Watakushi no myōji wa Yamada to iimasu.
3. Yamamoto San wa aru ginkō ni tsutomete imasu.
4. Ima Aoyama ni sunde imasu.
5. Akambō wa mada futatsu desu.
6. Kanai wa rusu desu.

B. What is the Japanese equivalent of each of the following sentences?
1. This is Tarō, the eldest son.
2. My elder brother who is serving in a bank is very busy now and works till late.
3. I have just come; I don't know anything.
4. This baby will be (=become) just two years old on the 8th of February.
5. His sister is older than I by two years.
6. His father is an old man and lives in the country.
7. Saburō San, Mr. Yamamoto's father, is fairly old, but is very healthy.
8. Michiko is married and lives in a city not very far from here.
9. My brother is a year younger than I, but looks older.
10. He got married two years ago and has a daughter.
11. I have two elder sisters, so I have many nephews and nieces.
12. My aunt is living with my cousin's family.

C. Mr. Yamamoto and Mr. Thomas are casual acquaintances and are talking about their families.

Mr. Thomas : Kyō wa okusan wa otaku dewa arimasen ka ?

Mr. Yamamoto : Hai, kanai wa kodomo o tsurete chichi no ie e ikimashita.

Mr. Thomas : Sō desu ka ? Anata wa kodomo-san ga ikunin arimasu ka ?

Mr. Yamamoto : Sannin arimasu. Futari wa musuko de hitori wa musume desu.

Mr. Thomas : Ichiban ōkii kodomo-san wa otokonoko desu ka, onnanoko desu ka?

Mr. Yamamoto: Ichiban ōkii no to chiisai no ga otokonoko desu.

Mr. Thomas: Ikutsu desu ka?

Mr. Yamamoto: Chōnan wa nanatsu de, chōjo wa itsutsu desu. Jinan wa kyonen umareta bakari de mada akambō desu. Anata mo kodomo-san ga arimasu ne.

Mr. Thomas: Ee, musuko to musume ga hitorizutsu arimasu.

Mr. Yamamoto: Ima Nippon ni imasu ka?

Mr. Thomas: Iie, kanai to issho ni Shikago (=*Chicago*) ni imasu.

Mr. Yamamoto: Anata wa otōsan ya okāsan ga arimasu ka?

Mr. Thomas: Chichi wa arimasu ga, haha wa mō nakunarimashita.

Mr. Yamamoto: Sō desu ka?

Mr. Thomas: Chichi wa kanari toshiyori desu ga genki de, inaka ni sunde imasu.

Mr. Yamamoto: Watakushi no haha mo inaka ni sunde imasu.

Mr. Thomas: Otōsan wa?

Mr. Yamamoto: Chichi ga kyonen nakunarimashita kara, haha wa ani no kazoku to issho ni sunde imasu.

Mr. Thomas: Sō desu ka?

Mr. Yamamoto: Ammari genki ja arimasen.

Mr. Thomas: Sore wa ikemasen nē.

Mr. Yamamoto: Desukara karada ni ki o tsukete imasu.

D. *Carry on a conversation along the following lines.*

Harada: *Good afternoon, Mr. Thomas.*

Thomas: *Good afternoon, Mr. Harada. How are you?*

Harada: *Fine, thank you. And you?*

Thomas: *I'm quite well, too. How is your wife?*

Harada: *She is sick now.*

Thomas: *That's too bad.*

Harada: *She has a headache, but she has no fever, so she will be all right soon.*

Thomas: *Please give her my regards.*

Nijū

(Main Text)

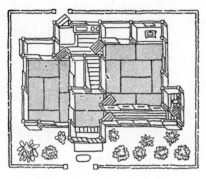 

A : Watakushi no ie wa Aoyama ni arimasu.

Densha ya basu no teiryūjō ni chikakute benri na tokoro desu.

Genkan o hairu to nijō no chiisana heya ga arimasu.

Sono heya no migi wa kyakuma de hachijō desu.

Kono heya no mae niwa engawa ga atte, sono mae wa niwa desu.

Niwa niwa iroiro no ki ga uete arimasu.

Benjo wa engawa no saki ni arimasu.

Nijō no heya no saki ni kaidan ga arimasu.

Nikai niwa heya ga futatsu arimasu.

Nijō no heya no hidari wa rokujō de chanoma desu.

Watakushitachi wa kono heya de shokuji o shimasu.

Taitei chabudai no mawari ni suwatte gohan o tabemasu.

Chanoma no mukō ni daidokoro ga arimasu.

Daidokoro niwa todana ya nagashi ya reizōko nado ga arimasu.

Daidokoro no soto ni ura no deiriguchi ga arimasu.

Genkan o tōranaide dehairi suru tame desu.

B : Watakushi no oji no ie wa Shibuya ni arimasu.

Ōkina mon no aru yōkan de, heya wa daidokoro ya furoba o nozoite jūshi'go arimasu.

Genkan o hairu to hiroi rōka ga arimasu.

Ikkai no ōsetsuma, kyakuma, shokudō nado wa yōma desu ga, jochūbeya wa nihomma de tatami ga shiite arimasu.

Nikai no shinshitsu wa yōma de shindai ga oite arimasu ga, hitotsu wa tokonoma no aru nihomma desu.

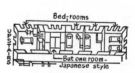

Nihonjin no okyaku o tomeru tame desu.

Nikai nimo semmenjo ya gofujō ga arimasu.

(A short Conversation)

A : Otaku wa dochira desu ka ?

B : Ōmori desu.

A : Eki kara tōi desu ka ?

B : Aruite gofun shika kakarimasen.

(For Memorizing)

1. [Teiryūjō] ni chikakute benri na tokoro desu.

   1. It's near the [streetcar- or bus-stop] and is in a very convenient place.

2. Niwa niwa iroiro no [ki] ga uete arimasu.

   2. Various [trees] are planted in the garden.

3. Watakushitachi wa kono heya de [shokuji o shimasu].

   3. We [have our meals] in this room.

4. [Chanoma] no mukō ni [daidokoro] ga arimasu.

   4. Beyond the [living-room] is the [kitchen].

5. [Genkan] o tōranaide dehairi suru tame desu.

   5. It's for going in and out without passing through the [front entrance].

6. Heya wa daidokoro ya furoba o nozoite [jūshi'go] arimasu.

   6. There are [fourteen or fifteen] rooms excluding the kitchen and the bathroom.

Hombun

Glossary

teiryūjō [------] *a streetcar- or bus-stop*

benri ['--] *(a-B) convenient*

genkan ['---] *(front) entrance; hall*

-jō [--] a classifier for counting **tatami**, *Japanese mats*

chiisana ['---] *(pre-noun) small*

kyakuma [---] *a guest-room:* **kyaku** means *guest*, and **ma**, *room.*

engawa [----] *a verandah; porch*

niwa [-'] *a garden; yard*

uete [---] from **ueru**, *to plant*

benjo [---] *a toilet.* This is the commonest term for a *lavatory* and is used throughout the country, but in Tokyo many people, particularly women, who consider that this word has already lost its former elegance prefer to use the word **gofujō** (literally meaning *unclean place*) or **(o)te-arai** (*hand-washing place*). One often hears in place of **benjo, habakari** (*place one hesitates to mention*) which sounds a little more polished.

saki [--] *the end; tip; ahead; beyond*

kaidan [----] *a staircase*

nikai [---] *the upper story; second floor* (See Grammar 171.)

chanoma [---] *a living- and dining-room.* This is the equivalent of a dining-room in a western-style house. It also serves as a living room, and is the place where family members assemble.

shokuji [---] *a meal.* **Shokuji o suru** means to have a meal. Don't say **shokuji o taberu.**

chabudai [----] *a low dining-table*

mawari [---] *around*

suwaru [---] *to squat down; sit*

daidokoro [-----] *a kitchen*

todana [---] *a cupboard; closet*

nagashi [---] *a sink*

reizōko [--'--] *an icebox; refrigerator*

nado ['-] *etc.*

ura [-'] *the back; rear*

deiriguchi [-----] *an entrance :* **deguchi** means *exit* and **iriguchi,** *entrance.*

dehairi [----] *going in and out*

tame [-'] *for (the purpose)* (See Grammar 172.)

ōkina ['---] (pre-noun) *large ; big*

mon ['-] *a gate*

furoba [--'] *a bathroom* (not a toilet)

nozoite [----] from **nozoku**, *to exclude*

jūshi'go [----] *fourteen or fifteen*

rōka [---] *a hallway ; corridor ; passage*

ikkai [----] *the first floor*

ōsetsuma [-----] *a reception room*

yōma [---] *a western-style room*

jochūbeya [-----] *a maids' room :* **jochū** means *a maid*, and **beya** (= **heya**), *a room.*

nihomma [----] *a Japanese-style room*

tatami [---] *a mat laid in a Japanese house*

shiite [---] from **shiku**, *to spread*

shinshitsu [----] *a bedroom*

shindai [----] *a bed*

tokonoma [----] *an alcove*, the recess in a Japanese room in which scrolls are hung

Nihonjin [-----] =**Nipponjin**, *a Japanese*

okyaku [---] *a guest*, **o** is an honorific

tomeru [---] *to give a shelter ; keep a person for the night*

semmenjo [-----] *a washroom*

gofujō [----] *a toilet ; lavatory*

Grammar

"Jō"—a Classifier for Counting Tatami

169. There are straw mats called **tatami** laid in a Japanese-style room. The size of **tatami** is usually 6 feet by 3 feet, and the size of a Japanese-style room is measured by the number of **tatami** laid in it. Most usual size of a Japanese-style room is **yojōhan** ($4\frac{1}{2}$ mats), **rokujō, hachijō,** or **jūjō.**

" Ōkina " and " Chiisana "

170. Ōkina and **chiisana** are pre-nouns derived from true adjectives. They naturally come before nouns, but are never used predicatively.

Kore wa ōkina machi desu. *This is a large town.*

but, **Kono machi wa ōkii desu.** *This town is large.*

" Kai "—a Classifier for Floors or Stories

171. Kai is a numeral classifier used for floors or stories.

ikkai, nikai, sangai, yonkai, gokai, rokkai, shichikai (or nanakai), hachikai (or hakkai), kukai (or kyūkai), jikkai......

Nikai is the second story or the second floor above the first floor (ground floor in British English) which we usually walk into from the street. In an ordinary circumstance **nikai** and upstairs correspond in meaning. But in such a case as when a person standing on the fifth floor is told to go to **nikai**, he will have to go down to the second floor instead of going upstairs which will be the sixth floor.

" Tame "—" Purpose "

172. This is a form noun and has several meanings, one of which is *for the sake of, on behalf of, in order to,* or merely *for.* It often takes **ni**, as **tame ni.**

Genkan o tōranaide dehairi suru tame desu.

It's for going in and out without passing through the front entrance.

Nippongo o narau tame ni kono gakkō ni hairimashita.

I entered this school in order to learn Japanese.

Mijikai Kaiwa

dochira [′– –] a polite word for **doko,** *where, in what place, in what direction,* or for **dotchi,** *which (of the two)*

Exercises

A. Answer the following questions.

1. Anata no otaku wa dochira desu ka ?
2. Otaku ni ichiban chikai basu no teiryūjō wa doko desu ka ?
3. Otaku wa yōkan desu ka ?
4. Otaku wa nikai ga arimasu ka ?
5. Yōma to nihomma ga ikutsuzutsu arimasu ka ?
6. Anata wa donna heya de shokuji o shimasu ka ?
7. Anata no benkyō-beya (= study room) wa nanjō desu ka ?
8. Otaku niwa niwa ga arimasu ka ?
9. Niwa niwa hana ya ki ga uete arimasu ka ?
10. Anata no shinshitsu wa nikai ni arimasu ka ?
11. Chanoma dewa nani o shimasu ka ?
12. Okyaku wa genkan kara hairimasu ka, ura no deiriguchi o tsukaimasu ka ?
13. Kyakuma wa nan no tame ni tsukaimasu ka ?
14. Doko de shokuji o koshiraemasu ka ?
15. Daidokoro niwa nani ga oite arimasu ka ?

B. What is the Japanese equivalent of each of the following sentences?

1. Somebody seems to have come to the entrance. Go and see (who it is), please.
2. A guest is waiting for you in the parlor.
3. There is one eight-mat room and one four-and-a-half-mat room on the second floor.
4. After dinner, we sometimes talk and sometimes watch (= look at) television (= *terebi*) in the living-room.
5. Mother is working by the sink in the kitchen.
6. All the rooms except the reception room are of Japanese-style.
7. There is no bed in a Japanese-style house; when people sleep, they spread bedding (= *futon*) on the mats.
8. Generally we sit around a dining-table in the living-room and have our dinner.
9. But sometimes we eat in the guest-room with guests.

10. We put guests in a Japanese-style room with an alcove for the night.
11. I should like to shave in the washroom. Have you got water?
12. My house is only five minutes' ride (by car) from the Ginza.

C. *What would you say when,*
1. you enter your friend's house?
2. you ask a visitor to sit down?
3. you ask where someone lives?
4. you show a guest into a room?
5. you give your regards to someone's wife?
6. you leave a sick person after a visit?

Nijū-ichi

(Main Text)

A : Watakushitachi wa me de mono o mimasu

Moshi me ga nakeraba nani mo miru koto
ga dekimasen.

Mekura no hito wa miru koto ga dekimasen.

Me ga mienai kara desu.

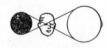

Watakushitachi wa akarukereba miemasu
keredomo, kurakereba yoku miemasen.

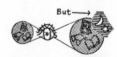

Makkura nara chittomo miemasen.

Yoru wa akari o tsukereba miemasu ga,
akari o keseba miemasen.

Desukara yoru wa akari ga irimasu.

Akari ga nakereba yoru hon o yomu koto ga dekimasen.

Desukara yoru wa dentō o tsukenakereba narimasen.

Moshi dentō ga kiereba rōsoku ya kaichū-dentō o tsukawanakereba narimasen.

Akari ga atte mo me o tojireba nani mo miemasen.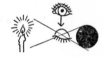

Shikashi me o akereba sugu ni miemasu.

B : Watakushitachi wa mimi de oto o kikimasu.

Moshi mimi ga nakereba nani mo kiku koto ga dekimasen.

Tsumbo no hito wa nani mo kiku koto ga dekimasen.

Mimi ga kikoenai kara desu.

Mimi ga atte mo sore o fusageba nani mo kikoemasen.

A : Eigo nimo Nippongo nimo takusan no kotoba ga arimasu.

Kotoba niwa minna imi ga arimasu.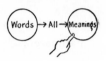

Desukara imi o shiranakereba kotoba o kiite mo wakarimasen.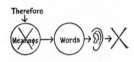

Bunshō o yonde mo imi ga wakarimasen.

Jibiki niwa kotoba no imi ga kaite arimasu.

Desukara jibiki o hikeba kotoba no imi ga wakarimasu.

(A Short Conversation)

B : Moshimoshi, Yamada San desu ka?

A : Denwa ga tōi desu ga.........

B : Kikoemasu ka ?

A : Kikoemasu. Chotto omachi kudasai.

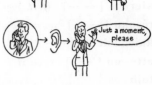

(For Memorizing)

1. Moshi [me] ga nakereba nani mo [miru] koto ga dekimasen.
   1. If we had no [eyes], we could not [see] anything.
2. Akarukereba miemasu keredomo, kurakereba miemasen.
   2. We can see if it is light, but we can't see if it is dark.
3. Yoru wa dentō o tsukenakereba narimasen.
   3. At night we must turn on the electric light.
4. Akari ga atte mo me o tojireba nani mo miemasen.
   4. Even if there is a light, we can't see anything if we close our eyes.
5. Imi o shiranakereba kotoba o kiite mo wakarimasen.
   5. If we don't know the meaning, we don't understand even if we hear a word.

Hombun

Glossary

moshi ['-] *if in case*
nakereba ['- - -] *if there is not......*, from **nai**, *non-existent*
mekura [- - -] *blind ; a blind person*
mie- [- -] from **mieru**, *can be seen ; be visible*. **Me ga mienai** means *to be blind*.
......keredomo ['- - -] *though*
makkura [- -'-] *(a-B) pitchdark*
chittomo [- -'-] *(not) at all* (with a negative)
akari [- - -] *a light*

tsukereba [-'--] *if we light*, from **tsukeru**, *to light*

keseba [-'-] *if we put out*, from **kesu**, *to put out* (a light)

dentō [----] *an electric light*

kiereba [----] *if it goes out*, from **kieru**, (a light) *goes out*

rōsoku [----] *a candle*

kaichū-dentō [----'---] *a flash-light*

atte mo ['---] *even if we have*, from **aru**, *to have*

tojireba [-'--] *if we close*, form **tojiru**, *to close*

tsumbo ['--] *deaf; a deaf person*

kikoe- [---] from **kikoeru**, *can be heard; be audible*

fusageba [----] *if we stop it up*, from **fusagu**, *to stop up*

kotoba [---] *a word; language*

imi ['-] *meaning*

shira- [--] from **shiru**, *to know*

kiite mo [----] *even if we hear*, from **kiku**, *to hear; listen to*

bunshō ['---] *a sentence*

yonde mo ['---] *even if we read;* from **yomu**, *to read*

(jibiki o) hikeba [-'-] *if we look up in* (the dictionary), from **hiku**, *to draw*

Grammar

"Aru" and "Nai"

173.　　**Me ga areba, miru koto ga dekimasu.**

　　　　We can see if we have eyes.

　　　　Mimi ga nakereba kiku koto ga dekimasen.

　　　　We could not hear if we had no ears.

　　　　Yoru wa akari ga areba miemasu ga, nakereba miemasen.

　　　　We can see at night if there is a light, but we cannot see if there isn't one.

　　Aru, *to exist* (*there is*), is a verb both in Japanese and English. *Not* in English is an adverb, whereas **nai** in Japanese is a true adjective. Therefore, **aru** conjugates as a verb and **nai** as an adjective.

　　In theory, the negative of **aru** should be "ara-nai," but instead of this form **nai** is generally always used.

　　The student is warned that this **nai**, which is a true adjective, is different from the adjective-like auxiliary **nai** which forms a negative by being tacked on to the negative base of a verb. Their apparent forms are the same, but the adjective **nai** is an independent word while the auxiliary **nai** is not.

Auxiliary:

> **Hon o yoma-nai deshō.** *Perhaps he will not read books.*
>
> **Kore o tabe-naide kudasai.** *Please don't eat this.*

True adjective:

> **Kitte ga nai to tegami o dasu koto ga dekimasen.**
>> *If we have no stamps, we cannot mail letters.*
>
> **Te ga nakute mo aruku koto ga dekimasu.**
>> *We can walk without hands.*

The Present Conditional

174. **Me ga nakereba miru koto ga dekimasen.**
> *If we had no eyes, we could not see.*

Me o tojireba nani mo miemasen.
> *If we close our eyes, we cannot see anything.*

Conditions which are usually expressed by *if such-and-such happens* or *if it is this way or that way* or *when so-and-so does*, or *provided that*, etc. are expressed by the conditional endings **ba** for verbs, and **kereba** for adjectives, attached to the present conditional base.

1. Verbs: Add **ba** to the fourth base, i.e. the form obtained by replacing the final vowel of the conclusive form (i.e. the 3rd base) by **e.**

(a)	**Yodan** verbs:	kak**u**	kak**e-ba**	*write*
		kik**u**	kik**e-ba**	*hear*
		yom**u**	yom**e-ba**	*read*
		ar**u**	ar**e-ba**	*be*
		kau	ka**e-ba**	*buy*
		fusag**u**	fusag**e-ba**	*close*
(b)	**Ichidan** verbs:	aker**u**	aker**e-ba**	*open*
		taber**u**	taber**e-ba**	*eat*
		tojir**u**	tojir**e-ba**	*shut*
		okir**u**	okir**e-ba**	*get up*
(c)	**Irregular** verbs:	kur**u**	kur**e-ba**	*come*
		sur**u**	sur**e-ba**	*do*

2. Adjectives: Add **kereba** to the stem (or the conditional base, i. e. the base without the final **i** of the dictionary form).

na**i**	na-**kereba**	*not*
akaru**i**	akaru-**kereba**	*light*
kura**i**	kura-**kereba**	*dark*

When the idea of provision is to be strongly expressed like *if in case,* **moshi** is placed at the beginning of a sentence.

Moshi mimi ga nakereba...... *If in case we had no ears......*

A concession expressed by *even if* is described with **mo** added to the **te**-form.

Mimi ga atte mo sore o fusageba nani mo kikoemasen.

Even if we have ears, we can't hear if we stop them up.

Te ga nakute mo hanashi o suru koto ga dekimasu.

Even if there were no hands, we would be able to talk.

"Mieru" and "Kikoeru"

175.   **Kurakereba miemasen.**   *We cannot see if it is dark.*

Mimi o akereba kikoemasu.   *We can hear if we open our ears.*

Mieru and **kikoeru** are intransitive verbs corresponding to the transitive verbs **miru**, *to see* and **kiku**, *to hear.*

Mieru means *to be visible, to appear, can see, can be seen,* etc. and **kikoeru** means *to be audible, can hear, can be heard,* etc.

An important thing about these verbs is the fact that, because they are intransitive, they follow **wa** or **ga**, never the objective particle **o**.

Takai yama ga miemasu.   *A high mountain is visible.*

Sono oto wa koko kara kikoemasen.

That sound isn't audible from here.

Me ga mienai (*blind*) and **mimi ga kikoenai** (*deaf*) are collocations. In these collocations **ga** is used for the purpose of clarifying ambiguity of the predicate, which was explained in Lesson 13, Grammar 97.

"Ma-"—a Prefix meaning "Really," "Truly"

176.   **Ma** is a prefix attached to some adjectives (true or quasi-) and adverbs, meaning *really, truly.*

masshiroi or **masshiro na**	*snow-white*
makkurai or **makkura na**	*pitch-dark*
maue ni	*right above*
maushiro ni	*right behind*

"Nakereba narimasen"—"Must"

177. Necessity or obligation expressed by *must, should,* etc. is usually expressed by negative conditionals.

Nakereba narimasen literally means *if one does not......, it won't do,* which boils down to *one must......*

Dentō o tsukenakereba narimasen.
We must turn on the electric light.

Mō ikanakereba narimasen. *I must go now.*

Tabenakereba narimasen. *I must eat.*

Mijikai Kaiwa

moshimoshi ['---] an attention caller meaning *I say, look here, listen, excuse me,* etc. This is commonly used in telephoning.

denwa [---] *a telephone.* **Denwa ga tōi** means *the voice is indistinct.*

omachi [---] from **matsu**, *to wait,* with **o**, honorific

Exercises

A. Practise converting from one form to another rapidly and fluently.

Conversion Table 8

Dictionary Form	If	Even if	Meaning
(verbs)			
iu	ieba	itte mo	*say*
aruku	arukeba	aruite mo	*walk*
kesu	keseba	keshite mo	*put out (light)*
matsu	mateba	matte mo	*wait*
yobu	yobeba	yonde mo	*call*
hairu	haireba	haitte mo	*enter*

aru	areba	atte mo	*have ; exist*
tōru	tōreba	tōtte mo	*pass*
iku	ikeba	itte mo	*go*
tsukeru	tsukereba	tsukete mo	*put on (light)*
kieru	kiereba	kiete mo	*go out (light)*
tojiru	tojireba	tojite mo	*close ; shut*
kuru	kureba	kite mo	*come*
suru	sureba	shite mo	*do*
(true-adjectives)			
nai	nakereba	nakute mo	*non-existent*
kurai	kurakereba	kurakute mo	*dark*
yoi, ii	yokereba	yokute mo	*good*
warui	warukereba	warukute mo	*bad*
akarui	akarukereba	akarukute mo	*light*
tōi	tōkereba	tōkute mo	*far*

B. *Answer the following questions.*

   1. Watakushitachi wa nan de oto o kikimasu ka ?

   2. Mimi ga nakereba nani o suru koto ga dekimasen ka ?

   3. Naze tsumbo no hito wa nani mo kikoemasen ka ?

   4. Naze yoru wa akari ga irimasu ka ?

   5. Me ga mienai hito o nan to iimasu ka ?

   6. Mimi ga areba itsumo kikoemasu ka ?

   7. Kotoba no imi ga wakaranakereba bunshō o yonde mo imi ga wakari-masen ka ?

   8. Okane ga nakute mo kau koto ga dekimasu ka ?

   9. Anata wa jibiki o hikeba Nippongo no shimbun o yomu koto **ga** dekimasu ka ?

  10. Anata wa hima ga areba itsumo benkyō shimasu ka ?

C. *Combine* (a) *and* (b) *into a sentence, making necessary changes.*

   Example : (a) Me ga **nai** desu.

           (b) Miru koto ga dekimasen.

                Me ga **nakereba** miru koto ga dekimasen.

           (a) Okane ga **nai** desu.

(b) Hairu koto ga dekimasu.

Okane ga **nakute mo** hairu koto ga dekimasu.

1. (a) Kuroda San ga kimasu.
   (b) Hanashimasu.

2. (a) Ame ga furimasu.
   (b) Dekakemasen.

3. (a) Yoku benkyō shimasu.
   (b) Wakarimasen.

4. (a) Ano hito no uchi ga tōi desu.
   (b) Watakushi wa ikimasen.

5. (a) Sono hon wa takai desu.
   (b) Watakushi wa sono hon o kaimasu.

D. *What is the Japanese equivalent of each of the following sentences?*

1. If I haven't 3,000 yen, I can't buy those shoes.
2. Even if I called him, he couldn't hear me. He seems to be deaf.
3. Even if you send it by airmail, it won't reach there before Christmas
    (=*Kurisumasu*).
4. If it is bad, please correct it.
5. If it rains, he won't come.
6. If you read newspapers, you will understand.
7. If I have time, I'd like to go.
8. If you go there in the evening, you must use the flashlight.
9. If the electric lights go out, I'll use these candles.
10. Even if Japanese is difficult, you'll be able to become good at it if
    you study hard.
11. Can you see Mt. Fuji (=*Fujisan*) over there?
12. I have to go to Mr. Tanaka's today even if it rains.
13. If there are words which you don't know, you have to look them up
    in the dictionary.
14. The sun has set. It has become dark. Turn on the light, please.

Nijū-ni

(Main Text)

A : Anata wa kudamono wa suki desu ka, kirai desu ka ?

B : Daisuki desu.

A : Donna kudamono ga osuki desu ka ?

B : Ringo, biwa, momo, nashi, kaki, mikan nado nan demo suki desu.

A : Kudamono wa futsū doko de utte imasu ka ?

B : Kudamonoya de utte imasu ga, yaoya demo kau koto ga dekimasu.

A : Yaoya dewa nani o urimasu ka?

B : Jagaimo, hōrensō, kabu, ninjin, kyabetsu nado no yasai o urimasu.

A : Hoka no shinamono wa donna mise de
kaimasu ka?

B : Pan wa pan'ya de, sara wa setomonoya
de, gyūniku ya butaniku wa nikuya de
kaimasu.

A : Gyūniku to iu no wa nan desu ka?

B : Ushi no niku desu.

A : Nikuya dewa toriniku ya tamago mo
utte imasu ka?

B : Taitei utte imasu.

A : Shio ya satō ya biiru ya sake nado
ga hoshii toki niwa donna mise e ikanakereba narimasen ka?

B : Shokuryōhin'ya e ikanakereba narimasen.

A : Nani ka hoshii toki niwa itsumo jibun de kai ni ikanakereba narimasen ka ?

B : Iie, sō shinakute mo ii desu.

Denwa ga areba denwa de chūmon shite mo ii desu. Jochū o kai ni yatte mo ii desu.

(A Short Conversation)

A : Dotchi o agemashō ka ?

B : Dotchi demo kamaimasen.

A : Kore wa ikaga desu ka ?

B : Sore wa suki ja arimasen. Kō iu no ga hoshii desu.

(For Memorizing)

1. Anata wa [kudamono] wa kirai desu ka ?

2. Daisuki desu.

3. [Gyūniku] to iu no wa nan desu ka ?

1. Do you dislike [fruit] ?

2. I like it very much.

3. What is meant by [beef] ?

4. [Shio] ya [satō] ga hoshii toki niwa donna mise e ikanakereba narimasen ka ?	4. When we want [salt] or [sugar], what sort of shop must we go to ?
5. [Shokuryōhin'ya] e ikanakereba narimasen.	5. We must go to the [provision store].
6. Sō shinakute mo ii desu.	6. You needn't do so.
7. Denwa de chūmon shite mo ii desu.	7. You may order it by telephone.

Hombun

Glossary

kudamono [-'--] *fruit*

suki [-'] (*a–B*) *pleasing ; liking*

kirai [---] (*a–B*) *disliking*

daisuki ['---] (*a–B*) *very fond of*

osuki [---] (*a–B*) **o**, honorific and **suki**, *pleasing ; liking*

biwa ['-] *a loquat*

momo [--] *a peach*

nashi [--] *a pear*

kaki [-'] *a persimmon*

mikan ['--] *a tangerine ; mandarine orange*

nan demo ['---] *anything ; everything ; all*

utte [---] from **uru**, *to sell*

kudamonoya [-----] *a fruit-shop*

yaoya [---] *a greengrocer*

jagaimo [----] *Irish potatoes*

hōrensō [--'---] *spinach*

kabu [--] *a turnip*

ninjin [----] *a carrot*

kyabetsu ['--] *cabbage*

yasai [---] *vegetables*

hoka no [---] *other ; another*

shinamono [----] *an article ; object*

mise [-'] *a store; shop*
pan ['-] *bread*
pan'ya ['--] *a baker; bakery*
sara [--] *a plate; dish*
setomonoya [-----] *a china-shop*
gyūniku [----] *beef*
butaniku [----] *pork*
nikuya [-'-] *a butcher; meat-shop*
ushi [--] *a cow; ox*
niku [-'] *meat*
toriniku [----] *chicken meat*
tamago [-'- or ---] *an egg*
shio [-'] *salt*
satō [-'-] *sugar*
biiru ['-- or ---] *beer*
sake [--] *liquor; spirits; wine*
hoshii [-'-] *(a-A) desirous of having; want* (an object)
shokuryōhin'ya [-------] *a provisions store*
nani ka ['--] *something; anything*
jibun de [----] *(by) oneself*
kai ni [---] *for buying,* kai, *from* kau, *to buy*
-te mo ii *may; be permitted to......*
chūmon suru [------] *to order*
jochū [---] *a maid* (servant)
yatte [---] *from* yaru, *to send*

Grammar

"Suki" and "Kirai"

178. These are quasi-adjectives. Therefore, **suki na** and **kirai na** mean
pleasing and *displeasing* respectively.

> **suki na hito** *a pleasing person*, i.e. *a person whom one likes*
> or *a person who likes*
> **kirai na koto** *something* (abstract) *one dislikes*

Suki desu and **kirai desu** mean *it is pleasing* and *it is displeasing* respectively. Since these words are not verbs, the word order of the sentences differs from English sentences used in similar instances. In the Japanese sentences the object which one likes is in the nominative case with the particle **ga** or **wa** and the person who likes is followed by **wa**.

> **Watakushi wa sakana ga suki desu.** *I like fish.*
>
> **Anata wa kono e wa kirai desu ka?**
>
> *Do you dislike this picture?*

Nowadays we frequently hear the objective particle **o** used in place of **ga** or **wa**.

> **Kore o suki desu ka?** *Do you like this?*

"Ya"—a Dealer or a Shop

179. **Ya** is a suffix used after merchandise and indicates a dealer or a shop which handles such goods. **Kusuri** means *medicine* and **kusuriya**, *a druggist*. **Sakana** is *a fish* and **sakanaya**, *a fish dealer*.

Sometimes **san** is used after it as **kusuriya-san, sakanaya-san,** etc. to show repect or kindly feeling.

"Hoshii"—"Desirable"

180. **Hoshii** is a true adjective and corresponds more or less to *desirable* or *wanted* rather than the verb *to want*. Therefore, the thing one wants is in the nominative case.

> **Anata wa nani ga hoshii desu ka?** *What do you want?*
>
> **Watakushi wa ringo ga hoshii desu.** *I want some apples.*

181. In Lesson 16, Grammar 135 we had the desiderative **tai** which also means *to want to*. The difference is that **tai** is an auxiliary and is always used with a verb while **hoshii** means *to want something*.

> **Ringo ga tabetai desu.**   *I'd like to eat some apples.*
>
> **Nippongo ga naraitai desu.**   *I'd like to learn Japanese.*
>
> **Ikitaku wa arimasen.**   *I don't want to go.*
>
> **Kore ga hoshii desu ka?**   *Do you want this?*
>
> **Sore wa hoshiku wa arimasen.**   *I don't want that.*

Interrogative Words plus Particles

182. When interrogative words such as **nani, dare, doko, itsu, ikutsu, dotchi** are followed by such particles as **ka, mo, demo,** etc., they more or less form compound words and mean various combinations of *some, any* or *every*.

Interrogative Words plus "Ka"

183. Compare:

Nani ga hoshii desu ka?	*What do you want?*
Nani ka hoshii desu ka?	*Do you want anything?*
Dare ga ikimashita ka?	*Who went?*
Dare ka ikimashita ka?	*Did anyone go?*
Doko e okimashita ka?	*Where did you put it?*
Doko ka e okimashita.	*I put it somewhere.*
Itsu kakimasu ka?	*When will you write it?*
Itsu ka kakimashō.	*I'll write it some day.*

Interrogative Words plus "Mo" meaning "Every..."

184. In Lesson 12, Grammar 91 we had an example of an interrogative word plus **mo** followed by a negative word.

Nani mo arimasen. *I don't have anything; I have nothing.*

Doko emo ikimasen deshita.

I didn't go anywhere; I went nowhere.

When it is followed by **mo** in an affirmative sentence, it means *every* or *all*.

Itsumo kai ni ikimasu. *I always (=at all times) go to buy it.*

Dotchi mo suki desu. *I like both.*

Dono hon mo chiisai desu. *Every book is small.*

Doko mo kirei desu. *Everywhere is clean.*

Interrogative Words plus "Demo"

185.

Nan demo suki desu.	*I like anything* (or *everything* or *all*).
Itsu demo kekkō desu.	*Any time will do.*
Ikutsu demo agemasu.	*I'll give you any number of them.*
doko demo	*anywhere; everywhere*
dare demo	*anybody; everybody*
dotchi demo	*whichever*

"-nakute mo Ii" meaning "Need not"

186. **-nakute mo ii** which comes after the negative base of a verb means literally *all right even if...not*, hence, *need not*.

Tabenakute mo ii desu ka? *Is it all right even if I don't eat?*

Sō shinakute mo ii desu. *You needn't do so.*

"-te mo Ii" meaning "May"

187. The **te**-form of a verb or an adjective followed by **mo ii** means literally *it is all right even if you...*, hence, *may* (permission).

Denwa de chūmon shite mo ii desu.

It is all right even if we order it by telephone.

Eiga e itte mo ii desu. *You may go to the movies.*

Mijikai Kaiwa

kamaimasen [------] from **kamau**, *to mind; concern*

kō iu no [-----] *such a thing as this:* **kō, sō, ā** and **dō** respectively means *in this way, in that way,* and *in what way;* the differences among these correspond to those among **kore, sore, are** and **dore.** **Kō, sō, ā** and **dō** are adverbials. **Sō desu** literally means *It is like that* (=*what you have said*).

Exercises

A. Practice converting from one form to another rapidly and fluently.

Conversion Table 9

Dictionary Form	Must	Need not	May (all right even if it...)	Meaning
kau	kawanakereba narimasen	kawanakute mo ii desu	katte mo ii desu	*buy*
aruku	arukanakereba narimasen	arukanakute mo ii desu	aruite mo ii desu	*walk*
kesu	kesanakereba narimasen	kesanakute mo ii desu	keshite mo ii desu	*put out (light)*
matsu	matanakereba narimasen	matanakute mo ii desu	matte mo ii desu	*wait*
yobu	yobanakereba narimasen	yobanakute mo ii desu	yonde mo ii desu	*call*
yaru	yaranakereba narimasen	yaranakute mo ii desu	yatte mo ii desu	*send*
hairu	hairanakereba narimasen	hairanakute mo ii desu	haitte mo ii desu	*enter*

iku	ikanakereba narimasen	ikanakute mo ii desu	itte mo ii desu	*go*
tsukeru	tsukenakereba narimasen	tsukenakute mo ii desu	tsukete mo ii desu	*put on (light)*
miru	minakereba narimasen	minakute mo ii desu	mite mo ii desu	*see*
kuru	konakereba narimasen	konakute mo ii desu	kite mo ii desu	*come*
suru	shinakereba narimasen	shinakute mo ii desu	shite mo ii desu	*do*
yoi	yoku nakereba narimasen	yoku nakute mo ii desu	yokute mo ii desu	*be good*
takai	takaku nakereba narimasen	takaku nakute mo ii desu	takakute mo ii desu	*be expensive*

B. *Answer the following questions.*

1. Anata wa donna kudamono ga osuki desu ka ?
2. Kudamono wa doko de utte imasu ka ?
3. Yasai ga hoshii toki niwa donna mise e ikanakereba narimasen ka ?
4. Setomonoya to iu no wa donna mise desu ka ?
5. Nikuya dewa nani o utte imasu ka ?
6. Donna toki ni shokuryōhin'ya e ikanakereba narimasen ka ?
7. Anata wa mainichi hataraki ni ikanakereba narimasen ka ?

C. *What is the Japanese equivalent of each of the following sentences?*

1. "What do you want ?" "I don't want anything."
2. I want some sugar and salt.
3. Do you want to buy anything ?
4. No, I don't want to buy anything today. I'll come again tomorrow, if I want anything.
5. Must we wait so long (=*nagaku*) ?
6. No, you don't need to wait so long.
7. If he doesn't come in the morning, you don't have to wait (for him) any longer (=*mō*).
8. I want some dishes, but where can I buy them ?
9. You will be able to buy them at the chinaware shop in your neighborhood.
10. As I like home-made bread (=bread made at home), you don't need

to buy it at the bakery.

11. Must I go out now ? It's raining heavily (=a lot).

12. No, you don't need to go now. Go tomorrow morning.

D. Carry on, in Japanese, the following conversation between the mistress and the maid.

Mistress : Jagaimo wa takusan arimasu ka ?

Maid : (*No, there isn't any.*)

Mistress : Dewa, kyō kaimashō. Hoka no yasai wa dō desu ka ?

Maid : (*Because there isn't much, we must buy some.*)

Mistress : Dewa kyabetsu to ninjin o katte kite kudasai.

Maid : (*Yes, ma'am. Madam, we haven't any fruit, either.*)

Mistress : Dewa kaki to mikan o katte kite kudasai. Kyō wa gyūniku mo butaniku mo kawanakereba narimasen nē.

Maid : (*Well then, I'll go to the butcher's.*)

Mistress : Iie, ikanakute mo ii desu; denwa de chūmon shimasu kara. Pan ga arimasen deshō ?

Maid : (*No, there isn't.*)

Mistress : Dewa pan'ya e ikanakereba narimasen nē; asuko niwa denwa ga arimasen kara.......

Maid : (*Yes, I must go there.*)

Review (Lessons 13—22)

Vocabulary Check-up :

A. Fill in each blank with an appropriate word.

		( ) airplane	( ) automobile	( ) steam train	( ) electric train	( ) bicycle	( ) boat
1	Vehicles	( ) airplane	( ) automobile	( ) steam train	( ) electric train	( ) bicycle	( ) boat
2	Verbs	noru ( )	tsuku ( )	iku ( )	kuru ( )	kaeru ( )	tōru ( )
3	Places	sora ( )	michi ( )	yama ( )	kaigan ( )	shima ( )	umi ( )
4	Modi-fiers	semai ( )	hiroi ( )	mijikai ( )	nagai ( )	usui ( )	atsui ( )
		( ) width		( ) length		( ) thickness	

5	Houses & Shops	yōkan ( )	( ) Japanese-style room	( ) hospital	( ) post office	( ) bank	( ) church
		kudamo-noya ( )	yaoya ( )	nikuya ( )	pan'ya ( )	shokuryō-hin'ya ( )	( ) any other shop
6	Food	( ) fruit	( ) vegetables	( ) beef	( ) pork	( ) sugar	( ), salt
7	Fruit	( ) apple	( ) tangerine	( ) persimmon	( ) loquat	( ) pear	( ) peach
8	Vege-tables	jagaimo ( )	hōrensō ( )	kabu ( )	ninjin ( )	kyabetsu ( )	( ) any other vegetable
9	Part of a House & Furni-ture	genkan ( )	deiriguchi ( )	rōka ( )	engawa ( )	kaidan ( )	entotsu ( )
		ōsetsuma ( )	kyakuma ( )	shokudō ( )	chanoma ( )	shinshitsu ( )	daidokoro ( )
		jochūbeya ( )	semmenjo ( )	furoba ( )	nihomma ( )	yōma ( )	gofujō; benjo ( )
		tokonoma ( )	tatami ( )	todana ( )	shindai ( )	reizōko ( )	nagashi ( )
		chabudai ( )	ikkai ( )	nikai ( )	niwa ( )	mon ( )	mado ( )
10	Mail & Com-muni-cation	kozutsumi ( )	tegami ( )	kawase ( )	kakitome ( )	sokutatsu ( )	kōkūbin ( )
		dempō ( )	denwa ( )	rajio ( )	posuto ( )	hagaki ( )	kitte ( )
11	Family & Rela-tives	( ) father	( ) mother	( ) elder brother	( ) younger brother	( ) elder sister	( ) younger sister
		( ) grand father	( ) grand mother	( ) uncle	( ) aunt	( ) nephew	( ) niece
		( ) grandchild	( ) parents	( ) cousin		( ) boy	( ) girl

B. Pick up a suitable numeral classifier for each of the following objects; count from one to ten each.

Numeral classifier

   a. hon b. mai c. satsu d. nin e. ken f. sō g. dai

   1. kippu   2. jibiki   3. mannenhitsu

4.	hito	5.	empitsu	6.	jitensha
7.	kami	8.	yaoya	9.	satsu
10.	hari (*of watch*)	11.	fune	12.	yōkan
13.	jidōsha	14.	ki	15.	hon

C. *See if you know the meanings of each of the following words.*

1.	ōfuku	6.	asobu	11.	gaikokujin	16.	kinjo
2.	koshiraeru	7.	tōku	12.	omote	17.	haru (-')
3.	kin	8.	issho	13.	soshite	18.	tsukareru
4.	bin	9.	kumoru	14.	dōka	19.	tsumbo
5.	taihen	10.	atama ga itai	15.	goshujin	20.	mekura

D. (1) *A Conversation:*

See if you understand the following conversation between X and Y.

X: Anata no otaku wa yōkan desu ka ?

Y: Iie, Nihon no ie desu.

X: Heya wa ikutsu arimasu ka ?

Y: Ikkai niwa genkan, chanoma, kyakuma no mittsu ga atte, nikai niwa shinshitsu ga futatsu arimasu. Minna de itsutsu desu.

X: Koko kara tōi desu ka ?

Y: Gojikkiro gurai arimasu.

X: Koko e kuru no ni nani o tsukaimasu ka ?

Y: Kisha de kimasu.

X: Kisha de dono gurai kakarimasu ka ?

Y: Kinjo no eki kara ichijikan gurai kakarimasu.

X: Kisha wa ichijikan ni nando gurai desu ka ?

Y: Sando gurai desu.

X: Otaku wa eki kara tōi desu ka ?

Y: Eki kara aruite jūgofun gurai desu.

X: Dewa aruku no o irete, otaku kara koko made ichijikan jūgofun kakarimasu ne. Eki kara wa densha ga arimasu ka ?

Y: Iie, densha wa arimasen. Keredomo basu ga arimasu.

X: Anata no otaku no kinjo ni ōkina ie wa arimasen ka ?

Y: Arimasu. Ōkii kyōkai ga arimasu.

X: Otaku wa sono kyōkai no tonari desu ka ?

Y: Iie, sō ja arimasen. Kyōkai no mae ni chiisana yūbinkyoku ga arimasu.

Watakushi no ie wa sono yūbinkyoku no soba desu.

X: Anata no kazoku wa nannin desu ka?

Y: Watakushi o ireru to gonin desu. Ani to imōto ga hitorizutsu arimasu.

X: Dewa anata wa chōnan ja arimasen nē.

Y: Hai, chōnan ja arimasen; jinan desu.

X: Imōto-san wa ōkii desu ka?

Y: Iie, mada chiisai desu.

X: Otōsan wa nani o shite imasu ka?

Y: Byōin ni tsutomete imasu.

X: Isha desu ka?

Y: Hai, sō desu.

(2) *Pattern Practice:*

All the sentences in "For Memorizing" and "A Short Conversation" must be learned thoroughly. But, above all, the following sentences are so important that they should be given special attention to so that students can reproduce them rapidly and fluently. Try and do so.

1. Kono jibiki wa haba ga semai desu.

   This dictionary is narrow.

2. Kono empitsu wa onaji nagasa desu ka?

   Are these pencils of the same leugth?

3. Ippon wa nagakute mō ippon wa mijikai desu.

   One is long and the other is short.

4. Ikura haitte iru deshō?

   Do you know how much there is in it?

5. Soredewa akete mimashō.

   Then, let's open it and see.

6. Ichien to goen to jūen no naka de dore ga ichiban ōkii desu ka?

   Which is the largest, a one-yen piece, a five-yen piece, or a ten-yen piece?

7. Gin wa kin gurai takai desu ka?

   Is silver as expensive as gold?

8. Gin wa kin hodo takaku wa arimasen.

   Silver is not so expensive as gold.

9. Ie no chikaku de kodomo ga asonde imasu.

   Some children are playing near the house.

10. Ie no mae e kuru tokoro desu.

    It's coming in front of the house.

11. Onnanohito no yō desu.

    It seems to be a woman.

12. Shima no soba o fune ga tōtte imasu.

    A boat is passing by the island.

13. Jidōsha o unten shite iru hito o ireru to ikunin desu ka?

    How many people are there including the one who is driving the car?

14. Kono michi wa Ginza e ikimasu ka?

    Does this road go to the Ginza?

15. Ginza made dono gurai arimasu ka?

    How far is it from here to the Ginza?

16. Iku tsumori deshita ga, byōki deshita.

    I had intended to go, but I was sick.

17. Densha de iku to ichijikan gurai de tsukimasu.

    We (can) get there in about one hour by electric train.

18. Eki kara wa aruku hō ga ii deshō.

    From the station it'll be better to walk.

19. Iku koto ga dekiru ka dō ka wakarimasen.

    I'm not sure whether I can go or not.

20. Watakushi wa maiasa rokuji ni okimasu.

    I get up at six o'clock every morning.

21. Basu ya densha ni noranaide takushii de iku koto mo arimasu.

    Instead of taking a bus or a streetcar, I sometimes go by taxi.

22. Tegami o kaitari hito ni attari shite hiru made hatarakimasu.

    I work until noon, sometimes writing letters and sometimes seeing visitors.

23. Kinō kozutsumi o dashi ni yūbinkyoku e ikimashita.

    I went to the post office to send a package yesterday.

24. Kono kozutsumi o dashitai no desu ga ikura kakarimasu ka?

    I'd like to send this package; how much will it cost?

25. Futsū de kekkō desu.

Ordainary mail will do.

26. Suzuki to iu no wa myōji de namae wa Haruo to iimasu.

    Suzuki is his surname and his first name is Haruo.

27. Niisan wa Suzuki San yori toshi ga futatsu ue desu.

    His elder brother is Suzuki's senior by two years.

28. Goshujin wa otaku desu ka?

    Is the master at home?

29. Niwa niwa iroiro no ki ga uete arimasu.

    Various trees are planted in the garden.

30. Genkan o tōranaide dehairi suru tame desu.

    It's for going in and out without passing through the front entrance.

31. Heya wa daidokoro ya furoba o nozoite jūshi'go arimasu.

    There are fourteen or fifteen rooms excluding the kitchen and the bathroom.

32. Aruite gofun shika kakarimasen.

    It's only five minutes' walk.

33. Moshi me ga nakereba nani mo miru koto ga dekimasen.

    If we had no eyes, we could not see anything.

34. Akarukereba miemasu ga, kurakereba miemasen.

    We can see if it is light, but we can't see if it is dark.

35. Yoru wa dentō o tsukenakereba narimasen.

    At night we must turn on the electric light.

36. Imi o shiranakereba kotoba o kiite mo wakarimasen.

    If we don't know the meaning, we don't understand even if we hear a word.

37. Anata wa kudamono ga kirai desu ka?

    Do you dislike fruit?

38. Gyūniku to iu no wa nan desu ka?

    What is meant by beef?

39. Sō shinakute mo ii desu.

    You needn't do so.

40. Denwa de chūmon shite mo ii desu.

    You may order it by telephone.

(Main Text)

A : Anata wa mō Nippongo o dono kurai benkyō shimashita ka ?

B : Mō nikagetsu benkyō shimashita.

A : Kanari jōzu ni hanasemasu ka ?

B : Iie, mada desu.   Yoku wa hanasemasen.

A : Nippongo no hon ga yomemasu ka ?

B : Iie, mada jōzu ni yomemasen.   Tabitabi machigaimasu.

A : Nippongo wa muzukashii to omoimasu ka ?

B : Iie, kanari yasashii to omoimasu.

A : Nippongo no hatsuon wa Eigo no yori zutto yasashii desu.

Nippongo dewa kanji ya kana o tsukaimasu.

Anata wa kanji ga kakemasu ka ?

B : Iie, mada kakemasen.

A : Mō takusan no kotoba o oboemashita ka ?

B : Iie, mada tarimasen.

A : Ikutsu gurai shitte imasu ka ?

B : Yoku wakarimasen.

Takusan naraimashita ga sugu wasuremasu kara.

Tabun shi'gohyaku oboete imashō.

A : Nippongo no kotoba wa oboenikui desu ka ?

B : Oboenikui kotoba mo oboeyasui kotoba mo arimasu ga, yoku benkyō shinakereba dame desu.

A : Teiryūjō to iu no wa dō iu imi desu ka ?

B : Densha ya basu no tomaru tokoro to iu imi desu.

(A Short Conversation)

B : Motte itte mo ii desu ka ?

A : Iie, oitette kudasai.

B : Airon o kakemashō ka ?

A : Sō shite kudasai. Kore o hoshite kudasai.

(For Memorizing)

1. Kanari jōzu ni [hanasemasu] ka ?
2. Nippongo no [hon] ga yomemasu ka ?
3. Iie, mada jōzu ni [yomemasen].
4. Kanari [yasashii] to omoimasu.
5. Nippongo no hatsuon wa [Eigo] no yori zutto yasashii desu.
6. Ikutsu gurai shitte imasu ka ?
7. Tabun [shi'gohyaku] oboete imshō.
8. Benkyō shinakereba dame desu.
9. [Teiryūjō] to iu no wa dō iu imi desu ka ?

---

1. Can you [speak] it fairly well ?
2. Can you read Japanese [books]?
3. No, I can't [read] them well yet.
4. I think it is fairly [easy].
5. Japanese pronunciation is much easier than that of [English].
6. About how many do you know ?
7. Probably I remember about [four or five hundred].
8. It's no good if we don't study hard.
9. What is meant by a [streetcar or bus-stop]?

Hombun

Glossary

mō [-- or '-] *already ; till now*

dono kurai [----- or '---] = **dono gurai**, *about how long; about how much* (See Grammar 188.)

jōzu ni [----] *skilfully ; well*

hanase- [---] from **hanaseru**, *can speak*

yome- [--] from **yomeru**, *can read*

tabitabi [----] *often ; frequently*

machigai- [----] from **machigau**, *to make a mistake*

......**to omoimasu** *I think that......*

hatsuon [----] *pronunciation*

zutto [- - -] *by far*

kanji [- - -] *a Chinese character*

kana [- -] *the Japanese syllabary*

kake- [- -] from **kakeru**, *can write*

tari- [- -] from **tariru**, *to be enough ; be sufficient*

tabun ['- -] *perhaps ; probably*

shi'gohyaku [- - - -] *four or five hundred*

oboenikui [- - - -'-] (*a–A*) *hard to learn*

oboeyasui [- - - -'-] (*a–A*) *easy to learn*

dame [-'] (*a–B*) a word that expresses disapproval, dissatisfaction, or hope-
lessness, so that it may mean *no good, hopelsss, useless, impossible*, etc.

dō iu ['- - -] *what sort of*

tomaru [- - -] *to stop*

Grammar

"Dono kurai" meaning "About how much" "About how long"

188. **Dono** belongs to the same category of pre-nouns as **kono**, **sono**, and
ano. It always comes before a noun, but not as the predicate of a sentence.

> **dono tsuki**   *which month*
>
> **dono hito**   *which person*

Kurai (or **gurai**) corresponds in meaning to the English word *about*,
approximately, or *as much as* (cf. Lesson 15, A Short Conversation), so
dono kurai means *about how much.*

> **Koko kara otaku made dono kurai arimasu ka ?**
>
> *About how much (=far) is it from here to your house?*
>
> **Kono omosa wa dono kurai arimashō ka ?**
>
> *What is the weight of this?*

Potential Verbs

189. We have already learned that potentiality can be expressed by adding
koto ga dekimasu to the 3rd (i.e. the conclusive) base.

There is another way of expressing the same idea by replacing the final **u**
of the conclusive form of a **Yodan** verb by **e**.

> **hanasu**   **hanase-**   *speak*

— 235 —

yomu	yome-	*read*
narau	narae-	*learn*
hataraku	hatarake-	*work*
yasumu	yasume-	*rest*
kaku	kake-	*write*

Nippongo ga hanasemasu ka? *Can you speak Japanese?*

Nippongo no hon ga yomemasu. *I can read Japanese books.*

Mada kanji ga kakemasen. *I cannot write characters yet.*

It is important to remember that these potential verbs are formed only from **Yodan** verbs and conjugate exactly the same as **Ichidan** verbs. Therefore, if you are in doubt as to whether a verb is **Yodan** or **Ichidan**, it is safe for you to use **koto ga dekimasu** instead of trying to form a new **Ichidan** potential verb, since **koto ga dekimasu** can be used with the conclusive form of any verb.

Yodan :	**Yomemasu ka?**	*Can you read?*
	Yomu koto ga dekimasu ka?	*Can you read?*
Ichidan :	**Taberu koto ga dekimasen.**	*I cannot eat (it).*
	Miru koto ga dekimasen.	*I cannot see.*

190. Another point worth remembering is that these potential verbs are preceded by the particle **ga** or **wa** instead of **o**, even though the word before **ga** or **wa** appears to be in the objective case.*

Kono hon ga yomemasu ka? } *Can you read this*
Kono hon o yomu koto ga dekimasu ka? } *book?*

Nippongo ga hanasemasen. } *I cannot speak*
Nippongo o hanasu koto ga dekimasen. } *Japanese.*

" -yasui " and " -nikui " — Suffixes

191. **-yasui** and **-nikui** are adjectival suffixes meaning *easy to* and *hard to* respectively.

oboeyasui	*easy to remember*
oboenikui	*hard to remember*
kakiyasui	*easy to write*
kakinikui	*hard to write*

---

* This rule is beginning to be ignored by some of the younger generation.

"......nakereba Dame" — "Must"

192. **......nakereba** followed by **dame desu** has the same meaning as **......
nakereba narimasen**, but it is slightly weaker in meaning.

> **Yoku benkyō shinakereba dame desu.**
>
> Lit. *If you don't study well, it is no good,* hence, *You should study hard.*

> **Pen de kakanakereba narimasen.**
>
> Lit. *If you don't write it with a pen, it won't do,* hence, *You must write it with a pen.*

"......to iu (Imi)"

193. **......to iu** is idiomatic and is used in asking questions about things or their names.

> **Nan to iimasu ka?**   *What do you call it?*
> **Nan to iu imi desu ka?**
>
> *What meaning is it?; What's the meaning of it?*

Mijikai Kaiwa

motte itte [------] from **motte iku**, *to take away*
oitette [--'--] corruption of **oite itte** from **oite iku**, meaning literally *to place (something here) and go,* hence, *to leave behind*
airon [----] *an iron* (for pressing)
kake- [--] from **kakeru**, *to apply*
hoshite ['--] from **hosu**, *to air; hang up for drying*

Exercises

A. Practise converting from one form to another rapidly and fluently.

Conversion Table 10

Dictionary Form	Can	Cannot	Meaning
kau	kaeru	kaenai	*buy*
iu	ieru	ienai	*say*
kaku	kakeru	kakenai	*write*

hanasu	hanaseru	hanasenai	*speak*
matsu	materu	matenai	*wait*
yobu	yoberu	yobenai	*call*
yomu	yomeru	yomenai	*read*
yaru	yareru	yarenai	*send*
hairu	haireru	hairenai	*enter*
iku	ikeru	ikenai	*go*

B. *Answer the following questions.*

1. Anata wa Nippongo o dono kurai benkyō shimashita ka?
2. Nippongo ga jōzu ni hanasemasu ka?
3. Kanji ya kana ga yomemasu ka?
4. Nippongo de tegami ga kakemasu ka?
5. Nippongo to Eigo wa hatsuon wa dotchi ga muzukashii desu ka?
6. Anata wa Nippongo no kotoba o mō ikutsu gurai shitte imasu ka?
7. Nippongo wa narainikui desu ka?
8. Kanji wa kakiyasui to omoimasu ka?

C. *Convert the following sentences into their corresponding potential sentences.*

Example: Kono hon **o yomimasu**.

Kono hon **ga yomemasu**.

1. Watakushi wa Nippongo o yoku naraimasen.
2. Byōki desu kara yoku hatarakimasen.
3. Anata wa kanji o kakimasu ka?
4. Mō osoi desu kara kaeranai deshō.
5. Sono tokei wa takai kara kaimasen.

D. *You know that* -eru *(potenial verbs) can only be derived from yodan verbs. Turn the following sentences into the potential, using* **koto ga dekimasu** *only with those from which* -eru *cannot be derived.*

Example: Sore **o torimasu**.

Sore **ga toremasu**.

Kono sakana **o tabemasu** ka?

Kono sakana **o taberu koto ga dekimasu** ka?

1. Iroiro no mono o mimasu ka?
2. Kono yōfuku o kimasen.
3. Ano kata wa byōki ni narimashita ga yasumimasen.

4. Kono heya wa shimatte imasu kara hairimasen.

5. Kono kutsu wa mō hakimasen.

6. Anata wa Nippongo no jibiki o hikimasu ka?

7. Watakushi wa Nippongo no zasshi o mada yomimasen.

8. Komban wa benkyō shimasen.

E· What is the Japanese equivalent of each of the following sentences?

1. I have already studied Japanese for two months.

2. But I can't speak it well yet.

3. How many words can you learn a day?

4. Perhaps I can learn twenty words a day.

5. Can you read this book?

6. No, I cannot read it yet.

7. Can you go to school this afternoon?

8. This word is easy to pronounce, but hard to write.

9. Even if you learn many words, it's no good if you forget them soon.

10. Can you wait for a few more days?

11. What is meant by 'provisions'?

12. It means things to eat.

F. Read the following conversation and see if you can act out a similar one.

Stranger: Anata wa Nippongo ga jōzu desu nē.

Brown: Iie, dō itashimashite, mada heta desu.

Stranger: Dono gurai benkyō shimashita ka?

Brown: Ikkagetsu-han benkyō shimashita.

Stranger: Sō desu ka? Mō kana ga yomemasu ka?

Brown: Iie, mada yomemasen. Hanasu koto shika dekimasen.

Stranger: Nippongo wa kanari yasashii deshō?

Brown: Iie, taihen muzukashii desu.

Stranger: Sō desu ka? Mainichi dono gurai benkyō shimasu ka?

Brown: Gakkō de sanjikan, uchi de sanjikan gurai benkyō shimasu.

Stranger: Doyōbi mo desu ka?

Brown: Iie, doyōbi to nichiyōbi niwa gakkō e ikimasen.

Stranger: Dewa maishū itsukazutsu benkyō shimasu ne?

Brown: Sō desu. Keredomo tokidoki isogashikute benkyō dekimasen.

Nijū-shi

(Main Text)

A : Kinō wa kaisha ga yasumi datta node asanebō o shimashita.

Shimbun o yominagara asahan o tabete iru to yūbin'ya ga sokutatsu no tegami o motte kimashita. Suzuki San kara deshita.

Gogo watakushi o tazunete kuru hazu deshita ga, yōji ga atte kuru koto ga dekinai to kaite arimashita.

Asahan ga sunde kara Eikoku no tomodachi ni tegami o kakimashita.

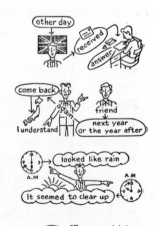

Konoaida moratta tegami no henji deshita.

Kono tomodachi wa rainen no owari ka sarainen mata Nippon ni kaette kuru sō desu.

Asa no uchi wa kumotte ite ame ga furisō deshita ga, jūji goro kara haresō ni narimashita.

Soshite hirusugi niwa sukkari harete ii tenki ni narimashita.

Suzuki San wa konai shi, hoka ni yakusoku mo nakatta node hiruhan no ato de sampo ni dekakemashita.

Ototoi ame ga hidoku futta tame to kaze ga amari nakatta tame ni hokori wa tachimasen deshita.

Kōkūbin o dasu tame ni tochū de yūbinkyoku e yottara, Hayashi San ni aimashita.

Dempō o uchi ni itta no da sō desu.

Chōdo Hayashi San mo hima datta node iroiro hanashinagara nimairu bakari saki no kōen made arukimashita.

Sanji goro ni naru to nodo ga kawaite onaka mo sukoshi suite kimashita.

Sokode oishisō na ryōri ya okashi nado o mado ni narabeta mise e haitte karui shokuji o shimashita.

Hayashi San wa goji goro no yakusoku ga atta tame soko kara basu de kaerimashita.

Watakushi wa basu ni noranaide hitori de aruite kaerimashita.

(A Short Conversation)

B : Kore wa doko-yuki desu ka ?

A : Yokosuka-iki desu.

B : Kono densha wa Atami e ikimasu ka ?

A : Ikimasen.

B : Doko de norikae desu ka ?

A : Kono tsugi desu.

B : Orimasu !

(For Memorizing)

1. Shimbun o yominagara [asa-han] o tabemashita.
2. [Gogo] watakushi o tazunete kuru hazu deshita.
3. Yōji ga atte [kuru] koto ga dekinai to kaite arimashita.
4. Kono tomodochi wa [sarainen] mata Nippon ni kaette kuru sō desu.
5. [Asa no uchi] wa kumotte ite ame ga furisō deshita.
6. Nodo mo kawaita shi, onaka mo sukimashita.

1. I ate my [breakfast] while reading newspapers.
2. He was to call on me [in the afternoon].
3. It said that he would not be able to [come] because of some business.
4. I understand that this friend will come back to Japan again [the year after next].
5. [During the morning] it was cloudy and looked like rain.
6. We became thirsty and hungry, too.

Hombun

Glossary

node ['-] *because* (See Grammar 194.)
asanebō[--'--] *a late riser ; sleepy head*
-nagara ['--] *while......ing* (See Grammar 195.)
yūbin'ya [-----] *a mailman*
tazunete [----] from **tazuneru**, *to visit :* **tazunete kuru** means *to visit.*
hazu [--] *is expected* (See Grammar 196.)
yōji [---] *business*
sunde ['--] from **sumu**, *to be over ; be finished*
Eikoku [----] *England ; United Kingdom*

konoaida [- - - - -] *the other day; a few days ago*

moratta [- - - -] the past form of **morau**, *to receive*

henji [- - -] *a reply; answer*

rainen [- - - -] *next year*

sarainen [- - - - -] *the year after next*

kaette [- - - -] from **kaeru**, *to return; come back:* **kaette kuru** means *to return.*

......**uchi** [- -] *while; during*

furisō [- -'-] *looks like rain*

hare- [-'] from **hareru**, *to clear up*

hirusugi [- - - -] *afternoon*

sukkari [- -'-] *completely*

yakusoku [- - - -] *a promise; appointment*

......**tame** (**ni**) [-'-] *because of; on account of* (See Grammar 200.)

kaze [-'] *wind*

hokori [- - -] *dust*

tachi- [- -] from **tatsu**, *to rise*

tochū [- - -] *on the way*

yottara [- -'-] *when I dropped in; if I (he, she) dropped in:* from **yoru**, *to drop in* (See Grammar 201.)

dempō [- - - -] *a telegram*

uchi ['-] from **utsu**, *to strike: knock:* **dempō o utsu** means *to send a telegram.*

mairu ['- -] *a mile*

bakari ['- -] *about; approximate*

kōen [- - - -] *a park*

nodo ['-] *the throat*

kawaite [-'- -] from **kawaku**, *to dry up:* **nodo ga kawaku** means *to become thirsty.*

suite [- - -] from **suku**, *to become empty:* **onaka ga suku** means *to be hungry;* **suite kuru**, *to become hungry*

sokode [- - -] *thereupon; and so*

oishi- [- - -] from **oishii**, *delicious; tasty:* **oishisō**, *delicious looking* (See Grammar 199.)

ryōri ['- -] *a dish; food; cooking*

okashi [-'-] **o**, honorific and **kashi**, *cake; candy; sweets*
narabeta [----] from **naraberu**, *to display; line up*
hitori de [-'--] *by oneself; alone*

Grammar

"Node" and "Kara"

194. A question arises as to the difference, if any, between **node** and **kara,**
since both of them denote cause or reason. They come after the present
form of a verb, adjective, or copula **desu** with practically the same meaning.

Kinō wa kaisha ga yasumi datta $\begin{Bmatrix}\textbf{node}\\\textbf{kara}\end{Bmatrix}$ **asanebō o shimashita.**

> *Yesterday, because we had a holiday at the company, I got
> up late.*

Gakkō e ikimasu $\begin{Bmatrix}\textbf{node}\\\textbf{kara}\end{Bmatrix}$ **jikan ga arimasen.**

> *As I go to school, I have no time.*

Suzushikatta $\begin{Bmatrix}\textbf{node}\\\textbf{kara}\end{Bmatrix}$ **benkyō shimashita.**

> *As it was cool, I studied.*

As can be seen in the above examples they are, in many cases, interchangeable. But when the contents of the second clause is the direct consequence of
those of the first clause, **node** is to be used.

> **Isogashii node, hima ga arimasen.**
> *I'm busy, and so I have no leisure.*

Kara is used to dedote a reason for the statement in the second clause
which has no direct connection with the statement in the first clause.

> **Isogashii kara ikanai deshō.** *Since he is busy, he will not go.*

This sentence means that the speaker wants to say that he won't go, giving
as a reason that he is busy.

Kara is often used as a reason or excuse in reply to a question or accusation.
In such a case **kara** comes at the end of a clause.

> **Naze shimasen deshita ka?**   *Why didn't you do it?*
> **Ammari muzukashii desu kara.**   *Because it is too difficult.*

After **desu**, kara is more frequently used. Different uses of **kara** such as

kara after a noun or after the **te**-form should not be confused with the **above.**
Kara may be used after **deshō**, or **mashō**, but **node** is not used.

> **Ame ga furu deshō kara, dekakemasen.**
>
> *As it may rain, I won't go out.*
>
> **Matte imashō kara, ikanakereba narimasen.**
>
> *As he may be waiting, I must go.*

" -nagara " — Two Simultaneous Actions

195. This is tacked on to the 2nd base, i.e. the continuative form of a verb and means two actions are performed simultaneously by the same person or persons.

> **Shimbun o yominagara asahan o tabemasu.**
>
> *I eat my breakfast while reading newspapers.*

Note that **nagara** cannot be used when two simultaneous actions are performed by different persons.

" Hazu " — " Reasonable Expectation "

196. **Hazu** is a form noun meaning reasonable expectation, and presupposes some previous arrangement or understanding. It should not be used when some moral obligation is to be expressed. For some reason, it is very common among the writers of books on the Japanese language to translate this word with *ought to*, but it is misleading, for the meanings of the word *ought* in the following two sentences are different.

(a) *You ought to be kind to people.* (moral obligation)

(b) *It's already three o'clock, so he ought to be here at any moment.*

(reasonable expectation)

Hazu corresponds to *ought to* in meaning only when it means reasonable expectation.

> **Suzuki San ga gogo watakushi o tazunete kuru hazu desu.**
>
> *Mr. Suzuki is to come to visit me this afternoon.*
>
> **Watakushi wa kinō Yokohama e iku hazu deshita ga, kaze o hiite ikemasen deshita.**
>
> *I was supposed to go to Yokohama yesterday, but as I caught a cold, I couldn't go.*

Modifying Phrases or Clauses (2)

197.   **Konoaida moratta tegami no henji deshita.**

It was an answer to a letter which I received the other day.

Dempō o uchi ni itta hito wa Hayashi San desu.

The person who went to send a telegram is Mr. Hayashi.

Mado ni okashi o narabeta mise ni yorimashita.

We dropped in at a shop where cake was displayed in a window.

Konoaida moratta tegami literally means *the-other-day-received-letter.*

Dempō o uchi ni itta hito literally means *to-send-a-talegram-went-person.*

Mado ni okashi o narabeta mise literally means *in-a-window-cake-displayed-shop.*

(a)   Kore wa **akai hon** desu.   (*red book*)

(b)   Kore wa **tomodachi no hon** desu.   (*friend's book*)

(c)   Kore wa **kinō katta hon** desu.   (*yesterday-bought-book*)

(d)   Kore wa **watakushi ga yomu hon** desu.   (*my-reading-book*)

(e)   Kore wa **watakushi ga yonda hon** desu.   (*my-having-read-book*)

See Lesson 15, Grammar 120.

"Te-form" plus "Iru" — a State

198.   **Asa no uchi wa kumotte imashita.**

It was cloudy in the morning.

Keredomo gogo wa harete imashita.

But in the afternoon, it was clear.

Kumoru, hareru, tsukareru (*to get tired*), **deru** (*to go out*), etc. are verbs which refer to changes of state. **Kumoru** means *to cloud up* and doesn't mean *to be cloudy.* The **te**-form of **kumoru** plus **iru** mean *to be in a state of having clouded up* or *to be cloudy.* So,

tsukarete iru	*to be tired*
dete iru	*to be out* (be in a state of having gone out)
kite iru	*to be here* (be in a state of having come)
......e itte iru	*to be there* (be in a state of having gone to)
onaka ga suite iru	*to be hungry*
oboete iru	*to remember*

" -sō " — a Suffix meaning Appearance

199. In Lesson 16, Grammar 124 we learned that **sō desu** after the conclusive base of a verb indicates given information.

Ame ga furu sō desu. *It is said it will rain.*

Sō which is combined with the 2nd base of a verb or the stem of a true or quasi-adjective as a suffix, means *to appear, look like.*

Ame ga furisō desu. *It looks like rain.*

Ano hito wa jōbusō desu. *He looks healthy.*

Yoi and **nai** become **yosasō** and **nasasō** respectively.

A verb or an adjective combined with **sō** acts as a quasi-adjective.

oishisō na okashi *delicious-looking cake*

ame ga furisō na tenki *the threatening weather*

jōbusō na hito *a healthy-looking man*

" Tame " — Cause or Reason

200. In Lesson 20, Grammar 172 we learned that **tame (ni)** means purpose.

Gaikokujin no okyaku o tomeru tame desu.

It is for foreign guests to pass the night.

Kōkūbin o dasu tame ni yūbinkyoku e yorimashita.

I dropped in at the post office to post an airmail.

Tame (ni) also means *because, on account of, due to,* etc.

Ame ga hidoku futta tame (ni) hokori wa tachimasen.

Because it rained heavily, dust doesn't rise.

Byōki no tame (ni) gakkō ni ikimasen deshita.

I didn't go to school because of sickness.

" -tara " — Subjunctive Use

201. **Yūbinkyoku e yottara Hayashi San ni aimashita.**

When I dropped in at the post office, I met Mr. Hayashi.

Dare ka kitara, byōki desu to itte kudasai.

If anyone should come, please say I am sick.

Tara is a subjunctive form of **ta.** It refers to the past, present, and future, so it is not the past form. The verbs, adjectives (e.g. **akakattara, ōki-kattara,** etc.), and copula (**dattara**), all ending in **tara** mean *if such-and-*

such had been the case, if such-and-such were the case, if such-and-such is the case, or *supposing such-and-such should happen.*

Besides this meaning of supposition or hypothesis, **tara** often means *when such-and-such happens* or *happened.* You have to judge from the context or the situation, whether the meaning is *if* or *when.*

Reference is made to the particle **to** after the present tense form. It means either *if* or *when.* (See Lesson 11, Grammar 83.)

The English subjunctive past, i.e. the supposition contrary to a past fact is commonly translated into Japanese with this **tara.**

> **Okane ga attara, ageta deshō (ga).**
>
> *If I had had money, I would have given it to him.*

Ga in the above sentence may be omitted. It means *but* indicating that *but as the fact was not so, I didn't.*

See the following examples:

> **Basu ga Ginza e kitara, orimashō.**
>
> *When the bus gets (comes) to the Ginza, let's get off.*
>
> **Motto ii no o kattara dō desu ka?**
>
> *How would it be if you bought a better one?*

" ...no da "

202. **Da** is the plain form of **desu.** So **Dempō o uchi ni itta no da (sō desu)** means almost the same as **Dempō o uchi ni itta no desu (sō desu).**

In comparing the following two sentences,

(a) **Dempō o uchi ni ikimashita.**

(b) **Dempō o uchi ni itta no desu.**

(b) is more emphatic than (a). The following will illustrate the force of the two sentences.

A: **Tōkyō e ikimashita ka?**   *Did you go to Tokyo?*

B: **Ee, ikimashita.**   *Yes, I did.*

A: **Anata ga jibun de itta no desu ka?**   *Did you go yourself?*

B: **Ee, watakushi ga jibun de itta no desu.**

                      Yes, I did go myself.

It may happen, however, that **no desu** is used when emphasis does not seem noticeable, but it is there just the same.

Itsu iku no desu ka?   *When is it that you go?*

One should not confuse this **no desu** with that of **watakushi no desu,** etc., which is **desu** accidentally coming after **watakushi no** meaning mine.

Mijikai Kaiwa

doko-yuki(-iki) [----] **doko**, where and **yuki**, *going:* **yuki** (or **iki**) is from **yuku** (usually **iku** nowadays) and is used as a suffix meaning *bound for*.

norikae [----] **nori**, *ride* and **kae**, *change*, hence *changing cars*

tsugi [-′] *next (one)*

ori- [--] from **oriru**, *to get down; get off:* **orimasu** is an expression used as a sign to conductors and others that one wants to get off.

Exercises

A. Answer the following questions.

1. Anata wa yasumi no hi niwa asanebō o shimasu ka?
2. Tomodachi kara moratta tegami niwa itsu henji o kakimasu ka?
3. Anata wa michi o arukinagara nani ka tabemasu ka?
4. Kyō wa harete imasu ka, kumotte imasu ka?
5. Ame ga fureba hokori wa tachimasen ka?
6. Sokutatsu ya kōkūbin o dasu tame niwa yūbinkyoku e ikanakerebe **nari-masen** ka?
7. Anata wa kinjo no kōen made itsumo sampo ni ikimasu ka?
8. Sampo no tochū de onaka ga suitara dō shimasu ka?
9. Anata wa kyō no yūgata tomodachi ni au yakusoku ga arimasu ka?
10. Tōkyō-eki kara Yokosuka-iki no densha ga demasu ka?

*B. **Kuru** or **iku** after the **te**-form of certain verbs add the idea of progression. Therefore the verb that can be used in this case is the one which has the meaning that requires a certain length of time to perform the action, e.g.,*

Nodo ga **kawakimashita.**

I have become thirsty. (a statement of having become thirsty)

Nodo ga **kawaite kimashita.**

I am getting thirsty. (a statement of gradual change into thirstiness)

Read the following sentences aloud, paying special attention to the difference in meaning.

1. (a) Kumotte imashita ga ima haremashita.
   (b) Kumotte imashita ga ima harete kimashita.
2. (a) Yoku benkyō shimashita node sukoshi jōzu ni narimashita.
   (b) Yoku benkyō shimashita node sukoshi jōzu ni natte kimashita.
3. (a) Kanari aruita node onaka ga sukimashita.
   (b) Kanari aruita node onaka ga suite kimashita.
4. (a) Kusuri o nomimashita node byōki ga yoku narimashita.
   (b) Kusuri o nomimashita node byōki ga yoku natte kimashita.
5. (a) Atsuku natta node takusan no hito ga umi ya yama e ikimasu.
   (b) Atsuku natte kita node takusan no hito ga umi ya yama e ikimasu.

C. *What is the Japanese equivalent of each of the following sentences?*

1. Because it rained very heavily last night and there isn't much wind now, no dust rises.
2. During the morning, it still looked like rain, but it is now clearing up.
3. Today is Sunday and besides it's a fine day, so he has gone out for a walk.
4. Because no guest is coming and I have no business (to do) this afternoon, I will go out for a walk.
5. On the way I met Mr. Tanaka, who (told me that he) went to visit his English teacher.
6. Mr. Tanaka and I went together to the station while talking about various things.
7. We dropped in at the shop where delicious-looking food was displayed in a window, and had a light meal.
8. I got up late this morning, so I had to go to the office by bus instead of walking.
9. The letter I received this morning from a friend of mine says that he is coming to see me this week-end (=end of this week).
10. I was to write a reply immediately, but I had some business and couldn't.

11. I must send my maid to the post office to send him a special delivery letter.

12. If the special delivery letter won't arrive there before Friday, I must send him a telegram.

13. Because I have an appointment to see a friend on the Ginza at 3 p.m., I must go there by taxi.

14. Since there's no bus bound for the Ginza, you have to change buses at Tokyo station.

15. I'm waiting for a taxi while talking with my friend.

D. *What would you say when,*

1. you want to know where to change trains?
2. you want to say you can't hear well on the phone?
3. you want to find out which of the two someone wants?
4. you want to say either will do?
5. you want to ask if you can take it along?
6. you want to ask the maid to iron your trousers?

Nijū-go

(Main Text)

A : Howaito San wa jimusho e dekakeru
   mae ni jochū no Hana San to hanashite
   imasu.

Howaito : Kyō no otenki wa dō deshō ?

Hana : Zuibun oatsū gozaimasu ne.

Ima wa sukoshi kumotte orimasu ga
ato de hareru rashū gozaimasu yo.

Howaito : Sō desu ka ?

Hana : Kesa wa nanji ni odekake desu ka ?

Howaito : Mō jippun bakari de dekakemasu.

Rusu ni dare ka kitara, shichiji sugi
de nakereba kaeranai to itte kudasai.

Hana: Kyō wa ichinichijū jimusho desu ka?

Howaito: Gozenchū Yokohama e itte ohiru-sugi de nakereba kaerimasen.

Sorekara moshi ka suru to Suzuki San kara denwa ga kakaru kamo shiremasen ga, moshi denwa ga attara, asu no ban wa tsugō ga warukute dame desu kara asatte no ban kuru yō ni itte kudasai.

Hana: Nanji goro irassharu yō ni iimashō ka?

Howaito: Shichiji sugi nara itsu demo kekkō desu to itte kudasai.

Shikashi kuru mae ni denwa o kakeru yō ni tanonde kudasai.

Hana: Gogo daiku-san ga kuru hazu desu ga, naosu tokoro wa yoku shitte iru deshō ka?

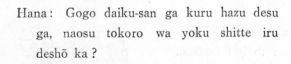

Howaito : Konoaida yoku hanashite okimashita kara machigai wa nai to omoimasu.

Moshi wakaranakattara denwa de kiku
yō ni itte kudasai.

Hana : Waishatsu ga kanari yogorete ita
node sentaku ni dashite okimashita ga,
yoroshū gozaimashō ne.

Howaito : Ee, kekkō desu.

Sorekara shashin o haru nori ga naku-
natta node hitotsu katte oite kudasai.

Hana : Kashikomarimashita.

Kono mae kaimashita no wa ōkyū gozaimashita ga, sukoshi takō gozaimashita
ne.

Howaito : Nedan wa kamaimasen kara yosasō
na no o katte oite kudasai.

Ii no ga nakereba kawanaide kudasai.

— 255 —

Hana : Kashikomarimashita. Dewa itte irasshai mase.

(A Short Conversation)

A : Kore kara dekakemasu.

B : Nanji ni okaeri desu ka ?

A : Tabun osoku narimasu. Komban shokuji o shimasen.

B : Sayō desu ka ?

A : Matanaide kudasai.

(For Memorizing)

1. Zuibun [oatsū] gozaimasu ne.
2. [Kesa] wa nanji ni odekake desu ka ?
3. Rusu ni dare ka kitara, [shichiji] sugi de nakereba kaeranai to itte kudasai.
4. Moshi ka suru to [Suzuki San] kara denwa ga aru kamo shiremasen.

1. It's terribly [hot], isn't it ?
2. At what time will you go out [this morning]?
3. If anyone should come during my absence, please tell him that I won't be back before [seven o'clock].
4. There may be a telephone call from [Mr. Suzuki].

5. Denwa ga attara [asatte] no ban kuru yō ni itte kudasai.	5. If he telephones, please tell him to come [the day after tomorrow] in the evening.
6. Hitotsu katte oite kudasai.	6. Please buy some (and keep it for me).

Hombun

Glossary

jimusho [- - -] *an office*

zuibun [' - - -] *considerably ; very (much)*

oatsū [- - - -] the polite form of **atsui**   (See Grammar 204.)

ori- [- -] from **oru**, *to be :* polite word meaning the same as **iru**. (See Lesson 7, Grammar 49.)

ato de [' - -] *later ; afterwards*

rashū [' - -] from **rashii**, *to seem to ; appear*   (See Grammar 204.)

yo [-] a familliar emphatic particle used at the end of a sentence

odekake [- - - -] **o** honorific and **dekake** from **dekakeru**, *to go out*

bakari [' - -] *about ; approximate*

dare ka [' - -] *somebody ; anybody :* **dare** means *who*.   (See Lesson 22, Grammar 183.)

kitara [- ' -] from **kuru**, *to come*

gozenchū [- - - - -] *in the morning*

ohirusugi [- - - - -] **o**, honorific and **hirusugi**, *afternoon*

moshi ka suru to *might*   (See Grammar 208.)

kakaru [- ' -] *to hang (v.i.).* **Denwa ga kakaru** means *someone calls me* (on the phone).

asu [- -] *tomorrow*

tsugō [- - -] *convenience :* **tsugō ga warui** means *inconvenient*.

......**yō ni** [- - -] *in such a way as......*   (See Grammar 209.)

irassharu [- - - - -] *to come* (honorific)

kakeru [- ' -] *to hang (v.t.).* **Denwa o kakeru** means *to telephone; ring up*.

tanonde [- ' - -] from **tanomu**, *to request*

daiku [' - -] *a carpenter*

naosu [- ' -] *to repair ; mend*

-te oku *to do something in advance*   (See Grammar 211.)

yogorete [- - - -] from **yogoreru**, *to get dirty*

sentaku [- - - -] *laundry; washing*

dashite ['- -] from **dasu**, *to send out*

shashin [- - -] *a photograph; picture*

nori [-'] *paste; starch*

nakunaru [- - - -] *to run out; disappear*

kashikomari [- - - - -] from **kashikomaru**, *to sit solemnly*, hence, *to pay attention*. **Kashikomarimashita** means *Very well, sir* or *madam; certainly; with pleasure.*

nedan [- - -] *price*

yosasō [- - - -] *seems to be good*   (See Lesson 24, Grammar 199.)

irasshai [- - - - -] from **irassharu**, *to come; go; stay* (honorific). **Itte irasshai** literally means *Go and come back*, an expression used as a sort of farewell greeting to a person who is leaving.

mase ['-] *please*, used only to superiors

Grammar

Gozaimasu

203. **Gozaimasu** is more polite than **desu** although the latter is already polite. Therefore, **gozaimasu** is used mostly in the speech of women, merchants, salesmen, etc., or when men want to be very polite. Of course set conversational expressions such as **Arigatō gozaimasu**, **Ohayō gozaimasu**, etc. are used by all.

Euphonic Changes before "Gozaimasu"

204. Before **gozaimasu** (from an old verb **gozaru** meaning *to be*) and **zonjimasu** (a polite verb meaning *I think*), true adjectives take an adverbial form with **k** dropped off for euphonic reasons.

Ai changes into **aku**, then **k** drops off and turns into **au** which is pronounced in the same way as **ō**.

-ai $\begin{cases} \text{hayai} & \text{hayaku} \rightarrow \text{hayau} \rightarrow \text{hayō} \\ \text{arigatai} & \text{arigataku} \rightarrow \text{arigatau} \rightarrow \text{arigatō} \end{cases}$

Likewise, **ii, ui** and **oi** change as follows:

-ii	ōkii	ōkiku	→	ōkiu	→	ōkyū
	yoroshii	yoroshiku	→	yoroshiu	→	yoroshū
	hoshii	hoshiku	→	hoshiu	→	hoshū
-ui	kikinikui	kikinikuku	→	kikinikuu	→	kikinikū
	furui	furuku	→	furuu	→	furū
-oi	shiroi	shiroku	→	shirou	→	shirō
	kuroi	kuroku	→	kurou	→	kurō

205. The adjective **ii**, good, seems like an exception because it becomes **yō gozaimasu** instead of **yū gozaimasu**. But when one realizes that it comes from **yoi**, one will see that its euphonic form **yō** is no exception.

The negative construction, consisting of the euphonic form of a true adjective and **gozaimasen**, is seldom used in Tokyo speech. In such a case the adverbial form of a true adjective is used instead.

> **Yoku wa gozaimasen.**   *It is not good.*
>
> **Takaku wa gozaimasen.**   *It is not high* (or *expensive*).

Honorific Form of Verbs

206. When speaking of an action of a superior, one may use an honorific form of a verb. There are a few different honorific forms. One of them is to use the construction pattern **o** x [second base of a verb] x **desu**.

> **Nanji ni odekake desu ka?**   *At what time will you go out?*
>
> **Otomodachi o otazune deshita ka?**   *Did you visit a friend?*

In the case of a verb of Chinese origin which takes **go** for honorific, the construction pattern **go** x [Chinese verb without **suru**] x **desu** is used. **Go** in this case may be omitted, but it makes it less polite.

> **Nani o gobenkyō desu ka?**   *What are you studying?*
>
> **Gosampo desu ka?**   *Are you taking a walk?*

Whether a verb takes **o** or **go** for honorific must be determined individually, because some common verbs of Chinese origin often take **o**.

"......de Nakereba......masen" — "Not Before"

207.   **Shichiji sugi de nakereba kaerimasen.**

      I won't be back before seven o'clock.

This is a case of double negatives. It literally means *If it is not after seven o'clock, I won't be back,* which comes to mean *I won't be back before seven.*

Ashita de nakereba wakarimasen.

I shall not know before tomorrow.

Sen'en de nakereba urimasen.

I won't sell it for less than 1,000 yen.

" Moshi ka Suru to " — " Might "

208. This phrase suggests that it is not impossible to happen, and may be translated by *it may happen, it might be possible,* etc. It is usually followed by **kamo shiremasen**. (See Lesson 15, Grammar 116.)

Moshi ka suru to denwa ga kakaru kamo shiremasen.

There may be a telephone call.

Moshi ka suru to ame ga furu kamo shiremasen.

It may rain.

Whether there is **moshi ka suru to** or not doesn't very much affect the meaning so long as there is **kamo shiremasen**. If there is, the improbability is emphasized.

Indirect Discourse

209. **Nanji goro kuru yō ni iimashō ka?**

About what time shall I tell him to come?

Asatte no ban kuru yō ni itte kudasai.

Please tell him to come the day after tcmcrrow evening.

Instead of quoting the exact words, a gist of the speech may be given in indirect narration by using **yō ni**. In this case the word that comes before **yō ni** is only the dictionary form of a verb as contrasted with any ending of a quoted sentence in direct discourse.

The answer to the above example may be written in direct discourse as:

(a) **Asatte no ban kite kudasai to itte kudasai.**

(b) **Asatte no ban ki nasai to itte kudasai.**

(c) **Asatte no ban koi to itte kudasai.**

Compare:

Irasshai to iimashita. (direct discourse)

He said, " *Please come.*"

Iku yō ni iimashita. (indirect discourse)

He told me to go.

Oagari kudasai to ii nasai. (direct discourse)

Tell him, " Please eat."

Taberu yō ni ii nasai. (indirect discourse)

Tell him to eat.

To iu is used in direct discourse to quote any statement as it is actually spoken whereas **yō ni iu**, etc. is used in indirect discourse to impart the meaning of what is said.

(N.B.) **Koi** is the imperative form of **kuru**.

"Irassharu" — Honorific Form

210. **Irassharu** is the honorific form of **iru**, *to be, stay, come* or *go.*

Komban anata wa otaku ni irasshaimasu ka?

Will you be at home this evening?

Watakushi no uchi e komban irasshatte kudasai.

Please come to my house this evening.

Anata wa ashita Suzuki San no otaku e irasshaimasu ka?

Will you go to Mr. Suzuki's house tomorrow?

"Oku" — a Terminal Verb

211. **Oku** as a principal verb means to put or to place or put aside, but when used as a terminal verb after the **te**-form of a verb, it indicates that there is a certain space of time between the time of doing and the time when the result of the action is needed. It literally means *to do something and put it aside for future use.* **Hanashite oku** means *to tell someone so that he will know about it when you see him again.*

Kaite okimashō.

I'll write it down (as it may be needed afterwards).

Koshiraete oite kudasai.

Please make it (so that it will be there when I call for it).

Doko e oite okimashō ka? *Where shall I put it?*

Koko e oitoite kudasai. *Please leave it here.*

(N.B.) **Oitoite** is the corruption of **oite oite.**

Mijikai Kaiwa

kore kara [- - - -] *from now on; now*
okaeri [- - - -] from **kaeru,** *to come back* (honorific)
sayō [- - -] *(a-B) so*

Exercises

A. Practice converting from one form to the other rapidly and fluently.

Conversion Table 11

Ordinary Form	Euphonic Form	Meaning
arigatai desu	arigatō gozaimasu	*grateful*
akai desu	akō gozaimasu	*red*
hayai desu	hayō gozaimasu	*early*
-tai desu	-tō gozaimasu	*want to......*
ii desu	yō gozaimasu	*good ; well*
yoroshii desu	yoroshū gozaimasu	*good*
ōkii desu	ōkyū gozaimasu	*large*
osoi desu	osō gozaimasu	*late*
hiroi desu	hirō gozaimasu	*wide*
shiroi desu	shirō gozaimasu	*white*
atsui desu	atsū gozaimasu	*hot ; thick*
samui desu	samū gozaimasu	*cold*
-nikui desu	-nikū gozaimasu	*hard to......*

B. Reconstruct the following sentences, adding **gozaimasu** *after the true adjectives and making other necessary changes.*

    Example :   Zuibun **oatsui desu.**

                 Zuibun **oatsū gozaimasu.**

   1.   Kore wa zuibun muzukashii desu nē.
   2.   Mō kaette mo yoroshii desu ka ?
   3.   Kyō wa tsugō ga warui desu.
   4.   Ano kata no otaku wa tōi desu.

5. Kinō wa taihen attakai deshita.

6. Ima itte mo ii desu ka?

C. *Turn the following sentences into more polite ones.*
    Example: **Dekakemasu** ka?
                   Odekake desu ka?

1. Kyō wa otomodachi o tazunemashita ka?
2. Anata wa kono hon o yomimashita nē.
3. Ima nani o hanashimasu ka?
4. Ashita no asa wa hayaku okimasu ka?
5. Tanaka San wa raishū kaerimasu.

D. *Change the following sentences using double negatives.*
    Example: Rokuji **ni** kaeri**masu.**
                Rokuji **de nakereba** kaeri**masen.**

1. Yūgata ni kaerimasu.
2. Yasukereba kaimasu.
3. Raigetsu wakarimasu.

E. *Change from direct to indirect speech.*
    Example: Sugu **ki nasai to** itte kudasai.
                Sugu **kuru yō ni** itte kudasai.

1. Kyō wa isogashii kara ashita kite kudasai to itte kudasai.
2. Kaette irasshattara watakushi ni denwa o kakete kudasai to hanashite kudasai.
3. Nanji ni motte ki nasai to iimashō ka?
4. Kyō rokuji ni kite kudasai to tanomimashita.
5. Sensei wa watakushi ni motto yoku benkyō shi nasai to iimashita.

F. The use of **aem** and **ato** after a verb corresponds to the English "*Before I go out*" and "*After I went out.*" Therefore, with **mae** the verb is always in the dictionary form. With **ato** the verb is in the past form.

This construction does not change to express "*Before I went out*" since the past tense is expressed in the final verb of the sentence.

Pay special attention to the difference in tense in the following cases, and try to express in Japanese the ideas suggested by the English sentences.

Example:
　Dekakeru mae ni yōji ga arimasu.
　I have some business before I go out.

　Dekakeru mae ni sō iimashita.
　He said so before he went out.

　Kaetta ato de hanashimashō.
　I'll tell you after he goes back.

　Kaetta ato de hanashimashita.
　I told him after he returned.

1. Do this before you go out.
2. I'll do that after the guest goes back.
3. I had lunch before I went out.
4. You must buy the book before school begins.
5. Shall we have dinner after we study ?

G. *What is the Japanese equivalent of each of the following sentences?*
　1. " Will you be at home all day ? "
　　" No, I shall be at school in the afternoon."
　2. I shall be out all morning. (Lit. I'll be absent unless it is in the afternoon.)
　3. There might possibly be a guest visiting me.
　4. Tomorrow morning is inconvenient and is no good for me.
　5. Please tell him to wait for me, as I am coming back very soon.
　6. Where shall I tell him to wait ?
　7. Tell him to call on me any day except Sunday.
　8. Any time after seven in the evening will be all right.
　9. Mr. Suzuki is expected to call on me this evening. If he should come before I come home, ask him to wait for me.
　10. I was to write to Mr. Kuroda, but I had some business and couldn't.
　11. Have you told the carpenter what to repair ?
　12. Please send a telegram to your friend (ahead of time).

Nijū-roku

(Main Text)

A : Guriin San wa Nippon no hanga ga suki
desu.

Beikoku ni ita toki furui mono o sukoshi
atsumemashita node, kondo wa atarashii no
o kaitai to omotte imasu.

Aruhi shiriai no Suzuki San ni atta toki
iimashita.

Guriin : Chotto onegai ga aru no desu ga......

Suzuki : Donna goyō desu ka ?

Guriin : Hanga o utte iru mise o gozonji
deshō ka ?

Suzuki : Hai, shitte imasu ga......

Guriin : Dewa goshōkai shite itadakenai deshō
ka ?

Suzuki : Kashikomarimashita.

Itsu demo goshōkai itashimasu.

Guriin : Sono mise wa dochira desu ka ?

Suzuki : Nishiginza desu.

Guriin : Sakki kono chizu o karimashita.

Tomodachi ga kashite kureta no desu.

Kono chizu de wakarimasu ka ?

A :   Suzuki San wa poketto kara meishi o
dashite nani ka kaite imashita ga, sono
chizu o mite iimashita.

Suzuki : Sono chizu dewa wakarimasen deshō kara watakushi ga kaite agemashō.

Nishiginza no wakariyasui tokoro desu.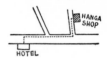

Hoteru o dete hantai no hō ni itte futatsume no kado o hidari e magatte iku to migigawa desu.

Guriin : Takushii de iku hō ga ii deshō ne.

Suzuki : Takushii nara sugu desu.

Kono chizu o untenshu ni misereba sugu tsurete itte kuremasu.

Guriin : Dewa kono chizu wa tomodachi ni kaeshimashō.

A : Sono hi no gogo Guriin San wa hoteru no mae de takushii o tsukamaete, Suzuki San ni kaite moratta chizu o misemashita.

Untenshu wa chizu o kaeshite "Wakari-mashita" to iinagara sugu ni kuruma o unten shite mise made tsurete ikimashita.

(A Short Conversation)

A : Hidari e magarimashō ka ?

B : Iie, massugu itte kudasai.

A : Kono hen desu ka ?

B : Koko de tomete kudasai.

Gokurōsama deshita.

(For Memorizing)

1. Chotto onegai ga aru no desu ga......
2. Donna goyō desu ka ?
3. Goshōkai shite itadakenai deshō ka ?
4. [Itsu demo] goshōkai itashimasu.
5. Chizu o [kaite] agemashō.
6. [Futatsu]me no kado o [hidari] e magatte iku to [migi]-gawa desu.
7. Suzuki San ni [kaite] moratta chizu o misemashita.

1. Excuse me, but I'd like to ask a favor of you......
2. What is it ?
3. I wonder if you can introduce me.
4. I'll introduce you [any time you wish].
5. I'll [draw] a map for you.
6. Turn to the [left] at the [second] corner; it's on the [right]-hand side.
7. He showed the map which Mr. Suzuki had kindly [drawn] for him.

Hombun

Glossary

hanga [‒‒‒] *woodcut print*

gaikoku [‒‒‒‒] *a foreign country*

atsume- [‒‒‒] from **atsumeru**, *to gather; collect*

kondo ['‒‒] *this time*

aruhi ['‒‒] *one day; a certain day*

shiriai [‒‒‒‒] *an acquaintance*

onegai [‒‒‒‒] **o**, honorific and **negai**, *reguest*

goyō [‒'‒] **go**, honorific and **yō**, *business*

gozonji [‒'‒‒] polite term for *to know*

goshōkai [‒‒‒‒‒] *introduction*: **go**, honorific and **shōkai**, *introduction*

itadake- [‒‒‒‒] from **itadakeru**, *to be able to receive* (humble) (See Grammar 215.)

itashi- [‒‒‒] from **itasu**, *to do* (humble)

chizu ['-] *a map*

kari- [--] from **kariru**, *to borrow; rent*

kashite [---] from **kasu**, *to lend; loan*

kureta [---] past form of **kureru**, *to give* (See Grammar 215.)

poketto [-'--] *a pocket*

meishi [---] *a calling card*

age- [--] *to give* (See Grammar 215.)

hoteru ['--] *a hotel*

hantai [----] *opposite*

-me [-] a suffix turning a cardinal number into an ordinal number. **Futatsu** means *two* (*pieces*), and **futatsume** means *the second.*

-gawa [--] a suffix meaning ......*side*

untenshu [--'--] *a driver; chauffeur*

tsurete itte [------] from **tsurete iku**, *to take* (a person) *along*

kaeshi- [---] from **kaesu**, *to return; give back*

tsukamaete [-----] from **tsukamaeru**, *to catch; get hold of*

moratta [----] past form of **morau**, *to receive* (See Grammar 215.)

mise- [--] from **miseru**, *to show*

kuruma [---] *a vehicle; wheel; car*

Grammar

" -tai to Omou " — " Want," " Would Like to "

212. (1) **Atarashii no o kaitai to omoimasu.** ⎱
    (2) **Atarashii no o kaitai desu.**   ⎰ *I want to buy a new one.*

There is not much difference in the meaning between (1) and (2). **-tai to omoimasu** softens a little the bluntness of **-tai desu.**

Verbs for Giving and Receiving

213. **Itadaku** and **morau** mean *to receive*; the former means *to receive from one's superior* while the latter, *to receive from one's equal or inferior.*

      Otōsan kara kono hon o itadakimashita.

        I received this book from my father.

      Tomodachi kara kono hon o moraimashita.

I received this book from my friend.

Similar distinction can be observed in the verbs which mean *to give*, i.e. **kudasaru**, **kureru** (*others give to me*) and **ageru**, **yaru**, (*I give to others*). See the following diagram and examples.

Diagram for Giving and Receiving

214.

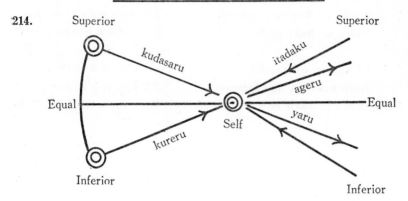

(◎ indicates the subject of a sentence; the arrow indicates the receiver of a favor.)

Giving

(a) | Superior | *gives* me* | Superior | **ga kudasaru**
(b) | Inferior | *gives* me* | Inferior | **ga kureru**
(c) | *I* give* | Superior | Superior | **ni ageru**
(d) | *I* give* | Inferior | Inferior | **ni yaru**

---

* *Self* in the diagram and *I* or *me* in the examples should be interpreted broadly and include not only the speaker but also those who are considered to be on the speaker's side such as his relatives, employees, etc. For instance, if a neighbor A gave a pencil to the speaker's brother B, the speaker will place A higher than B, e. g.

A San wa empitsu o B ni kudasaimashita.
Mr. A gave a pencil to B.

On the other hand if the speaker's father gave A a pencil, the relative position of one's own father and A depends on the speaker's opinion. If he thinks A is younger or lower in social standing than his father, he may use **yaru** instead of **ageru**, e. g.

Otōsan wa A ni empitsu o yarimashita.
Father gave a pencil to A.

— 271 —

Receiving

(e) *I* receive from* | Superior | | Superior | **ni** (or **kara**) **itadaku**

(f) *I* receive from* | Inferior | | Inferior | **ni** (or **kara**) **morau**

Examples:

(a) **Sensei ga kore o kudasaimashita.** *The teacher gave this to me.*

   Anata ga kudasatta no desu ka? *Did you give it to me?*

(b) **Jochū ga kureta no desu.** *The maid gave it to me.*

   Otōto ga kuremashita. *My younger brother gave it to me.*

(c) **Otōsan ni agemashō.** *I'll give it to father.*

   Kore o anata ni agemasu. *I'll give this to you.*

(d) **Jochū ni yaru hō ga ii deshō.** *You had better give it to the maid.*

   Inu ni yatte kudasai. *Please give it to the dog.*

(e) **Donata ni itadakimashita ka?** *From whom did you get it?*

   Okāsan ni itadakimashita. *I received it from mother.*

(f) **Dare ni moraimashita ka?** *Who did you get it from?*

   Yaoya ni moraimashita. *I got it from the greengrocer.*

"Kudasaru," "Kureru," "Ageru," "Yaru" and
"Itadaku," "Morau" — Terminal Verbs

215. The previous chart and examples show how to use **kudasasu, kureru, ageru, yaru** and **itadaku, morau**. All of these verbs are also used as terminal verbs with the meaning *one person does something as a favor to somebody else* or *one person receives a favor of other person's doing.*

(a) | Superior | *does somebody a favor of doing......*

   | Superior | **ga ......te kudasaru**

(b) | Inferior | *does somebody a favor of doing......*

   | Inferior | **ga ......te kureru**

(c) *Somebody does* | Superior | *a favor of doing......*

   | Superior | **ni ......te ageru**

(d) *Somebody does* | Inferior | *a favor of doing......*

Inferior ni ......te yaru

(e) *Somebody receives a favor of* Superior's *doing......*

Superior ni ......te itadaku

(f) *Somebody receives a favor of* Inferior's *doing......*

Inferior ni ......te morau

Examples:

(a) **Sensei ga imi o oshiete kudasaimashita.**

> *The teacher kindly taught the meaning to me.*

(b) **Jochū ga yaoya ni hanashite kuremashita.**

> *The maid spoke to the greengrocer for me.*

(c) **Kodomo wa ojiisan ni sore o yonde agemashita.**

> *The child read it for grandfather.*

(d) **Otōsan wa kodomo ni hon o katte yarimashita.**

> *Father bought a book for the child.*

(e) **Suzuki San ni goshōkai shite itadakimashita.**

> *I had Mr. Suzuki introduce me (to him). (Lit. I received the favor of Mr. Suzuki's introducing me to him.)*

(f) **Tomodachi ni katte moraimashita.**

> *I had my friend buy it for me. (Lit. I received the favor of my friend's buying it.)*

Mijikai Kaiwa

kono hen [-'-- or ----] *near here; around here*

tomete [---] from **tomeru**, *to stop*

Gokurōsama (deshita). [-'----] *Thanks for your trouble.* **Gokurōsama** literally means *hard work* and the whole sentence means **It was hard work**. Unlike **Arigatō**, this is used when one appreciates the effort of a person who is in one's employment or a person from whom such services can reasonably be expected.

Exercises

A. *Pick out the correct equivalent.*

— 273 —

1. Sensei ni goshōkai shite itadakimashita.

   a. My teacher kindly introduced me to him.

   b. I had my teacher introduce me to him.

   c. I was introduced to him by my teacher.

2. Tomodachi ni kashite moraimashita.

   a. A friend kindly lent it to me.

   b. I had a friend lend it to me.

   c. I borrowed it from a friend.

3. Beikoku no tomodachi ni katte agemashita.

   a. I bought it and gave it to my friend in the United States.

   b. I bought it for my friend in the United States.

   c. A friend of mine in the United States was kind enough to buy it.

4. Kodomo ni oshiete yarimashita.

   a. I was taught by a child.

   b. I taught it to a child.

   c. The child was taught by me.

5. Suzuki San ga tegami o kaite kudasaimashita.

   a. I had Mr. Suzuki write a letter for me.

   b. Mr. Suzuki wrote a letter and gave it to me.

   c. Mr. Suzuki wrote a letter for me.

6. Jimusho no hito ga kashite kuremashita.

   a. A person in the office lent it to me.

   b. I had it lent by a person in the office.

   c. A person in the office was kind enough to lend it to me.

B. Turn the following sentences into more polite ones.

   1. Anata wa ima yōji ga arimasu ka?

   2. Anata wa ii setomonoya o shitte imasu nē.

   3. Sono hito ni shōkai shite moraemasen ka?

   4. Watakushi ga tsurete itte yarimashō.

   5. Watakushi ni sono e o misete kuremasen ka?

C. What is the Japanese equivalent of each of the following sentences?

   1. He is very fond of stamps and has collected many old ones.

   2. I am thinking of collecting Japanese woodcut prints.

3. Do you know any American who will teach me English?
4. If you know one, can you introduce me?
5. Where is your house?
6. My house is near Shibuya Station and is very easy to find.
7. I borrowed this book from my friend but have to return it tomorrow.
8. Would you mind drawing a map for me?
9. If it is hard for you to find the house, it may be better to come by taxi from Shinagawa.
10. If you don't know that store, ask your friend to take you there.
11. I'll borrow (for you) the book you want to read.
12. My teacher kindly corrected the mistakes in the letter.
13. Go straight ahead and turn to the right at the third corner.
14. Please stop (the car) here, as this road is too narrow for the car (=this road is very narrow and the car can't pass).

D. *Mr. Suzuki and Mr. Jones know each other, but this is the first time for Mr. Jones to visit Mr. Suzuki. See if you can understand the following conversation.*

Mr. Jones :   Gomen kudasai. Kochira wa Suzuki San no otaku desu ka?

Mrs. Suzuki :   Hai, sayō de gozaimasu.

Mr. Jones :   Anata wa Suzuki San no okusan desu ka?

Mrs. Suzuki :   Sayō de gozaimasu.

Mr. Jones :   Hajimemashite. Watakushi wa Jonzu desu.

Mrs. Suzuki :   Onamae wa mae kara kiite orimashita. Chotto omachi kudasai.

    (Mr. Suzuki comes.)

Mr. Suzuki :   Jonzu San, yoku irasshaimashita. Dōzo oagari kudasai.

Mr. Jones :   Dewa gomen kudasai.

Mr. Suzuki :   Dōzo okake kudasai.

Mr. Jones :   Arigatō gozaimasu. Zuibun kirei na otaku desu nē.

Mr. Suzuki :   Dō itashimashite.

Mr. Jones :   Kyō wa chotto onegai ga atte maitta no desu ga......

Mr. Suzuki :   Donna goyō de......

E. *Carry on a conversation along the following outline.*

Harada : Good afternoon, Mr. Thomas.

Thomas :   Good afternoon, Mr. Harada.   How are you ?

Harada :   Fine, thank you.   And you ?

Thomas :   I'm quite well, too.   How is your wife ?

Harada :   She had a headache a few days ago.

Thomas :   That's too bad.

Harada :   But she is all right now.

Thomas :   That's good.

Harada :   (*seeing his friend*) May I introduce my friend, Mr. Yamada ?
(=I'll introduce Mr. Yamada) (*to Mr. Yamada*) This is Mr. Thomas.
Mr. Thomas is a school teacher.

Yamada :   How do you do ?

Thomas :   How do you do ?

Yamada :   Pleased to meet you.

Thomas :   The pleasure is mine.

Harada :   Mr. Yamada works in a bank. My cousin works in the same bank.

Thomas :   Is that so ?   I met your cousin the other day, didn't I ?

Harada :   That's right.   You met him when we went to my aunt's house.

Nijū-shichi

(Main Text)

A : Aburahamu Rinkan wa ima kara hyaku gojūnen hodo mae Amerika Gasshūkoku Kentakkii-shū de umaremashita.

Chiisai toki kara benkyō ga suki deshita ga, uchi ga hijō ni bimbō datta node, gakkō ni iku koto ga dekimasen deshita.

Shikashi hitori de yoku benkyō shimashita.

Ato de Rinkan wa hito ni yatowarete hataraitari, shōnin ni natte iroiro no shōbai o yattari shimashita.

Sorekara bengoshi ni natte dandan hito ni shirare, tōtō sen happyaku rokujūnen ni Beikoku no daitōryō ni erabaremashita.

Rinkan ga daitōryō ni natte ita toki yūmei na Namboku-sensō ga okotte minami no shū to kita no shū ga tatakaimashita.

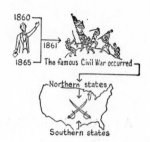

Kono sensō wa sen happyaku rokujū-ichinen kara rokujū-gonen made tsuzuita no desu ga, tōtō kita no shū ga katte minami no shū ga makemashita.

Desukara Rinkan wa hajime no uchi wa minami no shū no hitotachi niwa yoku omowaremasen deshita.

Mata aru hitotachi kara wa waruku iwaremashita.

Aru toki Rinkan ga Fōzuza to iu gekijō ni shibai o mi ni itta toki Jon Būsu to iu mono ni pisutoru de atama o utare-mashita.

Rinkan wa sugu ni chikaku no ie e okurarete isha no teate o ukemashita.

Keredomo tōtō sen happyaku rokujū-gonen shigatsu jūichinichi ni nakunari-mashita.

(A Short Conversation)

A : Dō shimashita ka?

B : Kega o shimashita.

A : Kusuri o tsukemashō ka?

B : Koko ni sawaranaide kudasai.

(For Memorizing)

1. Hito ni yatowarete hataraki-mashita.

1. He worked for other people.

2. Rinkan wa sen happyaku rokujūnen ni Beikoku no dai-tōryō ni erabaremashita.

2. Lincoln was elected President of the United States in 1860.

3. Aru hitotachi kara wa ⌊waruku⌋ iwaremashita.

3. He was spoken [ill] of by some people.

4. Rinkan wa pisutoru de [atama] o utaremashita.

4. Lincoln was shot in the [head] with a pistol.

Hombun

Glossary

Aburahamu [- - - - -] *Abraham*
Rinkan [- - - -] *Lincoln*
hodo [- -] *about; approximately*
Amerika [- - - -] *America*
gasshūkoku [- -ʹ- - -] *United States*
Kentakkii [- -ʹ- - -] *Kentucky*
shū [ʹ-] *a state; province*
hijō ni [- - - -] *exceedingly*
bimbō [ʹ- - -] *(a-B) poor* (not rich)
yatowarete [- -ʹ- -] from **yatowareru**, *to be employed*
shōnin [ʹ- - -] *a merchant; tradesman*
shōbai [ʹ- - -] *business; trade*
yattari [- -ʹ-] from **yaru**, *to do* (See Grammar 222.)
bengoshi [- -ʹ-] *a lawyer; attorney*
dandan [- - - -] *by degrees; gradually*
shirare [- - -] from **shirareru**, *to be known*
tōtō [ʹ- - -] *finally; at last*
happyaku [- - - -] *eight hundred*
daitōryō [- -ʹ- - -] *a president* (of a State)
erabare- [- - - -] from **erabareru**, *to be elected*
yūmei na [- - - - -] *(a-B) famous; well-known*
namboku [ʹ- - -] *south and north*
sensō [- - - -] *a war; battle*
Namboku-sensō [- - - -ʹ- - -] *American Civil War*
okotte [-ʹ- -] from **okoru**, *to start; break out*
minami [- - -] *south*

kita [-′] *north*

tatakai- [----] from **tatakau**, *to fight*

tsuzuita [----] past form of **tsuzuku**, *to last ; continue*

katte [′--] from **katsu**, *to win*

make- [--] from **makeru**, *to lose*

hajime no uchi [------] *at first*

omoware- [----] from **omowareru**, *to be thought of*

iware- [---] from **iwareru**, *to be spoken of*

aru toki [′---] *once*

Fōzuza [----] *Ford's Theater*

gekijō [----] *a theater*

shibai [---] *a play ; drama*

Jon Būsu [--′--] *John Booth*

mono [-′] *a person*

pisutoru [----] *a pistol*

utare- [---] from **utareru**, *to be shot*

okurarete [-----] from **okurareru**, *to be sent*

teate [′--] *treatment* (medical)

uke- [--] from **ukeru**, *to receive*

Grammar

The Gojūon (50 Sound) Table

216. The following is the **Gojūon** or the Fifty Sound Table used for conjugating verbs. Sounds in Base V become long when **Yodan** verbs in this base add another **o** i. e. **yomo-o = yomō.**

	Base I (Negative)	Base II (Continuative)	Base III (Conclusive)	Base IV (Conditional)	Base V (Volitional)	Base VI (Te-form)
—	a	i	u	e	o	—
kaku (*write*)	ka	ki	ku	ke	ko	ite
kasu (*lend*)	sa	shi	su	se	so	shite
tatsu (*stand*)	ta	chi	tsu	te	to	tte
shinu (*die*)	na	ni	nu	ne	no	nde
—	ha	hi	fu	he	ho	—

yomu (*read*)	ma	mi	mu	me	mo	nde
—	ya	i	yu	e	yo	—
toru (*take*)	ra	ri	ru	re	ro	tte
kau (*buy*)	wa	i	u	e	o	tte
fusagu (*close*)	ga	gi	gu	ge	go	ide
—	za	ji	zu	ze	zo	—
—	da	ji	zu	de	do	—
tobu (*fly*)	ba	bi	bu	be	bo	nde
—	pa	pi	pu	pe	po	—

Conjugation of Verbs

Yodan Verbs:

217. **Yodan** verbs conjugate in the first four rows as:

   I.   **kaka**-nai   (*I do not write*)

   II. **kaki**-masu   (*I write*)

   III. **kaku** koto ga dekimasu   (*I can write*)

   IV. **kake**-ba   (*if I write*)

Thus, they got the name of **Yodan** verbs. Bases V and VI are derived from Bases I and II respectively. Therefore, they were not considered different bases.

Base V, which has long sounds, is used for expressing volition or conjecture and Base VI is the **te**-form.

   V. **Kakō** to omoimasu.   *I think I'll write.*

   VI. **Kaite** kudasai.   *Please write.*

Base III is the plain, non-polite past form.

Ichidan Verbs:

218. The conjugation of **Ichidan** verbs is as follows:

   I.   **ki**-nai   (*I do not wear*)

   II. **ki**-masu   (*I wear*)

   III. **kiru** koto ga dekimasu   (*I can wear*)

   IV. **ki**-reba   (*if I wear*)

   I.   **tabe**-nai   (*I do not eat*)

   II. **tabe**-masu   (*I eat*)

   III. **taberu** koto ga dekimasu (*I can eat*)

   IV. **tabe**-reba   (*if I eat*)

Irregular Verbs:

219.

I.	**ko**-nai	(*I do not come*)
II.	**ki**-masu	(*I come*)
III.	**kuru** koto ga dekimasu	(*I can come*)
IV.	**ku**-reba	(*if I come*)
I.	**shi**-nai	(*I do not do*)
II.	**shi**-masu	(*I do*)
III.	**suru** koto ga dekimasu	(*I can do*)
IV.	**su**-reba	(*if I do*)

Bases V and VI of **Ichidan** and **Irregular** verbs are the same as Bases I and II respectively. **Yō** and **te** are used after these bases as:

V.	**Kiyō** to omoimasu.	*I think I'll wear it.*
VI.	**Kite** kudasai.	*Please wear it.*
V.	**Tabeyō** to omoimasu.	*I think I'll eat.*
VI.	**Tabete** kudasai.	*Please eat.*
V.	**Koyō** to omoimasu.	*I think I'll come.*
VI.	**Kite** kudasai.	*Please come.*
V.	**Shiyō** to omoimasu.	*I think I'll do it.*
VI.	**Shite** kudasai.	*Please do it.*

"Ukemi" or the Passive Voice

220. Compared with English, the use of the passive voice in Japanese is very much limited and the subject of a passive verb is, in most cases, a person or a living creature. Inanimate objects except when they are personified, seldom become the subject of a passive construction.

The passive voice is formed by adding **reru** to the negative base of Yodan verbs and **rareru** to that of Ichidan verbs and the irregular verb **kuru**. The irregular verb **suru** forms the passive irregularly.

Yodan Verbs:

yatou (*to employ*)	**yatowareru** (*to be employed*)
shiru (*to know*)	**shirareru** (*to be known*)
utsu (*to shoot*)	**utareru** (*to be shot*)

Ichidan Verbs and **Irregular Verb "kuru":**

taberu (*to eat*)	**taberareru** (*to be eaten*)

miru (*to see*)	mirareru (*to be seen*)
kuru (*to come*)	korareru (*to be visited*)

Irregular Verb " suru " :

suru (*to do*)	sareru (*to be done*)

The agent in the passive voice is indicated by the particle **ni**.

Rinkan wa dandan hito ni shiraremashita.

Lincoln was gradually known by people.

221. Strange as it may appear to English speaking people, intransitive verbs in Japanese such as **kuru** (*to come*), **shinu** (*to die*), etc., can form the passive with a certain difference in meaning. The meaning of a passive intransitive verb is that the subject receives the result of some other's action which was performed independently of the wishes of the subject.

Kinō watakushi wa tomodachi ni koraremashita.

This means *I received the (ill)-effect of a friend's coming*, hence, *a friend made a sudden visit and I was disturbed by his coming.*

" Yaru " — " to Do "

222. The verb **yaru** has the same meaning as the verb **suru**. It is widely used in spoken Japanese in a more familiar style.

Hayaku yari nasai. *Do it quickly.*

It must be remembered that there is another meaning of **yaru**, *to give*, which is often used as a terminal verb as shown in Lesson 26, Grammar 215.

Second Base as Continuative

223. When too many **te**-forms run together, the second base, which had the continuative function in the literary style, is sometimes used for this purpose for euphony's sake.

Sorekara bengoshi ni natte dandan hito ni shirare, tōtō Beikoku no daitōryō ni erabaremashita.

After that he became a lawyer and came to be known to people, and finally he was elected President of the United States.

Mijikai Kaiwa

kega [-'] *an injury; wound:* **kega o suru** means *to get hurt.*

tsukeru [-'-] *to put; apply* (medicine)

sawaranaide [- - -'- -] from **sawaru**, *to touch.* This ......**naide** plus **kudasai** means *Don't......* (See Lesson 17, Grammar 140.)

Exercises

A. Practise converting from one form to another rapidly and fluently.

Conversion Table 12

Dictionary Form	Passive Form	Passive Negative Form	Meaning
omou	omowareru	omowarenai	*think*
yatou	yatowareru	yatowarenai	*employ*
iu	iwareru	iwarenai	*say*
kiku	kikareru	kikarenai	*hear*
hanasu	hanasareru	hanasarenai	*speak*
utsu	utareru	utarenai	*shoot*
katsu	katareru	katarenai	*win*
erabu	erabareru	erabarenai	*elect*
tanomu	tanomareru	tanomarenai	*request*
yomu	yomareru	yomarenai	*read*
okuru	okurareru	okurarenai	*send*
shiru	shirareru	shirarenai	*know*
taberu	taberareru	taberarenai	*eat*
oboeru	oboerareru	oboerarenai	*remember*
wasureru	wasurerareru	wasurerarenai	*forget*
miru	mirareru	mirarenai	*see*
kuru	korararu	korarenai	*come*
suru	sareru	sarenai	*do*

B. Answer the following questions.

1. Rinkan wa ima kara nannen hodo mae ni umaremashita ka?
2. Rinkan wa chiisai toki kara nani ga suki deshita ka?
3. Naze Rinkan wa gakkō e ikemasen deshita ka?
4. Rinkan wa donna shigoto o shimashita ka?
5. Rinkan wa nannen ni daitōryō ni erabaremashita ka?
6. Rinkan ga daitōryō ni natte ita toki nani ga okorimashita ka?

7. Namboku-sensō dewa dare ga tatakatta no desu ka?

8. Kono sensō de dotchi no shū ga kachimashita ka?

9. Rinkan wa hajime no uchi demo minami no shū no hitotachi ni yoku omowaremashita ka?

10. Rinkan ga Fōzuza ni itta toki ni donna koto ga okorimashita ka?

C. *Turn the following sentences into the passive.*

   Example: Jon Būsu wa Rinkan **o** pisutoru de **uchimashita.**

   Rinkan wa Jon Būsu **ni** pisutoru de **utaremashita.**

   1. Ano mise wa Tarō o yatoimashita.

   2. Sono hitotachi wa ano hito o yoku omotte imasen.

   3. Jochū ga tegami o yomimashita.

   4. Ano kata ni tanomimashita.

   5. Ano hito no namae o wasuremashita.

   6. Seito o Beikoku no gakkō e okurimasu.

D. *What is the Japanese equivalent of each of the following sentences?*

   1. I was asked to teach English, but I have no time.

   2. I don't want to be seen when I am eating.

   3. In what state of the United States were you born?

   4. As he had no teacher, he had to study by himself.

   5. His books are known to many people.

   6. It will gradually get warmer from now on.

   7. His illness lasted for three months and he finally died.

   8. He is not thought well of by the people in his office.

   9. He was shot in the head with a pistol.

   10. Though he got medical treatment, he died on March 24, 1962.

   11. I have a sore throat; I think I'd better put some medicine on.

E. *What would you say when,*

   1. you tell your maid that you'll come home very late this evening and you won't eat at home?

   2. you tell your driver to go straight ahead?

   3. you want to thank your driver for his trouble?

   4. you want to say that you hurt yourself?

   5. you want to tell someone not to wait?

Nijū-hachi

(Main Text)

B : Suzuki San wa eiga ya shibai ga suki de tabitabi mi ni ikimasu.

Watakushi wa mada Nihon no shibai o mita koto ga arimasen kara zehi Kabuki o mitai to omotte imashita.

Suruto kinō Suzuki San ga kite Kabuki ni sasotte kuremashita.

Suzuki : Anata wa Kabuki o goran ni natta koto ga arimasu ka ?

Buraun : Iie, mada mita koto ga arimasen.

Suzuki : Dewa asu no ban mi ni irasshaimasen ka ?

Buraun : Arigatō gozaimasu ga myōban wa sen'yaku ga atte ikaremasen.

Suzuki: Zannen desu nē. Asatte wa ikaga desu ka?

Buraun: Asatte nara hima desu.

Suzuki: Dewa watakushi mo asatte ni shi-mashō.

Anata wa konoaida no ongakukai ni ikimashita ka?

Buraun: Ikitakatta n' desu ga kyaku ga derareatte ikaremasen deshita.

Suzuki: Watakushi mo kaze o hiite masen deshita.

Buraun: Yamada San ya Hayashi San wa itta deshō ne.

Suzuki: Yamada San wa itta sō desu ga, Hayashi San wa ikanakatta sō desu.

Buraun: Dōshite deshō?

Suzuki: Iku hazu deshita ga yōji ga dekite ikenakatta sō desu.

Buraun: Taihen yokatta sō desu ne.

Suzuki: Yamada san no hanashi dewa amari yoku nakatta sō desu.

Buraun: Sō desu ka?

Shimbun ni yoru to Katō San no uta wa taihen yokatta sō desu yo.

Suzuki: Sō deshita ka? Sore wa shirimasen deshita.

(A Short Conversation)

A: Sā, shitsurei itashimashō.

B: Mā, yoroshii deshō. Dōzo goyukkuri.

A : Matteru hito ga arimasu.

B : Soredewa mata dōzo.

Someone is waiting for m

Come again, please

(For Memorizing)

1. Watakushi wa mada Nihon no [shibai] o mita koto ga arimasen.

   1. I've never seen a Japanese [play].

2. Ikitakatta n' desu ga [kyaku] ga atte ikaremasen deshita.

   2. I wanted to go, but I couldn't, because I had a [visitor].

3. Yamada San no hanashi dewa [amari yoku nakatta] sō desu.

   3. According to Mr. Yamada it [wasn't so good].

4. Shimbun ni yoru to Katō San no [uta] wa taihen yokatta sō desu.

   4. According to the newspapers Miss Katō's [singing] was excellent.

Hombun

Glossary

zehi ['-] *by all means*

Kabuki [---] *Japanese classical play*

suruto [---] *then*

sasotte [----] from **sasou**, *to ask someone to do something together, such as going out for enjoyment, sightseeing, attending a theater, etc.*

goran ni naru [----'-] honorific term of **miru** (See Lesson 30, Grammar 235.)

sen'yaku [----] *a previous engagement*

ikare- [---] from **ikareru**, *to be able to go* (See Grammar 225.)

zannen [--'-] (*a-B*) *regrettable ; mortifying*

......**ni suru** [– – –] *to decide on*

ongakukai [– –´– – –] *a concert*

ikitakatta [– –´– – –] *wanted to go* (See Grammar 228.)

n' [–] contraction of **no**

kaze [–´] *a cold* (disease). **Kaze o hiku** means *to catch cold*.

derare- [– – –] from **derareru**, *to be able to go out* (See Grammar 225.)

ikanakatta [– –´– – –] *didn't go* (See Grammar 227.)

dōshite [´– – –] *why; how come*

dekite [´– –] from **dekiru**, *to come up*

ikenakatta [– –´– – –] *was unable to go* (See Grammar 227.)

yokatta [´– – –] *was good* (See Grammar 227.)

hanashi [– – –] *a story; talk*

......**no hanashi dewa** [– – – – – –] *according to......* (See Grammar 229.)

yoku nakatta [´–´– – –] *was not good* (See Grammar 227.)

......**ni yoru to** [– – – –] *according to......* (See Grammar 229.)

uta [–´] *a song*

Grammar

Past Experience

224. An experience in the past which is expressed by *have ever done such and such* is expressed by **koto ga aru** following the past form of a verb.

> **Shibai o mita koto ga arimasu ka?**
>
> > *Have you ever seen a play?*
>
> **Nippon e itta koto ga arimasen.**
>
> > *I have never been to Japan.*
>
> **Ano hito ni atta koto ga arimasen ka?**
>
> > *Haven't you ever met him?*

Koto ga aru literally means *there is a fact* and expresses the past experience only when it is preceded by the past form of a verb.

In Lesson 17, Grammar 141 we had **koto ga aru** following the dictionary form of a verb or a true adjective.

> **Osoku made kaisha ni nokoru koto ga arimasu.**
>
> > *I sometimes stay in the company till late.*
>
> **Atama ga itai koto ya onaka no itai koto ga arimasu.**
>
> > *I sometimes have headaches and stomach-aches.*

In this case **koto ga aru** may be interpreted as *have an occasion,* hence, *sometimes.*

The Passive in a Potential Sense

225.   **Myōban wa ikaremasen.**   *I cannot go tomorrow evening.*
      Kaze o hiite deraremasen deshita.
         I caught a cold and couldn't go out.

The Japanese passive is often used in a potential sense. To be exact, there is a form which denotes potentiality, and this form happens to be the same as the passive. Therefore, we have to use our judgement in determining whether the form is passive or potential.

      Kono yōfuku wa kiraremasen.

This may mean either *This suit is not worn* or *This suit can't be worn.* But the first meaning is unlikely since clothing is an inanimate object. Therefore, the second meaning must be the right one. Generally speaking, a potential sense is more usual in a sentence whose subject is inanimate.

      Sore wa iwaremasen.   *I can't tell you that.*
      Kore wa taberaremasu ka? *Can this be eaten? (Is this edible?)*

[Noun] x "ni Suru" — "Decide on"

226.   **Watakushi wa asatte ni shimashō.**
         I'll decide on the day after tomorrow.
      Watakushi wa akai no ni shimasu.
         I'll decide on (taking) the red one.

A noun plus **ni suru** means *to decide on*...... Instead of a noun, a noun equivalent may be used also before **ni suru.**

      Iku koto ni shimashita.   *I decided to go.* (**iku koto**=*going*)

The Past Form of "Tai" and "Nai"

227. Adjective-like auxiliaries such as **tai** and **nai** are conjugated like true adjectives.

present	past	te-form
tai-	**-takatta**	**-takute**

yokunai	yokunakatta	yokunakute
yoi	yokatta	yokute
kuroi	kurokatta	kurokute

The past form **takatta** was originally a combination of **taku** (the adverbial form of **tai**) and **atta** and in time the final **u** of the auxiliary was dropped.

[Conclusive Form of a Verb] x " n' Desu "

228. In Lesson 24, Grammar 202 we have learned that **no desu** after the conclusive form of a verb emphasizes the meaning. This **no** is sometimes shortened into **n**.

> **Ikitakatta no desu.**
> **Ikitakatta n' desu.** } *I wanted to go.*

The Te-form denoting a Reason

229.   **Yōji ga dekite ikenakatta sō desu.**

I hear that he, having some business, couldn't go.

Isogashikute hima ga arimasen deshita.

Being busy, I had no time to spare.

Ame ga futte michi ga warui desu.

Because it rained, the road is bad.

The **te**-form often denotes the reason for the statement that follows.

" No Hanashi dewa " and " ni Yoru to " — " According to "

230.   ......**no hanashi dewa**, which literally means *according to the talk of,* and ......**ni yoru to**, which means *if we depend on,* both correspond to *according to* in English. However, one very important difference is that the English sentence makes a definite statement, whereas the Japanese sentence has **sō desu** or some other words which express the idea of *I hear, I'm told,* etc., tacked on to the end of the statement.

> **Yamada San no hanashi dewa amari yoku nakatta sō desu.**
>
> *According to Mr. Yamada, it wasn't so good.*
>
> **Shimbun ni yoru to Katō San no uta wa taihen jōzu datta sō desu.**
>
> *According to the newspaper, Miss Kato's singing was excellent.*

Between the two expressions, **no hanashi dewa** is more colloquial. From the very meaning of *according to the talk of*, **no hanashi dewa** can only come after a person's name.

Mijikai Kaiwa

shitsurei [-'--] (*a-B*) *rude; impolite:* **Shitsurei itashimashō** literally means *I'll do rudeness* and is used when one takes a leave.

mā ['-] *well*

yoroshii deshō literally means *I suppose it's all right (for you not to leave so soon).*

Dōzo goyukkuri. ['-----'-] *Please take your time.*

matteru ['---] contraction of **matte iru**, *to be waiting*

Mata dōzo. [--'--] *Please (come) again.*

Exercises

A. Practise converting from one form to another rapidly and fluently.

Conversion Table 13

Polite Negative	Plain Negative	Past Experience	Meaning
iimasen	iwanai	itta koto ga arimasen	*say*
aimasen	awanai	atta koto ga arimasen	*meet*
kakimasen	kakanai	kaita koto ga arimasen	*write*
kikimasen	kikanai	kiita koto ga arimasen	*hear*
hanashimasen	hanasanai	hanashita koto ga arimasen	*speak*
kachimasen	katanai	katta koto ga arimasen	*win*
tobimasen	tobanai	tonda koto ga arimasen	*fly*
tanomimasen	tanomanai	tanonda koto ga arimasen	*request*
okurimasen	okuranai	okutta koto ga arimasen	*send*
ikimasen	ikanai	itta koto ga arimasen	*go*
tabemasen	tabenai	tabeta koto ga arimasen	*eat*
demasen	denai	deta koto ga arimasen	*go out*
mimasen	minai	mita koto ga arimasen	*see*
kimasen	konai	kita koto ga arimasen	*come*
shimasen	shinai	shita koto ga arimasen	*de*

Conversion Table 14

Dictionary Form	Desiderative	Past Desiderative	Meaning
au	aitai	aitakatta	*meet*
kau	kaitai	kaitakatta	*buy*
oku	okitai	okitakatta	*put*
kiku	kikitai	kikitakatta	*hear*
hanasu	hanashitai	hanashitakatta	*speak*
katsu	kachitai	kachitakatta	*win*
tobu	tobitai	tobitakatta	*fly*
yomu	yomitai	yomitakatta	*read*
nomu	nomitai	nomitakatta	*drink*
okuru	okuritai	okuritakatta	*send*
iku	ikitai	ikitakatta	*go*
taberu	tabetai	tabetakatta	*eat*
miru	mitai	mitakatta	*see*
kuru	kitai	kitakatta	*come*
suru	shitai	shitakatta	*do*

Conversion Table 15

Dictionary Form	Plain Past	Plain Past Negative	Meaning
chiisai	chiisakatta	chiisaku nakatta	*small*
semai	semakatta	semaku nakatta	*narrow*
akai	akakatta	akaku nakatta	*red*
ii	yokatta	yoku nakatta	*good*
ōkii	ōkikatta	ōkiku nakatta	*large*
isogashii	isogashikatta	isogashiku nakatta	*busy*
osoi	osokatta	osoku nakatta	*late*
kuroi	kurokatta	kuroku nakatta	*black*
warui	warukatta	waruku nakatta	*bad*
samui	samukatta	samuku nakatta	*cold*
-nikui	-nikukatta	-nikuku nakatta	*hard to...*

B. Fill in each blank with an appropriate word.

1. Watakushi wa eiga ___ shibai ga daisuki ___ tabitabi mi ___ ikimasu.
2. Anata ga ashita iku nara, watakushi mo ashita iku koto ___ shimashō.

3. Konoaida no shimbun ___ yoru to, Takayama San no uta wa taihen jōzu ___ sō desu.

4. Kuroda San ___ hanashi dewa, amari yoku nakatta ___ desu.

5. Watakushi wa zehi Amerika e iki___ to omotte imasu.

C. *Convert the following into the past tense.*

1. Ikitai desu ga iku koto ga dekimasen.

2. Ashita no asa hayaku iku tsumori desu.

3. Nishimura San wa iku sō desu ga, Tamura San wa ikanai sō desu.

4. Iku hazu desu ga ikenai sō desu.

5. Yamada San no piano wa taihen ii sō desu.

D. *Combine each of the following pairs of sentences into one sentence, making necessary changes.*

1. (a) Yōji ga arimasu.
   (b) Ikaremasen.

2. (a) Kaze o hikimashita.
   (b) Gakkō e ikimasen deshita.

3. (a) Isogashii desu.
   (b) Deraremasen.

4. (a) Byōki desu.
   (b) Isha ni ikimashita.

5. (a) Kinō okyaku ga arimashita.
   (b) Benkyō dekimasen deshita.

E. *Read the following and then tell it in your own words.*

Watakushi wa ima kara yonkagetsu hodo mae ni Nihon e kimashita. Nihon e kuru mae kara Kabuki o mitai to omotte imashita ga mada mita koto ga arimasen. Suruto kinō Tanaka San ga kite, Kabuki ni sasotte kudasaimashita. Watakushi wa issho ni ikitakatta n' desu ga, tomodachi no uchi e iku yakusoku ga atta node iku koto ga dekimasen deshita. Raishū no getsuyō nara hima desu kara, Tanaka San mo getsuyō ni shite, gogo goji goro sasoi ni kite kureru hazu desu.

Watakushi wa tokidoki ongakukai emo ikimasu. Senshū no ongakukai ewa okyaku ga atte ikaremasen deshita ga, Tanaka San mo kaze o hiite ikenakatta sō desu. Kono ongakukai e itta Kuroda San no hanashi dewa amari yoku nakatta sō desu ga, shimbun ni yoru to Takayama San no piano wa taihen jōzu datta sō desu.

E. What is the Japanese equivalent of each of the following sentences?
1. Have you ever been to Kyōto?
2. I have not been there yet.
3. But I am anxious to go (literally, I have been thinking of going there by all means.)
4. Would you like to go out for a walk this afternoon?
5. No, I wouldn't, as I expect to go to see movies.
6. I intended to go to Mr. Tanaka's house on Sunday, but as a guest came, I couldn't go.
7. Will you be able to come here the day after tomorrow?
8. No, as I have to go to a friend's house, I shall not be able to come.
9. I wanted to buy a dictionary, but I had no money.
10. Did Mr. Katō become sick?
11. No, he didn't, but I hear his wife caught a cold.
12. I was supposed to write a letter to Mr. Kuroda, but I had some business and couldn't.
13. He wanted to learn Japanese, but he couldn't.
14. I was supposed to go to a show last night, but having had some business I couldn't. So I expect to go tomorrow afternoon.
15. According to what Mr. Tanaka says, his piano (playing) isn't very good.
16. But according to the paper, he is excellent.
17. I hear she sang very well.
18. According to yesterday's paper, the president of the United States will go to England next year.

F. Complete in Japanese the following conversation between Mr. Brown and Mr. Yamada along the line suggested in English.

(*Mr. Brown meets Mr. Yamada on the street.*)

Brown: (*Good day, Mr. Yamada. It's a fine day, isn't it?*)

Yamada: Konnichi wa. Ii otenki desu nē. Kaze wa nai shi yoku harete ite.

Brown: (*That's why I came out for a walk.*)

Yamada: Sō desu ka? Watakushi wa yōji ga atte eki no chikaku made kimashita.

Brown: (*Then, you are on your way home, aren't you? Are you busy now?*)

Yamada: Iie, kyō wa mō yōji ga arimasen.

Brown: (*Is that so? Then, won't you take a little walk with me?*)

Yamada: Sō desu ne. Goissho ni arukimashō.

Brown: (*What's that large house near the bakery?*)

Yamada: Jidōsha ga mon no mae ni tomete aru uchi desu ka?

Brown: (*No, (I mean) the two-storeyed house in front of which many bicycles are placed.*)

Yamada: Wakarimashita. Are wa atarashiku dekita gekijō desu.

Brown: (*What's "gekijō"? I don't know the word.*)

Yamada: Shibai o miseru tokoro desu. Tokidoki Kabuki mo shimasu.

Brown: (*I understand. Have you ever been to that theater?*)

Yamada: Ni'sando itta koto ga arimasu. Senshū asuko de ongakukai ga arimashita.

Brown: (*Did you go?*)

Yamada: Ikitakatta n' desu ga yōji ga atte ikaremasen deshita. Shimbun ni yoru to raishū mata ongakukai ga aru sō desu.

Brown: (*Is that so? If it is a good one, I'd like to go. Do you expect to go, too?*)

Yamada: Iku tsumori desu. Moshi ohima nara issho ni ikimasen ka?

Brown: (*If it is Wednesday or Thursday, I shall be free.*)

Yamada: Dewa suiyōbi ni shimashō. Kyō uchi e kaettara sugu kippu o kaimashō.

Brown: (*Please do. We have walked a lot. I am a bit tired. Aren't you?*)

Yamada: Ee, sukoshi. Dewa mō kaerimashō ka?

Brown: (*Let's do so. It's nearly four o'clock. And I'm a bit thirsty and hungry, too.*)

Yamada: Watakushi no uchi e itte ocha o nomimashō.

Brown: (*Thank you.*)

Nijū-ku

(Main Text)

A : Suzuki San no ie niwa jochū ga hitori imasu.

Kotoshi jūshichi de, inaka kara kita bakari desu.

Kono musume no uchi wa hyakushō desu.

Katei no koto o narawasetai to omotte Suzuki San ni tanonda no desu.

Oyatachi wa hatachi ka nijū-ichi gurai made tsutomesasetai to itte imasu.

Mada Tōkyō ni narete imasen kara tōku ni tsukai ni yaru koto wa dekimasen ga, konogoro kinjo ni kaimono ni ikaseru koto ga dekiru yō ni narimashita.

Ryōri wa okusan ga shimasu ga, jochū mo tetsudaimasu.

Sono zairyō wa okusan ga kai ni iki-masu ga, isogashii toki niwa denwa o kakete motte kosasetari, kono jochū o tori ni ikasetari shimasu.

Akachan no sewa mo okusan ga shi-masu ga tokidoki kono jochū ga akachan no gyūnyū o attametari sore o nomasetari shimasu.

Sono hoka heya no sōji ya sentaku o sasetari niwa o hakasetari shimasu.

(A Short Conversation)

B : Oyobi desu ka ?

A : Kore wa tsumetai desu. Attamete kudasai.

B : Dōmo omatase itashimashita.

A : Kono sara wa yogorete imasu kara torikaete kudasai.

(For Memorizing)

1. Oyatachi wa [hatachi] gurai made tsutomesasetai to itte imasu.

    1. Her parents are saying that they want to have her work until she is about [twenty years old].

2. Mada [Tōkyō] ni narete imasen.

    2. She is not accustomed to [Tokyo] yet.

3. [Kaimono] ni ikaseru koto ga dekiru yō ni narimashita.

    3. It became possible to let her go [shopping].

4. [Isogashii] toki niwa denwa o kakete motte kosasemasu.

    4. When she is [busy], she telephones (to the shops) and lets them bring it.

Hombun

Glossary

musume [- - -] a girl

hyakushō [- -'-] a farmer; *peasant*

katei [- - -] *home; a family; household.* **Katei no koto** means *household matters.*

narawase- [- - - -] from **narawaseru**, *to let......learn* (See Grammar

231.)

hatachi ['--] *twenty years old*

tsutomesase- [-----] from **tsutomesaseru**, *to let......work in*

(ni) narete ['--] from **nareru**, *to get accustomed to*

tsukai [---] *an errand; mission*

konogoro [----] *nowadays; these days*

ikaseru [----] *to let......go*

ryōri ['--] *cooking*

tetsudai- [----] from **tetsudau**, *to help; assist*

zairyō [--'-] *(raw) material*

motte kosase- ['-----] from **motte kosaseru**, *to let......bring. To bring* is **motte kuru**.

tori ni ikase- ['-----] from **tori ni ikaseru**, *to let......go and get; send......to get something.*

akachan ['---] *a baby*

sewa [-'] *care*

gyūnyū [----] *(cow's) milk*

attame- [----] from **attameru**, *to warm*

nomase- [---] from **nomaseru**, *to let......drink*

sōji [---] *sweeping; cleaning* (of a room, etc.)

sase- [--] from **saseru**, *to let......do*

hakase- [---] from **hakaseru**, *to let......sweep*

Grammar

The Causatives

231. The fundamental idea of the causative is that a person causes some other person or animal, etc. to do something regardless of the latter's wishes. It naturally follows the one who causes an action to be performed is superior or in authority. The causative may generally be translated into English by *make, let, have* or *get.*

When one requests another to do something, **morau** or **itadaku** after the **te**-form is used as explained in Lesson 26, Grammar 215.

The causative may have two meanings: (a) *to cause to do* and (b) *to allow something to be done.*

(a) **Oyatachi wa musume ni katei no koto o narawasemasu.**

The parents have their daughter learn domestic work.

Jochū ni gyūnyū o attamesasete kudasai.

Please let the maid warm the milk.

(b) **Kodomo ni kore o tabesasete wa ikemasen.**

Don't let the child eat this.

The causative form of Yodan verbs is formed by adding **seru** to the first base, i. e. the negative base, and that of Ichidan verbs and the irregular verb **kuru** by adding **saseru** to the negative base.

The irregular verb **suru** is an exception. We might say that **saseru** itself is the causative form of **suru**.

Yodan verbs:

narau (*to learn*)	narawa-**seru** (*to cause to learn*)
nomu (*to drink*)	noma-**seru** (*to cause to drink*)
haku (*to sweep*)	haka-**seru** (*to cause to sweep*)
matsu (*to wait*)	mata-**seru** (*to cause to wait*)

Ichidan verbs:

attameru (*to warm*)	attame-**saseru** (*to cause to warm*)
tsutomeru (*to work in*)	tsutome-**saseru** (*to cause to work in*)
miru (*to see*)	mi-**saseru** (*to cause to see*)

232. The person caused to act is expressed by **ni** or **o**, but very often the recipient is not mentioned.

Taitei jochū ni ikasemasu. *I usually let the maid go.*

Jochū o tori ni ikasemashita. *I sent the maid to get it.*

Seito ni tegami o kakasemasu. *I let the students write letters.*

233. The causative is sometimes used when the causation is purely imaginary.

Furasetaku nai desu nē.

I hope it won't rain. (Lit. *I do not wish to cause rain to fall.*)

Ii hito o shinasemashita.

We have lost a good man. (Lit. *We have caused a good man to die.*)

In case the causative is to be used in a passive construction, the passive comes after.

Mataserareru no wa kirai desu.

I don't like to be kept waiting. (Lit. *I don't like to be caused to wait.*)

Muzukashii koto o kotaesaseraremashita.

I was asked to answer a difficult thing.

"......ga Dekiru yō ni Naru" — "Become Possible to......"

234. **Yō ni iu** is used in Indirect Discourse (Lesson 25, Grammar 209).
Yō literally means *manner, way,* so **yō ni** literally means *in a manner.*
When **yō ni** comes before **naru**, it means *it turns into a manner that......*

Kaimono ni iku koto ga dekiru yō ni narimashita.

It has become possible for her to go shopping. (Lit. *It has turned into a manner that she can go shopping.*)

Mijikai Kaiwa

oyobi [- - -] **o**, honorific and **yobi** from **yobu**, polite form for *to call.*
Oyobi desu ka means *Do you want me? Did you call me?*
tsumetai [- - - -] (*a-A*) *cold* (of an object). *Cold* of weather is **samui**.
Omatase itashimashita. a humble expression meaning *I am sorry to have kept you waiting.*
torikaete [- - - - -] from **torikaeru**, *to exchange; change*

Exercises

A. Practise converting from one form to another rapidly and fluently.

Conversion Table 16

Present	Causative	Passive Causative	Meaning
tetsudaimasu	tetsudawa-semasu	tetsudawase-raremasu	*help*
naraimasu	narawa-semasu	narawase-raremasu	*learn*
kaimasu	kawa-semasu	kawase-raremasu	*buy*
hakimasu	haka-semasu	hakase-raremasu	*sweep*
kikimasu	kika-semasu	kikase-raremasu	*hear*
machimasu	mata-semasu	matase-raremasu	*wait*
yobimasu	yoba-semasu	yobase-raremasu	*call*

nomimasu	noma-semasu	nomase-raremasu	*drink*
shirimasu	shira-semasu	shirase-raremasu	*know*
ikimasu	ika-semasu	ikase-raremasu	*go*
tsutomeru	tsutome-sasemasu	tsutomesase-raremasu	*work*
naremasu	nare-sasemasu	naresase-raremasu	*accustomed*
attamemasu	attame-sasemasu	attamesase-raremasu	*warm*
mimasu	mi-sasemasu	misase-raremasu	*see*
kimasu	ko-sasemasu	kosase-raremasu	*come*
shimasu	sasemasu	sase-raremasu	*do*

B. Turn the following sentences into the causative.

1. Seito wa yoku benkyō shimasu.
2. Watakushi no ato o tsukete iimasu.
3. Kudamono o katte kudasai.
4. Kutsu o migakimashō.
5. Tagami o kaku koto mo arimasu.
6. Mizu o motte kimashō ka ?
7. Isha o sugu yobimasu.
8. Kodomo ga kusuri o nomimasu.

C. What is the Japanese equivalent of each of the following sentences?

1. As I have studied Japanese for about half a year, it has become possible for me to talk with my Japanese friends.
2. I have just come to Japan and don't know much about Japan.
3. The parents want to have their daughter learn domestic work at a respectable (=*rippa na*) home.
4. Please let me read by myself.
5. When the students can't answer (=*kotaeru*) I have them repeat after me.
6. I'm very thirsty; please have the maid bring me a cup of (=*ippai*) tea.
7. I usually have my maid buy things, but sometimes I go to buy things myself.
8. I'm hungry; I'd like to have something to eat.
9. When I visited him yesterday, I was made to wait for one hour.
10. Please have the maid clean my room.

Sanjū

(Main Text)

Yamada : Yoku irasshaimashita. Dōzo oagari kudasai.

Hayashi : Shitsurei itashimasu.

Itsumo gobusata bakari itashite orimasu ga minasan okawari mo gozaimasen ka ?

Yamada : Arigatō gozaimasu. Okagesama de. Otaku dewa ?

Hayashi : Shujin ga sukoshi byōki de gozaimashita ga, mō hotondo naorimashita.

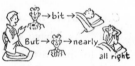

Yamada : Sayō de gozaimashita ka ? Chittomo zonjimasen deshita. Dō nasatta no desu ka ?

Hayashi : Kaze o hikimashita no desu kara taishita koto wa gozaimasen.

Sorede kyō wa shujin no kawari ni Suzuki San no tokoro e agaru tokoro de gozaimasu.

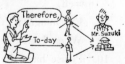

Yamada : Sayō de gozaimasu ka?

Watakushi wa Suzuki San niwa shibaraku ome ni kakarimasen ga oai ni narimashitara yoroshiku osshatte kudasaimasen ka?

Hayashi : Kashikomarimashita. Mōshiagemasu. Amari gobusata itashimashita node chotto goaisatsu ni ukagaimashita.

Soredewa oitoma itashimashō.

Yamada : Mā yoroshii dewa gozaimasen ka? Mō sukoshi asonde irasshatte kudasai.

Hayashi : Goyō ga oari no tokoro o taihen ojama itashimashita.

Yamada : Iie, dō itashimashite. Dōzo goshimpai naku.

Soreni mō ohiru desu kara, nani mo gozaimasen ga gohan o agatte irasshatte kudasaimasen ka?

Hayashi : Arigatō gozaimasu ga, kyō wa shitsurei itashimasu.

Mata kono tsugi ni chōdai itashimasu.

Yamada : Sayō de gozaimasu ka ? Dewa mata oide kudasai.

Hayashi : Arigatō gozaimasu. Chikai uchi ni mata ojama ni ukagawasete itadaki-masu.

Yamada : Sayōnara.
Hayashi : Sayōnara.

(A Short Conversation)

B : Dōzo meshiagatte kudasai mashi.

A : Itadakimasu.

Gochisōsama deshita.

B : Osomatsusama de gozaimashita.

Hombun

Glossary

yoku irasshaimashita *Glad to see you*, expression used when welcoming a visitor : **yoku**, the adverbial form of **yoi**, *good*

oagari [- - - -] **o**, honorific, and **agari** from **agaru**, *to come (go) up ; rise*. This word is used for *coming (going) into a Japanese house*.

gobusata [- - - -] **go**, honorific, and **busata**, *neglecting to call or write ; silence*

bakari ['- -] *only ; nothing but*

minasan [-'- -] *all of you ; everybody*

okawari [- - - -] **o**, honorific, and **kawari**, *change*

naori- [- - -] from **naoru**, *to recover*

zonji- [- - -] from **zonjiru**, polite term of *to know*

nasatta [-'- -] the past tense of **nasaru**, honorific term for *to do*

taishita ['- - -] *serious*

sorede [- - -] *therefore ; then*

kawari [- - -] *substitute :* **kawari ni** means *in place of.*

agaru [- - -] the humble term for *to go (come)*

shibaraku [-'- -] *for some time*

ome ni kakari- [- - - - - -] from **ome ni kakaru**, humble term for *to meet*

oai [- - -] **o**, honorific, and **ai** from **au**, *to meet :* **oai ni naru** means *to meet.* (honorific)

osshatte [- -'- -] from **ossharu**, honorific term for *to say*

mōshiage- [- - - - -] from **mōshiageru**, humble term for *to say*

goaisatsu [-'- - -] **go**, honorific, and **aisatsu**, *greeting*

ukagai- [- - - -] from **ukagau**, humble term for *to visit*

oitoma suru [- - - - - -] *say good-bye ; to take leave :* **o**, honorific, and **itoma**, *leave*

oari [- - -] **o**, honorific, and **ari** from **aru**, *to have*

ojama suru [- - - - -] **o**, honorific, and **jama**, *disturbance : to disturb*

goshimpai [- - - - -] **go**, honorific, and **shimpai**, *worry*

soreni [- - -] *in addition to that ; besides*

mō [- -] *now*

agaru [- - -] *to eat* (honorific)

chōdai suru [– – – – – –] humble term for *to receive ; eat*

In a familiar polite imperative sentence such as **Mizu o chōdai, it** means *please give me.*

oide [– – –] honorific term for *to go, come, be*

chikai uchi ni [–'– – – –] *before long*

ukagawasete [– – – – – –] from **ukagawaseru**, *to cause to visit*

itadakimasu [– – – – – –] from **itadaku**, *to receive* (*a favor*)

Grammar

Honorific and Humble Words

235. The Japanese, like Chinese and other Oriental peoples, make frequent use of honorific and humble expressions in order to distinguish in their speech the actions and things of the first person from those of the second or the third person. In speaking to a superior, honorific forms are used about the superior's action while plain forms are employed when speaking to an equal or an inferior.

Besides these forms there are honorific words which are used in speaking of a superior and humble words which are used in speaking of oneself or of an inferior.

There is also another group of words which might be called polite words which are used in making a sentence polite regardless of whether one may be speaking of a person or a thing.

Therefore, the words may have four categories, i.e. plain, polite, humble, and honorific. Speaking broadly, humble words are used for the first person or a person who is under him, honorific words for the second person or his people, and plain words for the third person. This differenece helps greatly to reduce the repetition of personal pronouns.

1. Honorific forms and words are used:

(a) About actions or things of the second person of higher social standing than the speaker or those related to the second person.

(b) About actions or things of a third person of higher social standing than the speaker or those related to the third person. However, when one speaks of a third person impersonally and objectively such as in the case of one speaking about the action of cabinet ministers, this may or may not apply. Characters in history are spoken of without the honorifics unless they are in some way related to the addressee.

(c) About the members of the Imperial family or things related to them.

(d) By women of higher social standing.

2. Humble forms and words are used:

(a) About the actions or things of the first person when speaking to his superior.

(b) When shopkeepers and tradesmen, workmen, etc. speaking to their customers.

(c) By students in addressing their teachers.

236. The following lists will give an idea of the common, polite, honorific, and humble verbs.

Plain	Polite	Honorific	Humble
aru (*be*)	**gozaru**	**irassharu**	—
au (*meet*)	—	**oai ni naru**	**oai suru;** **ome ni kakaru**
iku (*go*)	**mairu**	**irassharu**	**agaru; ukagau**
iru (*be; stay*)	**oru**	**irassharu**	—
iu (*say*)	**mōsu**	**ossharu**	**mōshiageru**
kariru (*borrow*)	—	**okari ni naru**	**okari suru;** **haishaku suru**
kasu (*lend*)	—	**okashi ni naru**	**okashi suru;** **goyōdateru**
kiru (*wear*)	—	**omeshi ni naru**	—
kiku (*hear*)	—	**okiki ni naru**	**okiki suru;** **uakgau;** **uketamawaru**
kureru (*give*)	—	**kudasaru**	—
kuru (*come*)	**mairu**	**irassharu**	**agaru; ukagau**
kuu (*eat*)	**taberu**	**(meshi)agaru**	**itadaku**
miru (*see*)	—	**goran ni naru**	**haiken suru**
miseru (*show*)	—	**omise ni naru**	**omise suru;** **ome ni kakeru**
morau (*receive*)	—	**omorai ni naru**	**itadaku;** **chōdai suru**
omou (*think*)	**zonjiru**	**oboshimesu**	—

shiru (*know*)	**zonjiru**	**oshiri ni naru**	—
suru (*do*)	**itasu**	**nasaru; asobasu**	—
yaru (*give*)	—	**oyari ni naru**	**(sashi)ageru**
yobu (*call*)	—	**oyobi ni naru; mesu**	**oyobi suru**

About the Use of the Plain Style

237. You have already learned about the polite and plain or non-polite styles. However, you have not actually used the plain style yet, because what you have been studying is the normal polite style of the standard Japanese used by educated people in speaking to strangers, acquaintances as well as to superiors. It can be used both by men and women. The style of speech treated in Lesson 30 is more or less the style used by women in the Tokyo area in their formal conversation. Women in the country use less polite forms. Therefore, the style in this Practical Japanese is about the middle between the plain, intimate and ceremonious styles.

In this normal polite style, the ending of a sentence must be in the polite style, but the verbs, adjectives and copulas in the middle of a sentence may be in the plain style.

The plain style is that which employs the plain forms at the end of a sentence such as:

Sō da.	*That's right.*
Nan da?	*What is it?*
Dame da.	*It's no good.*

But you are strictly warned not to fall into the temptation of using these sentences yet, because the wrong use of them may cause unnecessary friction by making the hearer feel insulted.

The plain style is used among brothers, close friends, classmates, or when speaking to social inferiors such as tradesmen, workers, and people who are much younger. However, it is better to speak in the polite style even when you feel their social standing is lower, because they feel honored if you speak to them with respect.

"Bakari" — "Only"

238.   **Gobusata bakari itashite orimasu.**

I did nothing but neglecting to call on you. (=*I haven't been to see you for a long time.*)

Bakari means *nothing but* or *just.* It is used after a noun with or without a particle, a verb, or a **te**-form.

Shiranai hito bakari desu.	*They are all strangers.*
Kanji bakari (o) kaite kudasai.	*Please write only characters.*
Benkyō suru bakari deshita.	*He was only studying.*
Asonde bakari imasu.	*He is just loafing.*

"Taishita Koto wa Gozaimasen."

239. **Kaze o hikimashita no desu kara taishita koto wa gozai-masen.**

> *As he only caught a cold, it's not serious.*

Watakushi no uchi wa koko kara aruite gofun desu kara, taishita koto wa arimasen.

> *Since my home is five minutes' walk from here, it is not very far.*

One may feel that it is more logical to say **taishita koto ja arimasen.** In fact, this is often used as,

Kono byōki wa taishita koto ja arimasen.

This sickness is nothing serious.

Sonna koto wa taishita koto ja arimasen.

Such a thing is not very important.

Taishita koto wa arimasen literally means "*There isn't any serious question (about it).*" and the whole sentence means "*It's easy, trifling, a cinch, no trouble, nothing remarkable, etc.*"

It is a difference of viewpoint.

Hyakuen no chigai desu kara taishita koto ja arimasen.

> *Since it is a difference of 100 yen, it isn't anything serious* (=not worth making a fuss).

Hyakuen no chigai desu kara taishita koto wa arimasen.

> *Since it is a difference of 100 yen, it isn't very important* (=the difference is very small).

"Shibaraku" — "for Some Time"

240. **Shibaraku** means either *a short time* or *a long time.* The context

— *313* —

decides which the word means.

Shibaraku deshita nē. Ogenki desu ka?

It's a long time since I saw you last. How are you?

Shibaraku omachi kudasai; sugu mairimasu kara.

Wait a little while, please; as he is coming very soon.

Another Honorific Form of Verbs

241. In addition to what was mentioned in Lesson 25, Grammar 206, there is another general form of making a verb honorific. It is to use the construction patterns

(a) **o** x [second base of a verb] x **ni naru** or

(b) **o** x [second base of a verb] x **nasaru**

(a) **Suzuki San ni oai ni narimashitara, yoroshiku osshatte kudasai.**

When you see Mr. Suzuki, please give my best regards.

Nan de okaki ni narimashita ka?

What did you write with?

(b) **Nippongo de ohanashi nasaimasu ka?**

Will you speak in Japanese?

Mado o oshime nasaru hō ga yoroshū gozaimasu.

You'd better shut the window.

In fact the polite imperative form using **nasai** at the end of a sentence is nothing other than the imperative form of this construction pattern.

Otachi nasai.	*Stand up, please.*
Koko e oide nasai.	*Come here, please.*
Heya no naka e ohairi nasai.	*Go into the room, please.*

242. If the verb to be used is a Chinese compound with **suru** such as **benkyō suru, sampo suru,** etc., the following construction patterns are used.

(a) **go** x [Chinese verb without **suru**] x **ni naru**

(b) **(go)** x [Chinese verb without **suru**] x **nasaru**

In the case of (b) the honorific **go** may be omitted.

(a) **Kyō wa gosampo ni narimasu ka?**

Will you go out for a walk today?

Doko de gobenkyō ni narimashita ka?

Where did you study?

— *314* —

(b) **Okāsan ga (go)shimpai nasaru deshō.**

Your mother will be worried.

Anata ga (go)unten nasaimasu ka?

Will you drive?

In the case of such a short honorific word as **goran** in which **go** is a part of the word, **go** cannot be omitted.

Kore o goran nasai.   *Look at this.*

"......no Tokoro" — "When......"

243. As you learned in Lesson 15, Grammar 114, **tokoro** meaning *a place* or *a scene*, has a derivative meaning of *about to* or *just*.

Suzuki San no tokoro e agaru tokoro desu.

I'm going to call on Mr. Suzuki. (Lit. *I am in the scene of going to Mr. Suzuki's place.*)

Kono hon o yonda tokoro desu.

I have just read through this book. (Lit. *I am in the scene of having read this book.*)

Nippongo o benkyō shite iru tokoro desu.

I am just studying Japanese. (Lit. *I am in the scene of studying Japanese.*)

It may not be hard to understand the use of **tokoro** in the following sentences.

Goyō ga oari no tokoro o taihen ojama itashimashita.

I'm afraid I have taken up a lot of your time when you have so much work.

Hon o yonde iru tokoro e tomodachi ga tazunete kimashita.

When I was reading a book, a friend came to visit me.

This **tokoro** usually comes after a verb and is followed by the particles **e** or **o**, which is determined by the main verb. If one comes or goes to a place or a scene, **e** is usually used.

"Te-form" plus "Irassharu" — "Do Something before One Goes"

244.   **Mō sukoshi asonde irasshatte kudasai.**

Please stay a little longer.

Irassharu here means *to go*. The sentence means *Enjoy yourself a little more before you leave.*

> **Gohan o agatte irasshatte kudasai.**
>> *Please have lunch with us.* (Lit. *Have a meal before you go.*)

Causative used in Polite Speech

245.   **Mata ojama ni ukagawasete itadakimasu.**

The literal translation of the above sentence is:

> *I'll have you cause me to come to disturb you again.*

As you can see from the above, to frame a sentence in such an indirect way so as to show that it is not due to my wish but your command that I call on you, is a mark of great respect. This practice is popular among women who are polite in their speech or when shopkeepers courteous to their customers.

> **Ojama sasete itadakimasu.**
>> *Pardon me for intruding.* (= *I'll stay here awhile, if I may.*)
>
> **Chotto denwa o kakesasete itadakimasu.**
>> *Please let me use your telephone.*

Mijikai Kaiwa

meshiagatte [------] from **meshiagaru**, *to eat* (very polite)

mashi ['-] *please:* polite ending, not so formal as **mase** (See Lesson 25.)

Itadakimasu. [------] an expression used before eating

Gochisōsama (deshita). [------] an expression used when one finishes eating: **gochisō** means *a feast*, **sama** adds politeness.

osomatsu [-'--] **o**, honorific and **somatsu** (*a-B*), *course, rough*. **Osomatsusama** is an expression used by the host or hostess to the guest.

Exercises

A. *Fill in each blank with an appropriate word.*

1. Watakushi wa Suzuki San ___ shibaraku ome ___ kakarimasen ga, **oai** ni ___ yoroshiku ___ kudasaimasen ka ?

2. Mō ohiru ___ kara nani mo ___ ga, gohan o agatte ___ kudasai.

3. Goyō ga oari ___ tokoro ___ taihen ojama ___.

4. Chikai uchi ____ mata ojama ____ ukagawasete itadakimasu.

B. Give the corresponding polite expressions.
1. Sō desu.
2. Suzuki San ni aimasu.
3. Kono tsugi ni moraimasu.
4. Ii ja nai desu ka?
5. Nani mo arimasen.
6. Chittomo shirimasen deshita.
7. Mō kaerimashō.
8. Yōji ga aru deshō.
9. Gohan o tabete itte kudasai.
10. Yoroshiku itte kudasai.

C. There are set Japanese expressions that express the following ideas. Give them from your memory.
1. I'll say good-bye now.
2. Don't hurry away (Lit. Isn't it all right to stay?)
3. Please stay a bit longer.
4. Is your family quite well? (Lit. Isn't there any change in your family?)
5. Would you mind remembering me to Mr. Kaneko?
6. I haven't anything particular to offer you, but please have dinner.
7. I'll get it next time I come.
8. Before long I'll be calling on you.
9. What's the matter with you?
10. I have neglected to call on you for such a long time.
11. Glad to see you.
12. We are all fine, thank you.

D. Turn the following into polite forms, making necessary changes.
Example : Nan de **kakimashita** ka ?
Nan de **okaki ni narimashita** ka ?
1. Suzuki San ni attara dōzo yoroshiku.
2. Kyō wa sampo shimasen ka ?
3. Kinō Shinagawa made ikimashita ka ?

4. Rokuji made ni kite kudasai.

5. Kono kotoba wa oboeru hō ga ii desu.

E. *What is the Japanese equivalent of each of the following sentences?*

1. Shall I offer you tea or coffee ?

2. Saying that he had some business to attend to do on the way, he left the office early.

3. I was a little sick, but I am nearly all right now.

4. As it's only a slight stomach-ache, it's not serious.

5. Since my father has caught a cold, I'm going to call on Mr. Suzuki for him today.

Review (Lessons 23—30)

Vocabulary Check-Up:

A. *Do you recognize all the words charted? Put down the meaning in brackets.*

1	shōbai ( )	daitōryō ( )	bengoshi ( )	isha ( )	untenshu ( )	daiku ( )	hyakushō ( )
2	somatsu ( )	yūmei ( )	bimbō ( )	zannen ( )	taihen ( )	hijōni ( )	zuibun ( )
3	tsugō ( )	yōji ( )	goyō ( )	yakusoku ( )	rusu ( )	shōkai ( )	sewa ( )
4	mise ( )	kaisha ( )	jimusho ( )	gekijō ( )	Kabukiza ( )	ongakukai ( )	katei ( )
5	gochisō ( )	ryōri ( )	shokuji ( )	okashi ( )	zairyō ( )	gyūnyū ( )	ocha ( )
6	sugu ni ( )	aruhi ( )	kondo ( )	tsugi ( )	konogoro ( )	shibaraku ( )	tokidoki ( )

B. *Here are a few suffixes, i.e. words which are tacked on to other words. Put these suffixes to suitable words.*

____gawa,   ____me,   ____yuki (*or* iki),   ____yasui,   ____nikui, ____sō (appear)   ____nagara

C. Fill in each blank with an appropriate word.

Example: jibiki o **hiku** (to look up in a dictionary)

1.	dempō o _____	(to send a telegram)
2.	isha ni _____	(to consult a doctor)
3.	atama ga _____	(to have a headache)
4.	nodo ga _____	(to have a sore throat)
	_____	(to become thirsty)
5.	onaka ga _____	(to have a stomach-ache)
	_____	(to become hungry)
6.	denwa o _____	(to telephone)
7.	denwa ga _____	(to be called by telephone)
8.	ome ni _____	(to see a person)
9.	airon o _____	(to iron)
10.	kaze o _____	(to catch a cold)
11.	sewa o _____	(to take care)
12.	teate o _____	(to be treated)

D. Give the meaning and various forms of the following verbs.

Dictionary Form	Meaning	Desiderative	Passive	Causative
(Example) kaesu	*to return*	kaeshitai	kaesareru	kaesaseru
kasu				
matsu				
yatou				
shiru				
erabu				
katsu				
utsu				
narau				
iku				
tetsudau				
tsukamaeru				
makeru				
tsutomeru				
kuru				

E. (1) *A Conversation:*

Check if you understand the following conversation between Mr. Brown and Haru, his maid.

Haru: Oyobi desu ka?

Brown: Ee, kore wa Doitsu no tomodachi ga okutte kureta kozutsumi ni hatte atta kitte desu. Ashita Katō San ga kitara wasurenaide agete kudasai. Mae ni tanomareta mono desu.

Haru: Kashikomarimashita. Katō San wa nanji ni irassharu hazu desu ka?

Brown: Tegami ni yoru to ashita no asa irassharu rashii desu. Keredomo watakushi wa gozenchū wa rusu desu kara, kono kitte o agete, soshite dekireba gogo ni irassharu yō ni itte kudasai.

Haru: Gogo wa ouchi desu ka?

Brown: Gozenchū wa kaisha desu ga, gogo wa uchi desu.

Haru: Ashita wa nanji ni odekake desu ka?

Brown: Hachiji mae ni dekakeru tsumori desu.

Haru: Dewa shichiji goro ooki ni nareba yoroshū gozaimasu ne.

Brown: Iie, motto hayaku okitai desu; rokuji goro ni....... Sorekara kaimono ni iku tochū de daiku-san no tokoro e yotte, ashita no asa wa tsugō ga warui kara konai yō ni itte kudasai.

Haru: Dewa itsu kite moraimashō ka?

Brown: Isu o naoshitari chiisai hako o koshiraete morattari shitai kara, niji sugi nara nanji demo kekkō desu to itte kudasai.

(2) *You are supposed to know all of the following words and constructions. See if you understand all.*

Watakushi wa Marunouchi no aru ginkō ni tsutomete imasu. Maiasa rokujihan goro okite kao o aratte ha o migaite asahan o shichiji goro tabete, hachiji sukoshi mae ni uchi o demasu.

Densha no teiryūjō wa uchi no chikaku desu kara taihen benri de, aruite gofun gurai desu. Basu no hō ga sukoshi hayai desu kara tokidoki basu de ikimasu keredomo densha no hō ga yasui kara taitei densha de ikimasu.

Taitei kuji sukoshi mae ni ginkō ni tsukimasu. Soshite ocha o nonde kara hatarakimasu.

Jūniji kara ichiji made yasumimasu. Hiruhan no ato de taitei sampo o shitari kinjo no mise de kaimono o shitari shimasu. Kinō wa nekutai o ippon kaimashita.

Ichiji kara hataraite goji ni uchi e kaerimasu. Yūhan wa taitei rokuji goro desu. Yūhan no ato de hon o yominagara rajio o kikimasu ga, tokidoki eiga o mi ni dekaketari tomodachi o tazunetari shimasu.

Watakushi wa taitei jūjihan goro yasumimasu.

(3) *Sentence Patterns:*

All of the following sentences are picked up from among the sentences " For Memorizing " and from " A Short Conversation " so you should be able to give Japanese equivalents. Try to give the equivalents quickly and fluently.

Lesson 23

  1. Japanese pronunciation is much easier than that of English.
  2. It isn't good if we don't study hard.
  3. What is meant by a streetcar- or bus-stop ?
  4. May I take it away ?

Lesson 24

  5. I ate my breakfast while reading newspapers.
  6. He was supposed to call on me in the afternoon.
  7. I understand that this friend will come back to Japan again the year after next.
  8. During the morning it was cloudy and looked like rain.

Lesson 25 (*The equivalents should be in polite forms.*)

  9. It's terribly hot, isn't it ? (Use **gozaimasu**.)
  10. At what time will you go out this morning ?
  11. If anyone should come during my absence, please tell him that I won't be back before seven o'clock.
  12. There may be a telephone call from Mr. Suzuki.
  13. Please buy some (and keep it for me).
  14. Please don't wait for me.

Lesson 26

  15. Excuse me, but I'd like to ask a favor of you.
  16. I wonder if you can introduce me. (Use **itadakeru**.)
  17. I'll introdnce you any time you wish.
  18. I'll draw a map for you.
  19. Thank you for your trouble.

20. He worked for other people. (Lit. He was employed by other people and worked.)
21. Lincoln was elected President of the United States in 1860.
22. He was spoken ill of by some people.
23. Lincoln was shot in the head with a pistol.
24. What's the matter?
25. Please don't touch this.

Lesson 28

26. I've never seen a Japanese play.
27. I wanted to go, but I couldn't because I had a visitor.
28. According to Mr. Yamada, it wasn't so good.
29. According to the newspapers, Miss Kato's singing was excellent.
30. Well, I must be leaving.
31. Oh, stay a little longer. Don't hurry away.

Lesson 29

32. Her parents are saying that they want to have her work until she is about twenty years old.
33. It became possible to let her go shopping.
34. When she is busy, she telephones (to the shop) and let them bring it.
35. Did you call me?
36. I'm sorry to have kept you waiting.

Lesson 30

37. Please help yourself.
38. Thank you, I will.
39. I've had enough, thank you.
40. I apologize for our humble meal.

A Japanese-English Word List

bengoshi	an attorney; lawyer	27
benjo	a toilet	20
benkyō suru (*v. i.* & *v. t.*)	to study	8
benri(na) (*a-B*)	convenient	20
biiru	beer	22
bimbō(na) (*a-B*)	poor (not rich)	27
bin	a bottle	14
biwa	a loquat	22
-bon	=-hon	13
bōshi	a hat; cap	3
bunshō	a sentence	21
butaniku	pork	22
byōin	a hospital	18
byōki	illness; disease	12

C

chabudai	a low dining table	20
chairo (no)	brown	5
chanoma	a Japanese living- & dining-room	20
chichi	a father	19
chiisai (*a-A*)	small; little	2
chiisana	small; little	20
chikai (*a-A*)	near	18
~ uchi ni	before long	30
chikaku (de)	near	15
chittomo	(not)...at all	21
chizu	a map	26
chōdai suru (*v. t.*)	to receive; eat (humble)	30
chōdo	just; exactly	11
chōjo	the eldest daughter	19
chokki	a vest; waistcoat	3
chōmen	a notebook	8
chōnan	the eldest son	19
chotto	just; a short time	8
-chū	during; in the midst of	11
chūmon suru (*v.t.*)	to order	22

D

da	(plain form of **desu**)	10
dai	a stand	5
-dai	(classifier for vehicles)	15
daidokoro	a kitchen	20

daiku	a carpenter	25
daisuki(na) (*a-B*)	very fond of	22
daitōryō	a president (of a state)	27
dake	only	1
dame (*a-B*)	no good	23
dandan	gradually	27
dare	who	15
dare ka	someone; anyone	25
-dari	=-tari	17
dasu (*v. t.*)	to take out	8
	to send (a parcel, etc.); mail	18
	to send (to a laundry)	25
datta	(plain form of **de-shita**)	12
de	with (this much)	2
	in (language used)	5
	with; by (instrument or means)	6
	at; in (place)	15
de	in (time)	25
	is (are; am)... and; being... (continuative of **desu**)	4
dehairi	going in and out	20
deiriguchi	entrance	20
dekakeru (*v. i.*)	to go out; leave	12
dekiru (*v. i.*)	to be able to; can	8
	to be completed; be finished; be ready	12
	to come up (urgent business, etc.)	28
demo	even	16
dempō	a telegram	24
~o utsu	to send a telegram	24
densha	a streetcar; electric train	13
dentō	an electric light	21
denwa	a telephone	21
~o kakeru	to telephone	25
~ga kakaru	to have a phone call	25
derareru	to be able to go out	28
deru (*v. i.*)	to come (go) out	8
	to leave: start	16
deshita	(past form of **desu**)	8

		Lesson
deshō	(probable form of desu)	14
desu	is; are; am	1
desukara	therefore	11
dewa	well; well then; then	3
dewa	in; at (particle showing a place of action)	16
-do	...times	11
dō	copper	14
dō	how; in what way	16
Dō itashimashite.	Don't mention it; you're welcome.	1
~ iu	what...	23
doa	a door	1
dochira	where; what place (polite)	20
Doitsujin	a German	3
dōka	a copper coin	14
doko	where; what place	4
~-yuki(-iki)	where...bound for	24
dōmo	indeed; really	10
donata	who (polite)	3
~ no	whose (polite)	3
donna	what sort (kind) of	5
dono gurai (=**dono kurai**)	how far (long, much, etc.)	15; 23
dore	which (of many)	14
dōshite	why	28
dotchi	which (of two)	9
	either	22
doyō(bi)	Saturday	10
dōzo	please	2

E

		Lesson
e	a picture	7
e	to; toward (particle showing direction)	8
ee	yes	2
eiga	movies	17
Eigo	English (language)	4
Eikoku	England; Great Britain; the United Kingdom	24
eki	a (railroad) station	15
empitsu	a pencil	1

		Lesson
en	yen	14
engawa	a Japanese verandah	20
entotsu	a chimney	15
erabu (*v. t.*)	to elect; select	27

F

		Lesson
fuku (*v. t.*)	to wipe	8
-fun	a minute	11
fune	a boat; ship	15
furoba	a bathroom	20
furu (*v. i.*)	to fall (rain, etc.)	9
furui	old (not new)	2
fusagu (*v. t.*)	to stop up	21
futari	two persons	15
futatsu	two	4
futsū (*ad.*)	usually; generally	12
~ no	ordinary; usual	18
futsuka	the 2nd of the month; two days	12
fuyu	winter	9

G

		Lesson
ga	(nominative particle)	4
...ga	but	7
gaikokujin	a foreigner	15
gaitō	an overcoat	3
gakkō	a school	10
garasu	glass (material)	14
gasshūkoku	the United States	27
-gawa	side	26
gekijō	a theater	27
genkan	a front entrance	20
genki(na) (*a-B*)	healthy; well; peppy	1
getsuyō(bi)	Monday	10
gin	silver	14
ginka	a silver coin	14
ginkō	a bank	19
go	five	5
(go)aisatsu	greetings	30
gobusata	neglecting to write or call; silence	30
Gochisōsama (deshita).	Thank you for your delicious food.	30
gofujō	=**benjo**, a toilet	20

		Lesson
gogatsu	May	9
gogo	afternoon; p. m.	11
gohan	meal; cooked rice	6
gojū	fifty	14
Gokurōsama (deshita).	Thanks for your trouble.	26
gomen (nasai)	pardon (me); excuse (me)	7
goran	(honorific imperative for miru, to see)	4
~ ni naru	to see (honorific)	28
goro	about; around (approximate point of time)	16
go'roppun	five or six minutes	18
(go)shimpai	worry	30
(go)shujin	a master; husband	19
(go)shōkai suru (v. t.)	to introduce	26
(go)yō	business (honorific)	26
(go)yukkuri	slowly	28
Dōzo ~.	Please take your time.	28
gozaimashita	(past form of gozaimasu)	1
gozaimasu	(polite term for desu)	1
gozen	forenoon; a. m.	11
~chū	in the morning	25
gozonji	(polite term for shiru, to know)	26
gurai (= kurai)	as...as	14
	about; approximately	23
gyūniku	beef	22
gyūnyū	cow's milk	29

H

ha	a leaf	5
ha	a tooth	17
haba	width; breadth	13
hachi	eight	8
hachigatsu	August	9
hachijū	eighty	14
hagaki	a postcard	1; 18
haha	a mother	19
hai	yes	1
hairu (v. i.)	to enter; come (go) in	8
hajime (no)	the beginning; first	9
hajimeru (v. t)	to begin; start	1
Hajimemashite.	How do you do?	3

		Lesson
hakkiri	clearly	3
hako	a box	1
haku (--) (v. t.)	to put on; wear (shoes, trousers, etc.)	7
haku ('-) (v. t.)	to sweep	29
hambun	a half	14
-han	half; thirty minutes	11
hana (-')	flower; blossom	5
hana (--)	nose	6
hanami	flower-viewing	16
hanaseru	to be able to speak	23
hanashi	a story; talk	28
...no ~ dewa	according to what ...told me about	28
hanasu (v. t.)	to speak; talk; tell	6
hanga	a woodcut print	26
hantai (no)	opposite; contrary	26
hareru (v. i.)	to clear up (of weather)	24
hari	a hand (of a clock or watch); needle	11
haru ('-)	spring (season)	9
haru (--) (v. t.)	to paste on; stick	14
hasami	scissors	1
hatachi	twenty years of age	29
hataraku (v. i.)	to work	7
hatsuka	the 20th of the month; twenty days	12
hatsuon	pronunciation	23
hayaku	quickly	8
hazu	supposed to; expected to	24
henji	an answer; reply	24
heta(na) (a-B)	poor at	5
heya	a room	1
hi	a day	10
	the sun	11
hidari	left (not right)	7
hidoi (a-A)	serious (illness); hard	17
higashi	the east	11
hige	moustache; beard	17
hijō ni	exceedingly; very	27
hikōki	an airplane	7
hiku (v. t.)	to look up in (a dictionary)	21
hiku (v. t.)	to catch (cold)	28

		Lesson
hikui (*a-A*)	low	2
hima(na) (*a-B*)	time to spare ; leisure	11
hiroi (*a-A*)	wide	13
hiru	noon	17
hiruhan	a lunch ; noon meal	17
hiruma	daytime	11
hirusugi	afternoon	24
hito	a person	7
hitobito	people	16
hitomawari	one round	11
hitori	one person ; alone	15
～ de	by oneself ; alone	24
hitotsu	one	4
hō	direction ; side	7
...no ～ ga (ōkii)	...is (larger)	9
...～ ga ii	to be better ; had better	16
hodo	(not) so...as ; as...as	14
	about ; nearly ; approximately	27
hoka (no)	other ; another	22
sono ～	besides ; in addition	6
hokori	dust	24
hon	a book	1
-hon	(classifier for long, cylindrical object)	11
hōrensō	spinach	22
hoshii (*a-A*)	desirous of having ; want (to have)	22
hosu (*v. t.*)	to air	23
hoteru	a hotel	26
hotondo	almost ; hardly (with negative)	17
hyaku	a hundred	14
hyakushō	a farmer ; peasant	29

I

ichi	one	1
ichiban	the most ; No. 1	14
ichido	once	17
ichigatsu	January	9
ichijikan	one hour	11
ichijitsu	1st of the month	12
ichiman	ten thousand	14
ichinen	one year	9
ichinichi	one day	11

		Lesson
ie	a house	15
Igirisujin	an Englishman ; Britisher	3
ii (*a-A*)	good ; nice ; fine	2
iie	no	1
ikaga	how (about)	1
ikareru	to be able to go	28
ikaseru	to cause to go	29
ikenai	no good	16
ikeru	to be able to go	28
-iki	bound for	24
ikkagetsu	one month	9
ikkai	the first floor	20
iku (*v. i.*)	to go	8
iku-	how many ; how much	13
～mai	how many sheets	13
～nichi	how many days	18
～nin	how many people	15
ikura	how much	14
ikutsu	how many	4
ima	now ; at present	7
imi	meaning	21
imōto	a younger sister	19
inaka	the country ; rural district	19
inki	ink	14
inu	a dog	6
ippon	one long, cylindrical object	13
irassharu	(polite term for to come, go, be)	25
ireru (*v. t.*)	to put in	14
	to include	15
iro	color	5
iroiro (no)	various ; various kinds of	5
iru (*v. i.*)	to need ; be needed	6
iru (*v. i.*)	to be (of an animate object)	12
(-te) iru	(construction to express an action in progress or a state)	7
isha	a doctor ; physician	17
isogashii (*a-A*)	busy ; engaged	11
isogu (*v. i.*)	to hurry	12
issatsu	one volume (of book)	13

kobosu (*v. t.*)	to spill	8
kochira	here; this way (polite)	19
kodomo	a child	7
kōen	a park	24
kōhii	coffee	6
koko	here; this place	4
kokonotsu	nine	4
kokonoka	9th of the month; nine days	12
kōkūbin	airmail	18
komban	this evening; tonight	3; 12
Komban wa.	Good evening.	3
kondo (wa)	this time	26
kongetsu	this month	9
konnichi	today	2
Konnichi wa.	Good day; good afternoon.	2
kono	this	2
konoaida	the other day	24
konogoro	these days; lately	29
kono hen	near here; around here	26
koppu	a glass	14
kore	this; this thing	1
kore kara	from now on; now	25
kosaseru	to cause to come	29
motte ～	to let someone bring	29
koshikakeru (*v. i.*)	to sit down (on a chair, etc.)	7
koshiraeru (*v. t.*)	to make; manufacture	14
koso	(particle for emphasis meaning the very)	3
koto	a fact; thing (abstract)	16
...～ ga dekiru	to be able to do	16
...～ ga (mo) aru	sometimes...	17
-ta ～ ga aru	have ever done such and such	28
kotoba	a word; language	21
kotoshi	this year	16
kozutsumi	parcel post; package	18
ku	nine	9
kuchi	a mouth	6

kudamono	fruit	22
kudamonoya	a fruit-shop	22
kudasai	please give me	4
(-te) kudasai	please do me a favor of ...ing	2
kugatsu	September	9
kumoru (*v. i.*)	to be (become) cloudy	16
kurai (*a-A*)	dark	11
kurai (=gurai)	as...as	14
	about; approximately	23
(-te) kureru	to do something for an inferior	26
kuroi (*a-A*)	black	2
kuru (*v. i.*)	to come	8
(-te) kuru	to do (something) and come back	17
	to become...	24
kuruma	a vehicle; car	26
kusa	grass	5
kusuri	a medicine; drug	17
kusuriya	a drugstore; druggist	17
kutsu	shoes; boots	3
kutsushita	stockings; socks	3
kyabetsu	cabbage	22
kyakuma	a parlor; guest-room	20
kyō	today	1
kyōdai	brothers and sisters	19
kyōkai	a church	18
kyonen	last year	16
kyū	nine	13

M

mā	well; oh!	28
machi	a town	19
machigai	a mistake; error	5
machigau (*v. i.*)	to make a mistake	23
mada (...nai)	(not) yet	7
made	to; as far as; until	3
mado	a window	1
mae	before	10
...no ～	in front of	15
magaru (*v. i.*)	to turn; bend	15
mago	a grandchild	19
mai-	every...	12
-mai	(classifier for flat	

moshimoshi	hello ; excuse me	21
motsu (*v. t.*)	to hold ; have	17
motte iku	to bring	17
	to take away	23
motte kuru	to bring	17
motto	more	14
muika	6th of the month ;	
	six days	12
mukō	the other side	
	(person, party)	15
murasaki (no)	purple	5
musuko	a son	19
musume	a daughter	19
	a girl	29
muttsu	six	4
mużukashii (*a-A*)	difficult	7
myōban	tomorrow evening	12
myōji	a surname	19

N

n	(contraction of **no**)	28
nado	and so forth ; etc.	20
nagai (*a-A*)	long	11
-nagara	while ...ing	24
nagasa	length	13
nagashi	a sink	20
-nai	(adverbial auxiliary	
	to form the plain	
	negative of a verb)	16
-naide	not... ; and... ;	
	without ...ing	17
naka	in ; inside	4
	among	14
nakereba (...nai)	if... (there is) not ;	
	unless	21
-~ naranai	must ; should	21
(...de)~(...nai)	if it isn't ; unless	25
nakunaru (*v. i.*)	to die ; pass away	
	(polite term for	
	shinu)	19
	to run short ; run out	25
-nakute mo ii	need not	22
namae	a name	8
namboku	the north and south	27
Namboku-sensō	American Civil War	27
nan	what	1

~ no	what...	13
~ demo	anything ; everything	22
nan-	what...	11
nanajū	seventy	14
nanatsu	seven	4
nangatsu	what month of the	
	year	9
nani	what	4
nani-	what...	10
nani ka	something ; anything	22
nani mo	nothing	4
naniyō(bi)	what day of the week	10
nanji	what time (o'clock)	11
nankagetsu	how many months	9
nannichi	what day of the	
	month ; how many	
	days	12
nanoka	7th of the month ;	
	seven days	12
nanuka	= nanoka	12
naoru (*v. i.*)	to be healed ; be cured	30
naosu (*v. t.*)	to correct	5
	to repair ; mend	25
...nara	if it is	18
naraberu (*v. t.*)	to arrange ; display	24
narau (*v. t.*)	to learn	7
narawaseru	to cause to learn	29
(...ni) nareru (*v. i.*)	to get accustomed	
	to	29
(...ni) naru (*v.i.*)	to become...	9
	(polite term for **suru**)	28
...nasai	(polite imperative	
	term for **suru**)	3
nasaru	(polite term for **suru**)	30
nashi	a pear	22
natsu	summer	9
naze	why	10
ne	isn't it ; you see	9
nē	isn't it ; you see	2
nedan	price	25
(...ni) negau (*v. t.*)	to request ; ask	18
neko	a cat	6
nekutai	a necktie	3
-nen	year(s) (classifier for	
	years)	9
nēsan	an elder sister	

～ ni hairu	to take a bath	17
ohairi	(honorific term of hairu, to enter)	7
Ohayō (gozaimasu). Good morning.		1
oi	a nephew	19
oide	(honorific term for iru, to be	19
	(honorific term for kuru, to come)	30
oishii (a-A)	delicious; tasty	24
oishisō(na)(a-B)	delicious-looking	24
oiteku (v. t.)	(corruption of oite iku, to leave behind)	23
oitoma suru(v.i.)	to take leave (polite)	30
ojama suru (v.i.)	to disturb (a person); intrude (polite)	30
oji	an uncle	19
ojiisan	a grandfather (honorific)	19
okaeri	(honorific term of kaeru, to return)	25
Okagesama de.	I'm quite well, thank you.	2
okake	(honorific term of (koshi)kakeru, to sit down)	19
okane	money	14
okāsan	a mother (honorific)	19
okashi	cake; candy; cookies; sweets	24
okawari	(honorific term of kawaru, to change)	30
ōkii (a-A)	large; big	2
ōkina	large; big	20
okiru (v. i.)	to get up	17
okoru (v. i.)	to break out; happen	27
oku (v. t.)	to put; place	8
(-te) oku	to do something in advance	25
okuru (v. t.)	to send	27
okusan	a wife; Mrs; mistress of a house (honorific)	3
(o)kyaku	a guest; visitor (polite)	20
omachi	(honorific term of	

matsu, to wait)		21
omatase suru	to cause to wait (honorific)	29
ome ni kakaru	to meet (humble)	30
omoi (a-A)	heavy	2
omote	the front; surface	14
omou (v. t.)	to think	11
(...to) ～	to think that...	23
omowareru	to be thought of	27
onaji	same	5
onaka	stomach; abdomen (polite)	17
～ ga suku	to be (become) hungry	24
(o)negai	a request	26
ongakukai	a concert	28
onnanohito	a woman; female person	7
onnanoko	a girl; female child	19
oriru (v. i.)	to get off	24
oru	(polite term of iru, to be)	19
ōsetsuma	a parlor; drawing room	20
oshieru (v. t.)	to teach	7
oshimai	the end	2
osoi (a-A)	late	17
Osomatsusama (deshita). It was nothing at all. (after offering dinner, etc.)		30
ossharu	(honorific term for iu, to say, tell)	30
(o)taku	(your) house (polite)	18
	at home	19
(o)tenki	weather (polite)	2
oto	a sound; noise	6
otokonohito	a man; male person	7
otokonoko	a boy; male child	19
otōsan	a father (honorific)	19
otōto	a younger brother	19
ototoi	the day before yesterday	10
ototoshi	the year before last	19
(o)tsuri	change (of money)	14
owari	the last; end	9

oya	a parent; parents	19
Oyasumi nasai.	Good night.	3
oyobi	(honorific term of yobu, to call)	29
(o)yu	hot water	6

P

pan	bread	22
pan'ya	a baker; bakery	22
pen	a pen	1
pisutoru	a pistol	27
poketto	a pocket	26
-pon	=-hon	11
posuto	a mail-box	18
-pun	=-fun	11

R

rai-	next...	9
raigetsu	next month	9
rainen	next year	24
raishū	next week	12
rajio	the radio	17
rashii	to seem; appear	7;16
reizōko	a refrigerator; ice-box	20
ringo	an apple	4
rippa(na) (a-B)	fine; splendid	5
rōka	a corridor; passage	20
roku	six	6
rokugatsu	June	9
rōsoku	a candle	21
rusu	absence; not at home	19
ryōhō (no)	both	11
ryōri	a dish; food	24
	cooking	29

S

sā	now; well	1
saifu	a purse; wallet	14
sakana	a fish	6
sake	wine; liquor	22
saki	the end; ahead; beyond	20
sakki	a little while ago	8
saku (v. i.)	to bloom	16
sakuban	last evening; last night	12

sakura	a cherry-tree; cherry-blossoms	16
sampo suru (v. i.)	to take a walk	7
samui (a-A)	cold (weather)	4
san	three	3
San	Mr.; Mrs.; Miss	3
sangatsu	March	9
sanjū	thirty	12
~-ichi	thirty-one	12
sara	a dish; plate	22
sarainen	the year after next	24
saseru	to cause to do	29
sasou (v. t.)	to invite; ask someone to do something	28
sasu (v. t.)	to point	11
satō	sugar	22
satsu	a bank-note; paper money	14
-satsu	(classifier for books, magazines, etc.)	13
sawaru (v. i.)	to touch	27
sayō	so (polite)	25
Sayōnara.	Good-bye.	1
seito	a student; pupil	3
seki	a place; seat	8
semai (a-A)	narrow	13
semmenjo	a washroom	20
sen	a thousand	14
sen-	last...	9
sengetsu	last month	9
sensei	a teacher	3
senshū	last week	12
sensō	a war	27
sentaku	laundry; washing	25
sen'yaku	a previous engagement	28
setomonoya	a china-shop	22
sewa	cares	29
shashin	a picture; photograph	25
shi	four	4
shi	and also (connective particle)	12;17
shibai	a (theatrical) play	27
shibaraku	for a short while	30
shibun-no-ichi	one-fourth; a quarter	14
shichi	seven	7

		Lesson
shichijū	seventy	19
shichigatsu	July	9
shigatsu	April	9
shi'gofun	four or five minutes	18
shi'gohyaku	four or five hundred	23
shigoto	work; business	17
shika	only (with negative)	18
shikaku (no)	square	5
shikashi	but; however	16
shiku (v. t.)	to spread	20
shima	an island	15
shimbun	a newspaper	4
shimeru (v. t.)	to shut; close	8
shinamono	an article; goods	22
shindai	a bed	20
shinshitsu	a bed-room	20
shio	salt	22
shirareru (v. i.)	to be known	27
shiriai	an acquaintance	26
shiroi (a-A)	white	2
shiru (v. t.)	to know	9
shita	under; below; beneath	4
	younger	19
shitsurei (suru)	discourtesy; rudeness	19
Shitsurei shimasu.	Excuse me.	19
Shitsurei itashimashō.	I'll say good-bye.	28
shōbai	business; trade	27
shōchi suru (v. t.)	to agree; consent	5
shokudō	a dining-room; restaurant	17
shokuji	a meal	20
shokuryōhin'ya	a provisions store	22
shōnin	a merchant; tradesman	27
shū	a state (of U. S. A.)	27
-shūkan	a week; weeks (classifier for weeks)	10
sō	so	1
... ~ desu	I hear; they say	16
-sō	(classifier for boats)	15
-sō (a-B)	seeming...; looking like...	24
soba	side	4
~ ni	by the side of; beside	4
sōji	cleaning (of room,	

		Lesson
etc.)		29
soko	there	4
sokode	thereupon; so; then	24
sokutatsu	special delivery	18
sonna	such; like that	17
sono	that	2
~ hoka	besides; in addition	6
~ koro	at that time; around then	16
sora	sky	7
sore	that; that thing	1
sorede	therefore	30
soredewa	then; in that case	14
sorekara	and then; after that	17
soreni	besides	30
soru (v. t.)	to shave	17
soshite	and	16
soto	outside	8
sue	the end (of month)	16
sugi	past (o'clock)	11
-sugiru	too...; excessively...	14
sugu	at once; immediately	16
...to ~	as soon as...	17
~ ni	at once; immediately	21
suiyō(bi)	Wednesday	10
suki(na) (a-B)	liking; fond of	22
sukkari	completely; entirely	24
sukoshi	a little; small amount	6
suku (v. i.)	to become empty; become hungry	24
Sumimasen.	I'm sorry.	10
sumu (v. i.)	to live	19
sumu (v. i.)	to finish	24
suru (v. t.)	to do	6
(...ni) suru	to decide on...; make it...	28
suruto	then; thereupon	28
suwaru (v. i.)	to squat down; sit	20
suzushii (a-A)	cool	9

T

taberu (v. t.)	to eat	6
tabitabi	often; frequently	23
tabun	perhaps; probably	23
-tachi	(plural suffix for persons)	6

tsukeru (*v. t.*)	to light; put on	21
tsukeru (*v. t.*)	to apply (medicine)	27
tsuki	a month	9
tsuku (*v. i.*)	to arrive	16
tsukue	a desk	1
tsumbo (no)	deaf; a deaf person	21
tsumetai (*a-A*)	cold (not hot)	29
tsumori	intention	16
tsureru (*v. t.*)	to take along (a person, animal, etc.)	7
tsurete iku	to take (a person) to a place	26
(...ni) tsutomeru (*v. i.*)	to serve at; work in	19
tsutomesaseru	to cause to serve at	29
tsuzukeru (*v. t.*)	to continue	12
tsuzuku (*v. i.*)	to continue; last	27

U

uchi	a house; home	1
uchi	during	24
asa no ~	in the morning	24
hajime no ~	at the beginning	27
chikai ~ ni	shortly	30
ue	on; upon	4
	above	7
	older; elder	19
ueru (*v. t.*)	to plant	20
ukagau (*v. i.*)	(humble term for to visit)	30
ukagawasete itadaku	to receive a favor of a visit (most humble)	30
ukeru (*v. t.*)	to receive	27
umareru (*v. i.*)	to be born	19
umi	sea	15
untenshu	a driver	26
unten suru (*v. t.*)	to drive	15
ura	the back; rear	20
uru (*v. t.*)	to sell	22
ushi	a cow; ox	22
usui (*a-A*)	thin (not thick)	2
uta	a song	28
utsu (*v. t.*)	to send (a telegram)	24
	to shoot	27
uwagi	a coat	3

W

wa	(nominative particle)	1
waishatsu	a shirt; dress shirt	3
wakaru (*v. i.*)	to understand	7
wakeru (*v. t.*)	to divide	11
warui (*a-A*)	bad	2
wasureru (*v. t.*)	to forget	10
watakushi	I	1
~ no	my; mine	3
~tachi	we	6

Y

ya	and (when enumerating more than two nouns)	5
yaku	about; approximately	10
yakusoku	engagement; appointment	24
yama	a mountain	15
yaoya	a greengrocer	22
yaru (*v. t.*)	to send (a person)	22
yaru (*v. t.*)	to give (something to an inferior)	26
yaru (*v. t.*)	to do	27
(-te) yaru	(to do a favor for an inferior)	26
yasai	vegetables	22
yasashii (*a-A*)	easy	7
yasui (*a-A*)	cheap	2
-yasui (*a-A*)	easy to...	23
yasumi	a holiday	10
yasumu (*v. i.*)	to go to bed; sleep	3
	to rest	7
Oyasumi nasai.	Good night	3
yatou (*v. t.*)	to employ; hire	27
yattsu	eight	4
yo	(emphatic particle)	25
yō (na) (*a-B*)	to seem; look like	15
...~ ni (iu)	to (tell) someone to...	25
...~ ni naru	to become...	29
yobu (*v. t.*)	to call	17
yōfuku	a western suit	7
yogoreru (*v. i.*)	to get soiled	25
yoi (*a-A*)	=ii, good; nice	28

		Lesson
yōji	business	24
yōka	8th of the month; eight days	12
yōkan	a western-style house	15
yokka	4th of the month; four days	12
yoku	well	7
Yoku irasshaimashita.	Glad to see you (when welcoming a visitor)	30
yōma	a western-style room	20
yomeru	to be able to read	23
yomu (*v. t.*)	to read	6
yon	four	10
yonin	four persons	15
yonjū	forty	14
yori	than	9
yoroshii (*a-A*)	(polite term of **ii**, **yoi**)	12
(Dōzo) yoroshiku.	Pleased to meet you.	3
(...ni) yoroshiku	give my best regards to...	19
yoru	night	11
(...ni) yoru (*v.i.*)	to drop in; stop at	24
(...ni) yoru to	according to...	28
yosasō	seems to be good	25
yottsu	four	4

		Lesson
yūbinkyoku	a post office	18
yūbin'ya	a mailman	24
yūgata	evening; dusk	11
yūhan	evening meal; supper; dinner	17
yuka	floor	4
yuki	snow	9
-yuki	bound for	24
yukkuri	slowly	2
yūmei(na) (*a-B*)	famous	27

Z

		Lesson
-za	a theater	27
zairyō	material; raw materials	29
zannen(na) (*a-B*)	regrettable; mortifying	28
zasshi	a magazine	6
zehi	by all means	28
zonjiru (*v. t.*)	to know (polite)	30
zōri	Japanese sandals	7
zubon	trousers	3
zuibun	considerably; very (much)	25
-zutsu	each	19
zutto	by far	23

An English-Japanese Word List

— 348 —

		Lesson
living- & dining room	**chanoma**	20
lodge	**tomeru** (*v. t.*)	20
long	**nagai** (*a-A*)	11
look	**miru** (*v. t.*)	6
	...**yō** (**na**) (*a-B*)	15
~ing like	**-sō** (**na**) (*a-B*)	24
~ up (in)	**hiku** (*v. t.*) (diction-	
	ary)	21
loquat	**biwa**	22
low	**hikui** (*a-A*)	2
lunch	(**o**)**bentō**	17
	hiruhan	17

M

magazine	**zasshi**	6
maid	**jochū**	22
~'s room	**jochūbeya**	20
mail	**dasu** (*v. t.*)	18
~-box	**posuto**	18
mailman	**yūbin'ya**	24
make	**koshiraeru** (*v. t.*)	14
~ it...	(...**ni**) **suru**	28
male	**otoko no**	
~ person	**otokonohito**	7
~ child	**otokonoko**	19
man	**otokonohito**	7
mandarin orange	**mikan**	22
manufacture	**koshiraeru** (*v. t.*)	14
many	**takusan** (**no**)	6
map	**chizu**	26
March	**sangatsu**	9
marry	(**kekkon suru**)	
get married	(...**to**) **kekkon suru**	
	(*v. i.*)	19
master	**shujin**	19
mat	**tatami** (Japanese)	20
material	**zairyō**	29
May	**gogatsu**	9
may	**kamo shirenai**	15
	(-**te**) **mo ii**	22
	moshi ka suru to	25
meal	**gohan**	6
	shokuji	20
meaning	**imi**	21
means		

		Lesson
by all ~	**zehi**	28
meat	**niku**	22
medical treatment	**teate**	27
medicine	**kusuri**	17
meet	**au** (*v. i.*)	17
	oai ni naru	
	(honorific)	30
	ome ni kakaru	
	(humble)	30
Pleased to ~ you.	**Dōzo yoroshiku.**	3
mend	**naosu** (*v. t.*)	25
mention	**iu** (*v. t.*)	1
Don't ~ it.	**Dō itashimashite.**	1
merchant	**shōnin**	22
metal	**kane**	14
middle	**mannaka** (**no**)	7
mile	**mairu**	24
milk	**gyūnyū** (cow's)	29
mind	**ki o tsukeru** (*v. i.*)	17
	kamau (*v. t.*)	22
mine	**watakushi no**	3
minute	**fun**	11
Miss	**San**	3
mistake	**machigai**	5
make a ~	**machigau** (*v. i.*)	23
mistress	**okusan** (of a house)	3
Monday	**getsuyō**(**bi**)	10
money	(**o**)**kane**	14
month	**tsuki**	9
this ~	**kongetsu**	9
what ~	**nangatsu**	9
more	**mō**	13
	motto	14
morning	**asa**	11
in the ~	**asa no uchi**	24
	gozenchū	25
moritfying	**zannen**(**na**) (*a-B*)	28
most	**ichiban**...	14
mother	**haha**	19
	okāsan (honorific)	19
motorcar	**jidōsha**	15
mountain	**yama**	15
moustache	**hige**	17
mouth	**kuchi**	6
Mr.	**San** (**no goshujin**)	3
Mrs.	**San** (**no okusan**)	3

		Lesson			Lesson
Saturday	doyō(bi)	10		(v. i.)	19
say	iu (v. t.)	2	seven	nanatsu	4
	mōshiageru (v. t.)			shichi	7
	(humble)	30	~ days	nanoka; nanuka	12
	ossharu (v. t.)		seventeen	jūshichi	12
	(honorific)	30	seventh	shichibamme (no);	
they ~...	...sō desu	16		nanabamme (no) (10)	
scent	nioi	6	~ of the month	nanoka; nanuka	12
school	gakkō	10	seventy	nanajū	14
scissors	hasami	1		shichijū	19
sea	umi	15	shave	soru (v. t.)	17
seashore	kaigan	15	ship	fune	15
seat	seki	8	shirt	waishatsu	3
second	nibamme (no)	10	shoes	kutsu	3
~ of the month	futsuka	12	shoot	utsu (v. t.)	27
~ floor	nikai	20	shop	mise	22
see	miru (v. t.)	6	shopping	kaimono	17
	au (v. i.)	17	short	miijkai (a-A)	11
	goran ni naru		shortly	chikai uchi ni	30
	(honorific)	28	should	-nakereba naranai	21
	oai ni naru (honor-		show	miseru (v. t.)	26
	ific)	30	shut	shimeru (v. t.)	8
	ome ni kakaru			tojiru (v. t.)	21
	(humble)	30	sick	byōki (no)	12
be ~n	mieru (v. i.)	21	side	soba	4
you ~	nē	2		hō	7
	ne	9		-gawa	26
seem	rashii	7; 16	by the ~ of	soba ni	4
	...yō (na) (a-B)	15	the other ~	mukō	15
~ing...	-sō (na) (a-B)	24	silence	gobusata	30
~s to be good	yosasō (a-B)	25	silver	gin	14
select	erabu (v. t.)	27	~ coin	ginka	14
sell	uru (v. t.)	22	since	kara	10
send	dasu (v. t.) (mail)	18		node	24
	yaru (v. t.) (a per-		sink	nagashi	20
	son)	22	sister	ane (elder)	19
	utsu (v. t.) (a tele-			nēsan (elder) (ho-	
	gram)	24		norific)	19
	dasu (v. t.) (to laun-			imōto (younger)	19
	dry)	25	sit	suwaru (v. i.)	20
	okuru (v. t.)	27	~ down	koshikakeru (v. i.)	
sentence	bunshō	21		(chair)	7
September	kugatsu	9		okake ni naru	
serious	hidoi (a-A)	17		(honorific)	19
	taishita	30	six	muttsu	4
serve (at)	(...ni) tsutomeru			roku	6

		Lesson			Lesson
~ days	**muika**	12	spread	**shiku** (*v. t.*)	20
sixteen	**jūroku**	12	spring	**haru** (′-)	9
sixth	**rokubamme no**	10	square	**shikaku (no)**	5
~ of the month	**muika**	12	squat down	**suwaru** (*v. i.*)	20
skilful	**jōzu(na)** (*a-B*)	5	staircase	**kaidan**	20
skilfully	**jōzu ni**	23	stand	**dai**	5
skin	**kawa**	14		**tatsu** (*v. i.*)	7
sky	**sora**	7	starch	**nori**	25
sleep	**yasumu** (*v. i.*)	3	start	**hajimeru** (*v. t.*)	1
slowly	**yukkuri**	28		**deru** (*v. i.*)	16
small	**chiisai** (*a-A*)	2	state	**shū** (U. S. A.)	27
	chiisana	20	station	**eki** (railroad)	15
~ amount	**sukoshi**	6	stay behind	**nokoru** (*v. i.*)	17
smell	**nioi**	6	stick		
	kagu (*v. t.*)	6	~ on	**haru** (--) (*v. t.*)	14
smoke	**kemuri**	15	stockings	**kutsushita**	3
snow	**yuki**	9	stomach	**onaka** (polite)	17
so	**sō**	1	stop	**tomaru** (*v. i.*)	23
	sokode	24		**tomeru** (*v. t.*)	26
	sayō (polite)	25	~ at	(...**ni**) **yoru** (*v. i.*)	24
(not) ~...as	**hodo** (...**nai**)	14	~ up	**fusagu** (*v. t.*)	21
socks	**kutsushita**	3	store	**mise**	22
(get) soiled	**yogoreru** (*v. i.*)	25	story	**-kai** (floor)	20
some	**aru**	16		**hanashi**	28
someone	**dare ka**	25	straight	**massugu(na)** (*a-B*)	15
sometimes	**tokidoki**	16	streetcar	**densha**	13
	...**koto ga (mo) aru**	17	~-stop	**teiryūjō**	20
	...**toki ga (mo) aru**	17	strong	**jōbu(na)** (*a-B*)	17
something	**nani ka**	22	student	**seito**	3
son	**musuko**	19	study	**benkyō suru** (*v. i.*	
eldest ~	**chōnan**	19		& *v. t.*)	8
song	**uta**	28	substitute	**kawari**	30
soon	**mō**	16	such	**sonna**	17
	mō sugu	16	(be) sufficient	**tariru** (*v. i.*)	23
as ~ as	(...**to**) **sugu**	17	sugar	**satō**	22
sore	**itai** (*a-A*)	17	summer	**natsu**	9
sorry			sun	**hi**	11
I'm ~.	**Sumimasen.**	10	Sunday	**nichiyō(bi)**	10
sound	**oto**	6	supper	**yūhan**	17
south	**minami**	27	supposed to	**hazu**	24
speak	**iu** (*v. t.*)	2	surface	**omote**	14
	hanasu (*v. t.*)	6	surname	**myōji**	19
special delivery	**sokutatsu**	18	sweep	**haku** (′-) (*v. t.*)	29
spill	**kobosu** (*v. t.*)	8	**T**		
spinach	**hōrensō**	22			
splendid	**rippa(na)** (*a-B*)	5	table	**tēburu**	4

W

wait	matsu (*v. t.*)	8
	omachi (kudasai)	21
be ~ing	matteru	28
cause to ~	omatase suru (humble)	29
walk	aruku (*v. i.*)	6
wall	kabe	2
wallet	saifu	14
want	-tai	16
	hoshii (*a-A*)	22
war	sensō	27
warm	attakai (*a-A*)	9
	attameru (*v. t.*)	29
wash	arau (*v. t.*)	17
	sentaku	25
~-room	semmenjo	20
watch	tokei	2
water	mizu	6
hot ~	(o)yu	6
way	michi	7
a long ~ off	tōi (*a-A*)	16
on the ~	tochū	24
this ~	kochira (polite)	19
we	watakushitachi	6
wear	haku (--) (*v. t.*) (shoes, etc.)	7
	kaburu (*v. t.*) (on head)	7
	kiru (*v. t.*) (clothes)	7
weather	(o)tenki	2
Wednesday	suiyō(bi)	10
week	shūkan	10
one ~	isshūkan	10
welcome		
You're ~.	Dō itashimashite.	1
well	genki(na) (*a-B*)	1
	yoku	7
I'm quite ~, thank you.	Okagesama de.	2
well	sā	1
	dewa	3
	mā	28
~ then	dewa	3
west	nishi	11

western	(yōfū no)	
~-style house	yōkan	15
~-style room	yōma	20
~ suit	yōfuku	7
what	nan	1
	nani	4
	nani-	10
	nan...	11
~...	nan no	13
	dō iu	23
~ sort (kind) of	donna	5
when	itsu	10
~...	...to	11
	...toki	22
where	doko	4
	dochira (polite)	20
whether or not	ka dō ka	16
which	dotchi (of two)	9
	dore (of many)	28
while		
~ (...ing)	...nagara	24
a little ~ ago	sakki	8
for a short ~	shibaraku	30
white	shiroi (*a-A*)	2
who	donata (polite)	3
	dare	15
whole...	-jū	12
whose	donata no (polite)	3
why	naze	10
	dōshite	28
wide	hiroi (*a-A*)	13
width	haba	13
wife	okusan (honorific)	3
	kanai (one's own) (humble)	19
win	katsu (*v. i.*)	27
wind	kaze	24
window	mado	1
wine	sake	22
winter	fuyu	9
wipe	fuku (*v. t.*)	8
with	de (quantity)	2
	de (instrument or means)	6
	...no aru	20
woman	onnanohito	7

		Lesson			Lesson
woodcut print	**hanga**	26	~ after next	**sarainen**	24
word	**kotoba**	21	~ before last	**ototoshi**	19
work	**hataraku** (*v. i.*)	7	last ~	**kyonen**	16
	shigoto	17	this ~	**kotoshi**	16
~ in	(...ni) **tsutomeru**		yellow	**kiiroi** (*a-A*)	5
	(*v. i.*)	19	yen	**en**	14
worry	(go)**shimpai**	30	yes	**hai**	1
wound	**kega**	27		**ee**	2
write	**kaku** (*v. t.*)	8	yesterday	**kinō**	10
			yet	**mada** (...**nai**)	7
	Y		you	**anata**	3
			your	**anata no**	3
year	**toshi**	19	younger	**shita** (age)	19
...~(s)	**-nen**	9			

GENERAL SUBJECT INDEX

The numbers refer to the numbered sections.

WORDS AND COLLOCATIONS EXPLAINED

The numbers refer to the numbered sections.

昭和37年12月10日　初版発行
昭和59年2月10日　重版発行

プラクティカル ジャパニーズ

著作者　　　長 沼 直 兄
　　　　　　森　　　清

　　　　　　東京都目黒区目黒4—6—21
発行者　　有限会社 長 風 社
　　　　　　代表者 田 口 和 男

　　　　　　東京都豊島区東池袋5—3—8
印刷者　　日之出印刷株式会社
　　　　　　代表者 長 沼 滋 雄

　　　　　　郵便番号　101
発売元　東京都千代田区神田猿楽町1-2-1
　　　　　　日 本 出 版 貿 易 株 式 会 社

Agent :
Japan Publications Trading Co., Ltd.
2-1, Sarugaku-cho 1-chome,
Chiyoda Ku, Tokyo, Japan

Ⓒ　　Printed in Japan

ジャパン・パブリ・・・

発行所　Japan Publications Trading Co., Ltd.

Agent:
Japan Publications Trading Co., Ltd.
2-1, Sarugaku-cho Ichome,
Chiyoda Ku, Tokyo, Japan